STRUCTURES OF PATRIARCHY

WOMEN AND THE HOUSEHOLD IN ASIA—VOL 2

STRUCTURES OF PATRIARCHY

State, Community and Household in Modernising Asia

Edited by
Bina Agarwal

Series Editor
Leela Dube

kali for women

Structures of Patriarchy: State, Community and Household in Modernising Asia
was first published in 1988

in India by
Kali for Women
A 36 Gulmohar Park
New Delhi 110 049

in the U K by
Zed Books Ltd.
57 Caledonian Road
London N1 9BU

First impression 1988

Reprinted 1991

ISBN 81-85107-06-8

Phototypeset by The Word, 807/95 Nehru Place,
New Delhi 110019
Printed at Crescent Printing Works (P) Limited,
P-14, Connaught Circus, New Delhi-110001

CONTENTS

ACKNOWLEDGEMENTS

This book is a product of the Conference on Women and the Household held in New Delhi on January 27-31, 1985. All the papers included here were presented in a series of panels I organised under the sub-theme: 'The State, the Household and Women,' with the exception of Joke Schrijvers' paper which was presented under another sub-theme.

The panel sessions were marked by lively and enriching interactions, and I would like to thank all those who participated in the discussions, and especially the paper writers, discussants and chairpersons, for their valuable contributions. Unfortunately, for varying reasons, including volume size and thematic unity, all the papers presented in these panels could not be accommodated in the book, although each one generated considerable interest and discussion in the sessions. This volume, it is hoped, will extend the process of interaction initiated during the Conference by generating further debate and analysis on the subject.

I would especially like to thank the authors in this volume for their contributions and their ready cooperation in revising their papers for publication. Joke Schrijvers' contribution, *Blueprint for Undernourishment,* first appeared in her book, *Mothers for Life: Motherhood and Marginalization in the North-Central Province of Sri Lanka* (Delft, Eburon, 1985); I am grateful to the publishers for permission to reproduce her article here. I appreciate Professor Leela Dube's involving me in the organisation of the Conference. I am grateful to Primila Lewis and Amrita Chhachhi, with whom discussions on several points while writing the introduction were most helpful. I also much appreciate the help provided by Ritu Menon of Kali for Women in the editing of the papers.

BINA AGARWAL

PREFACE

The Regional Conference for Asia on Women and the Household was held in New Delhi from January 27–31, 1985. Sponsored jointly by the Commission on Women of the International Union of Anthropological and Ethnological Sciences, Research Committee 32 ('Women in Society') of the International Sociological Association, and the Indian Association for Women's Studies, it brought together scholars and activists from the entire Asian region and gave them an opportunity to interact closely and share experiences with one another on five carefully selected sub–themes. Also present at the Conference were social scientists from other parts of the world—those who had a particular interest in the region and had carried out, or were involved in, research in Asia. The Conference thus proved to be an event in as much as it succeeded in bringing together scholars working on South Asia, South-east Asia, East Asia and West Asia, to explore various facets of a theme that has tremendous relevance for the Asian region as a whole.

The theme 'Women and the Household' must be explained for it may give the impression of being narrow and limited: or worse, of reinforcing existing norms and values. In speaking of the household, we do not suggest that it is woman's 'proper' place on account of biological determination: on the contrary, we assert that the household cannot be treated as a private entity separable from the context in which it is embedded. As the intimate experiences of life are structured by wider social relations, so in order to understand the position of women it is necessary to examine intra–household relationships, their dynamics and their historical, socio–economic and political contexts.

When we focus on the household in order to understand the predicament of women, we emphasise the necessity of seeing the various interlinkages between the individual household and the wider structures and processes of society. We deny, therefore, the existence of any such thing as an isolated individual household. As we question the wisdom of treating women as individual entities, ignoring in the process the households of which they form a part, in research as well as in programmes of action and development, so also we question the assumptions that underlie the treatment of a household as an undifferentiated unit in the study of social reality and in planning and action for bringing about social change.

The Asian region harbours a variety of production systems and diverse family and kinship systems and their variants. All the major religions of the world are represented here. There are significant differences between the various economies and polities. These constitute the contexts essential to an understanding of the lives of women and of the role and significance of the household in shaping, sustaining and changing them. In any society the ideological bases for the formation, organisation and functioning of the household seem to be explained by these contexts and their interplay.

The theme also exposes the erroneous but very commonly held view that there exists an undifferentiated *Asian* model of the position of women and of gender relations. Taking account of the subtle variations in basic conceptions of gender differentiation, in the ways in which women are viewed and treated, and in women's entitlements and rights to resources across the region, may help us towards a better understanding of gender relations in human society. It may also show us the ways in which exploitative mechanisms at the national and international levels make use of what we might call less extreme forms of gender differentiation in South-east Asia.

In order to understand the lives and predicaments of women, the centrality of the household as the entity in which the production and reproduction of social life in most societies is carried on, cannot be overemphasized. Women's experiences within the household vary by class, ethnic group, caste, culture and religion. We need to explore the differing principles and notions of family and kinship in different societies, because it is these that shape ideas about the normal composition of the household and its boundaries, about individual members' rights to its resource base, and about intra–household and inter–household relationships. In Asia, with its diverse production, family and kinship systems, the relationship between the household and the condition of women needs careful exploration in a cross–cultural perspective.

Is the household the site of gender subordination and sexual discrimination? Upon what are these based? Do relatively egalitarian relationships between the sexes in the household and the kinship group (as exist in some South-east Asian countries) always help women or do they, on the contrary, make them more vulnerable as participants in larger social processes? How do class differences interact with gender in defining intra-household relationships? What are the differences in the ideology of the household across cultures, groups and classes, and in what ways does ideology prove binding on women and limit their choices of action?

The household's relation to wider economic and political structures, and their use of it, raises a number of tangled issues for social scientists and activists. The policies of the State affect the household in diverse ways and require special consideration. Finally, we need to understand critically the manner in which the household is used as a unit of study in research and surveys and the possible implications of such treatment. The five collections of papers arising from the Conference deal with these various aspects.

Recent research has shown that by ignoring women as social actors who contribute to both continuity and change in society, the social sciences have seriously distorted their understanding of the total social reality. A balanced, 'bifocal' kind of analysis has now begun to be undertaken—men are not to be ignored, but definite focus on women must be maintained if we are to properly comprehend social and societal problems and processes. There is a new emphasis on the study of linkages, on the study of contexts. From this has emerged the consideration accorded to the household.

Structures of Patriarchy: State, Community and Household in Modernising Asia is the second of five collections of papers selected from among those presented at the Conference. The first volume, *Invisible Hands: Women in Home-based Production*, edited by Andrea Menefee Singh and Anita Kelles-Viitanen, was brought out by Sage Publications in 1987. The other three volumes that have been planned deal broadly with (*i*) the structural and cultural dimensions of intra-household relationships; (*ii*) interlinkages between structures of production and kinship systems, and between these and the household; and (*iii*) the household as the unit of data collection and analysis.

The editor of this volume, Dr. Bina Agarwal of the Institute of Economic Growth, Delhi, was also the organizer of the sub-theme on the State, the Household and Women at the Conference. She deserves commendation for having accomplished both tasks with imagination and efficiency. Some papers presented at her sessions could not be accommodated in this volume, but their exclusion does not in any way reflect on their quality.

The papers in this volume challenge, in various ways, the notion that State–directed development is gender–neutral. Together they provide a picture of the complex ways in which the State, the community and the household in Asia have upheld, to the detriment of women, what the editor calls patriarchal interests. The volume's focus on the gender implications of contemporary phenomena—strategies of agricultural and industrial development, population policies, the rise of religious fundamentalism, escalation of violence, and so on—makes it of considerable topical interest. The Introduction pulls together the main themes and arguments of the papers and offers a conceptual framework along with a cross–national perspective. The volume raises a number of new questions for research, discussion and introspection.

The Conference was the result of collective endeavour. It is our hope that these volumes—the responsibility for whose publication is being shared by Kali for Women and Sage—will carry forward the debates initiated at the Delhi Conference.

LEELA DUBE
Series Editor

Nehru Memorial Museum and Library
Teen Murti House
New Delhi 110011

PATRIARCHY AND THE 'MODERNISING' STATE

An Introduction

Bina Agarwal

What if the fence itself wrecks the field?
If the water itself ignites the fire?[1]

In the countries of Asia today, the role played by the State is assuming increasingly complex, multifarious and often pernicious forms. This role, already wide–ranging in terms of formulating and implementing developmental and related policies, is now being extended in many countries into the spheres of people's reproductive choices, religious beliefs, and (as in Islamic theocracies) even interpersonal relationships, dress and behaviour patterns. The class character and social basis of legitimacy of many Asian States has also been changing, in some cases quite radically, as in Iran, in others less dramatically and linked to long–term structural changes in the economy. Alongside, in several parts of the region, the State has emerged as the explicit supporter of particular religious, ethnic and communal interests. In the ensuing conflicts, any illusion that the economically and socially under–privileged may have harbored about the State as a protective fence, whether created by the socialist rhetoric of parliamentary democracies or the religious rhetoric of theocracies, is fast disappearing.

The specific gender implications of these emerging trends, and indeed of the overall development strategies followed in different countries are complex and varied, contingent in particular on the

[1] Taken from a Garhwali song by folk poet Ghan Shyam Shailani, sung by activists of the Chipko movement for forest protection in India.

assumptions underlying State policies and programmes about the household and its character (eg. whether seen as a unit of convergent or conflicting gender interests), and about the appropriate role of men and women in society; pre–existing customary norms; and the part played by the community (religious, ethnic, caste, clan, etc.) to which the household belongs, which is often a significant mediatory factor between the State and the household. Indeed the State, the community and the household could be seen as interacting structures embodying pulls and pressures which may, at specific junctures and in different country contexts, converge or move in contradictory directions—in the latter case providing spaces for the building up of countervailing resistances. What is apparent from the emerging literature, however, is that they are structures dominated by patriarchal interests and typically, the contradictions, as they have played themselves out, have tended to work to the detriment of women.

The papers in this volume trace some of the ways in which these structures are separately and interactively affecting the hold of patriarchy, and the economic and social position of women in present-day Asian societies. As most papers focus on individual country experiences and on specific aspects of State intervention, the following account seeks to pull together these aspects and experiences, and sketch some of the areas of cross–regional convergence or divergence, also bringing to bear on the issue additional relevant literature for this purpose. It focuses particularly on developments over the last two decades, including not only those on the economic front (in agriculture and industry, for instance) but also those relating to population policies, to legal, ideological and structural changes, and to grass–roots resistance.

On the agricultural front

A feature common to agricultural development strategies across Asia, especially over the past decade and a half, has been a concerted effort to increase productivity and agricultural surpluses through the introduction of new technologies and practices, embodied especially in the green revolution package of practices and in major irrigation and resettlement schemes. In non–socialist Asia, this preoccupation with growth and the neglect of both distributional and ecological considerations has led to the uneven emergence of capitalist development in agriculture, exacerbated class and regional inequalities (especially in South Asia where the radical components of land reform attempted in the immediate post–independence period were soon abandoned), and impinged in crucial (although as yet inadequately explored) ways on the political power balances, economic institutions and social fabric of these societies.

The *gender* effects of these strategies have been particularly complex and sometimes contradictory, depending especially on the initial condition of women's existence in these societies, the degree to which gender biases are an explicit part of the planned schemes as opposed to unplanned fallouts, and the extent of organised resistance to effected changes. One of the significant initial conditions on which these strategies have impinged is the strong son preference and even anti–female bias characterising much of Asia, and manifest (especially in South Asia) in gender–related intra–household inequalities in access to food and health care, and in extreme instances, female infanticide.

Agarwal's (Ch. 3) substantial evidence for India highlights the much lower caloric and protein intake levels of women relative to their needs, their higher levels of morbidity and malnutrition, and their greater neglect during illness, found especially, but by no means only, in poor households. As a result, despite their biological advantage over males there is at the all–India level an adverse sex ratio (females per 1000 males), and a lower female to male life expectancy at birth. Of note, however, are the considerable intra-country regional differences in the extent of these biases—which are much greater in the north–west than in the south (the sex ratio in 1981 ranged from 870 in Haryana to 1032 in Kerala). Agarwal's exploration into what underlies these regional differences points to a complex web of cultural and economic factors that have operated historically and been affected especially by recent State development policies. Among the economic variables, two are of particular significance: gender differentials in labour force participation rates (LFPR) and in earnings; and relative male/female marriage costs. In areas of visibly low female labour participation in agriculture and high dowry, such as north–west India, the view that girls are economic liabilities is especially strong and compounded, among other things, by long–distance patrilocal marriages that leave little scope for expecting help from married daughters.

While discriminatory food allocation and health care practices are also noted in other parts of South Asia, such as Sri Lanka (Schrijvers, Ch. 1) and Bangladesh (Agarwal) as well as in parts of South-east Asia (see Folbre, 1984, for the Philippines)[2], unlike the northern part of the Indian subcontinent—north India, Pakistan, Nepal—elsewhere this does not manifest itself in lower female life expectancy at birth or adverse sex ratios. As with intra–country differences, these cross–country variations need more in-depth probing, but pointers again appear to lie in a mix of the economic and cultural. For instance, both Sri Lanka and South-east Asia are characterised by higher female LFPRs in agriculture, a considerably greater access by women to productive resources such as land (e.g. bilateral inheritance has been the traditional norm among most communities in both regions), limited incidence of dowry, greater incidence of intra–village, close–kin marriages and higher female literacy than in much of South Asia. By logical extension, development strategies which adversely affect women's LFPRs or otherwise strengthen the view that they are an economic liability to the family (as due to dowry escalation) are likely to have long–term negative implications for the survival chances of female children. In this context, the trends highlighted in several papers in this volume, notably on India, Sri Lanka, Malaysia and China, become a particular cause for concern.

In the Indian context, Agarwal notes that agricultural growth strategies pursued since the mid-1960s have not only made an insignificant dent on the incidence of absolute poverty, but have increased male–female differentials in employment and earnings among the poor in many states of northern India where discrimination against females has also historically been high. Added to this, State policies have contributed significantly to the rapid depletion of the country's natural resources (water, forests, soils) and the increasing appropriation of what remains by a few. The permanent fall in the groundwater table in many areas (due to unmonitored private tubewell expansion, with the consequent drying up of shallower irrigation and drinking water wells);

[2] This is clearly an under-researched area on which a greater focus and more detailed data collection across Asia is needed.

escalating deforestation (especially due to commercial tree–felling, large–scale surface irrigation works, and agricultural expansion); soil erosion (due to loss of tree cover, canal–related water–logging, salinity, etc.); the decline in village commons (due to appropriation by large farmers, and government auctioning to private contractors); the barring of the poor from access to forest produce, have all created, on the one hand, severe shortages in the availability of fuel, fodder, water and gathered food items to poor women and, on the other, made questionable the long–term sustainability of agricultural yields under the present agricultural strategy. These macro–trends, coupled with the recent emergence of dowry–linked female infanticide in parts of South India and the growing popularity of foetal sex–determination tests followed by abortions of female foetuses in the north–west, portend ill for the future survival chances of female children in many parts of India.

Nor are these trends confined to India. Escalating dowry coupled with growing poverty and landlessness, with particularly negative effects on women, have been noted in Bangladesh (Jahan, Ch. 8). Again, ecological degradation associated with specific forms of agricultural and irrigation development has today emerged as a significant cause for concern across all of Asia including socialist China. Indeed, in China too, the pursuit of a high growth–oriented agricultural policy since the mid–1970s, with the decollectivisation of agriculture and the launching of the household contract system has had severe negative consequences for women, not dissimilar, in several respects, to those noted above as accompanying capitalist development in South Asian agriculture. Kelkar (Ch. 4) argues that the household contract system introduced in China in 1978, under which the production team contracts out land plots to peasant households for growing agreed quantities of specified crops, has substantially enhanced household productivity with rural women's labour, in particular, creating 'more wealth for the State, the collective and the family'. But, on the other hand, women's work burden has increased, there is no longer a State drive encouraging husbands to share in childcare (in fact, many social scientists are stressing the need to increase women's maternity and childcare leave to seven years), and able–bodied women are assumed to have 80 per cent of the strength of able-bodied men, thus perpetuating wage differentials in workpoints for the same work, and entitling women to only 1.6 mu of contract land relative to 2 mu for men. These gender differentials coupled with a thrust towards a one–child family (with maternity leave being given for only one child, and a penalty imposed for subsequent children) is associated with the revival of female infanticide: 'In case of a son one might pay a heavy penalty of upto 5000 yuan, but in the case of a daughter one might want to get rid of it.' Here, as Kelkar points out, son preference is not just a leftover of feudal ideology but is backed by sound economic reasons, stemming from the State's current agricultural and population policies.

While it can be argued that these effects represent the contradictory and unplanned (though not unforeseeable) consequences of State policies, in the schemes observed by Schrijvers, and Ng and Mohamed, the gender bias is direct and *integral* to their very conceptualisation. Schrijvers (Ch. 1) describes how ten years after the initiation of the Mahaweli irrigation and resettlement scheme (the biggest in Sri Lanka), planned to make the country self–sufficient in rice, the project region has the highest levels of chronic malnutrition in the country. Prior to the scheme, the villagers practiced both wet rice and swidden cultivation—the latter provided considerable food variety and cash incomes and, together with wet paddy, a greater security against hunger than the 2.5 acres of paddy and 0.5 acres of homestead land allotted per family under the scheme. Not only is the allotment inadequate for subsistence, but the cash from any crop sales remains with the men, and is spent at least in part on tobacco and liquor.

The scheme also specifically discriminates against women. Married women are not entitled to plots. Husbands are automatically assumed to be family heads and the allotted plots registered in their names. As the family can name only one heir, this is usually the son. Thus, contrary to Sinhala customary law and practice of bilateral inheritance whereby both sons and daughters have a right to the family's paddy land, and where married women too have independent and inalienable land ownership rights, in the scheme villages, wives are dependants. Also, without land titles, they have little access to agricultural extension information, institutional credit and cooperative membership. Women in the scheme thus find themselves working harder (on home gardens and paddy plots), without the help and emotional support of kin, the independent access to cash, and the free produce of the jungle that the old villages provided; they are also without access to information on new practices that would enable them to raise their productivity, with especially disadvantageous implications for female-headed households.

This scenario is in fact typical of the way in which most irrigation resettlement schemes are planned in the Third World. For instance, the Muda scheme in Malaysia and the Mwea scheme in Kenya were both planned assuming a nuclear family with a male head and a woman housewife-helper, ignoring existing customary practices which gave women relative autonomy as producers in these communities.

Ng and Mohamed's paper (Ch. 2) on West Malaysia again highlights a strong gender bias in the planning and implementation of development schemes. Contrary to the customary Malay law *(adat)* under which men and women had equal rights to paddy land, in new land settlements only young men have been given ownership rights to which, as in the Mahaweli project, only one heir (inevitably the son) can be nominated. In addition, peasant differentiation along class and gender lines has grown, as has the migration of young men and women to the cities for industrial employment, leaving behind a large percentage of older people, and especially households headed by divorced and widowed mothers, to work the paddy and rubber land, with unequal access to inputs, credit, labour and markets. Training programmes introduced by the State focus on handicrafts and embroidery (typical of many such training schemes in the Third World), while schemes to help rubber producers serve only male members, although a significant number of women are operating rubber plots on their own.

Paradoxically, this gender blindness and patriarchal bias in agricultural planning goes counter to the State's immediate goals of achieving higher agricultural productivity. But it could be seen (as implied by Ng and Mohamed) as playing a wider, although not necessarily planned role of keeping down the supply price of female labour for an expanding industrial sector.

On the industrial front

Since the 1960s, labour intensive, export-oriented industries (especially, though not always, based on multinational investment) have emerged as a significant new source of female employment in Asia, although largely confined to those countries and industries which were able to take advantage of the expansion in world trade in manufactures—electronics, garments and textiles being the main employers. Women's employment in electronics is noted to have grown from nil to 50,000 between 1971 and 1980 in Malaysia, and increased over six-fold in Singapore in the same period. In South Korea, one-third of the entire industrial labour force consists of women below 25 working in electronics, textiles and toy-making (Banerjee, 1985).

Over the past decade, a considerable literature has emerged on the work conditions and effects of such employment on the lives of the women, much of it focusing on the commonalities in these conditions across different South-east Asian countries, and typically emphasising the exploitative character of employment in these 'world market factories' (eg. Elson and Pearson, 1981). In several studies it was noted that the demand was for young, unmarried, relatively educated women assumed to have the manual dexterity ('nimble fingers') and docility needed for the tedious, repetitive and monotonous nature of the work. Given the considerable gender disparity in wages, women could also be recruited at relatively low cost. Such employment, while enabling a greater improvement in the material well-being of the women and their families than possible in other available jobs, also involved long hours of work, low pay relative to men, easy retrenchment, little scope for skill acquisition to enable easy job shifts, unhealthy work conditions, and strict supervision. Also women who migrated directly from the protected social environment of rural families (as in Malaysia) were an easy prey to sexual exploitation by young men in the cities, and suicides following unwanted pregnancies from pre-marital attachments that did not lead to marriage, were not uncommonly reported among certain ethnic groups, such as the Tamils in Malaysia.

Two decades have, however, elapsed since this form of industrialisation was initiated and most South-east Asian countries are today entering what some have termed the second phase. Emerging literature is now attempting to examine the changes over time in the conditions of work and recruitment in these factories within specific countries, as well as cross-country variations in experience. In particular, the substantial differences between countries in the overall labour market demand has made for a significant difference in the work conditions and wage rates commanded today by the women workers. Phongpaichit (Ch.5) in her paper focuses on some of these changes between what she terms the first and second phases of the industrialisation process in Singapore and South Korea, and the differences in their respective experiences.

She notes that in Singapore today, in contrast to the 1960s, women's conditions of work have improved radically. A tight labour market has led to a considerable increase in female employment, a narrowing of the male/female wage gap, State subsidy for childcare in some cases, and State support to both male and female workers for upgrading their skills. She further argues that family support for childcare in Singapore has been crucial for women to continue working after marriage by enabling them to acquire the necessary skills and tenure for moving up the industrial hierarchy, and hold their jobs when the industry moved towards more capital-intensive and skill-oriented production. In South Korea, by contrast, even in the second phase of industrialisation beginning in the mid-1970s, women workers still form a floating and peripheral workforce, having short industrial working lives, usually extending only upto the time they have children. Phongpaichit attributes the disadvantaged position of South Korean workers relative to those of Singapore, to the continuing slack in the labour market despite rapid industrialisation; their lack of family childcare support, given their rural-based families, which compel many to give up factory employment and take up domestic service jobs on marriage; and the virtual absence of State facilities for childcare, and for upgrading skills and educational levels, with private sector opportunities for vocational training and skill upgrading being concentrated on men. Indeed women export factory workers in Singapore and Hongkong today are noted to enjoy a considerably higher standard of living and better work conditions than their counterparts in most other Asian countries (Foo and Lim, 1987). In Singapore, recent observers have also found that workers are now able to defy management by carrying radios to work and taking frequent breaks. At the same time, however, the rise in labour costs is reported to have made both Singapore and Hongkong less attractive to multinationals, leading to relocations in the garment industry to other parts of South-east Asia and the Third World (Banerjee, 1985:15). The regional non-specificity of inputs and skills required in many of these export-oriented industries and hence the ease with which they can be relocated, underlines the basic long-term instability and insecurity of the employment they offer.

In contrast to South-east Asia, in South Asia the penetration of female-intensive, export-oriented factory production is very recent and limited. In countries such as India, import-substitution rather than export promotion has been the thrust of industrial policy, although there have been some shifts in direction recently. Also, unlike say Singapore where the industrial sector absorbs 40 per cent of the female labour force, and Hongkong where it absorbs 60 per cent, industry in general provides employment for a much smaller percentage of working women in South Asia (only 10 per cent in India)[3] where much of the expanding workforce in general, and female workforce in particular, is still dependent on peasant agriculture and the informal sector. However, export-oriented factories as a new and growing source of female employment in the region warrant closer examination.

In Sri Lanka, for instance, Free Trade Zones (FTZs) are of growing significance as employers of women workers who constituted an estimated 88 per cent of the total FTZ workforce in 1984 (ILO, 1984). Here, in a situation of persistently high unemployment, with limited alternative job openings for women, the workers, typically under 25 years of age, single, mostly from rural origins migrating for a first job, brought up in a relatively protected and conservative social milieu, face a much harsher economic and social climate than existed in the first phase of such employment in much of South-east Asia. Emerging studies indicate a higher incidence of illness among the workers of FTZs than those in other industries, strict work supervision, susceptibility to sexual exploitation by supervisors, low wages that allow for little saving after deducting boarding fees (for heavily overcrowded dormitory facilities) and other expenses, and the frequent imposition of fines for absence due to sudden illness or shortfall in

[3] Figures taken from Banerjee (1985).

production (Rosa, 1982; *Voice of Women,* 1982). Equally grim conditions of work and employment for women in FTZs are reported in India (see e.g. Trikha, 1985, on the Kandla FTZ).

At the same time, as in South-east Asia where various laws and enactments have curbed or banned labour agitation, in South Asia too the State, in its attempt to create a climate attractive to (especially foreign) investors, has effectively prevented unionisation in FTZs—in Sri Lanka by using its power to restrict the entry of outsiders into the zones and to withdraw the permits of workers who join a trade union or similar organisation, in India by methods such as depriving women of transport facilities and even by police action. Indeed with an upbringing where obedience and an unquestioning acceptance of authority are emphasised, the fact that this is often their first job, limited alternative job opportunities, the lack of an exposure to trade union activity, and time constraints in attending meetings after work, all serve as barriers to unionisation (Rosa, 1982; Trikha, 1985). Frequent complaints of illness and spontaneous mass work stoppages as methods of protest used by the Sri Lankans, are reminiscent of the mass hysteria and fainting fits resorted to by the South-east Asian women workers in the early 1970s. But given the overcrowded labour markets in South Asia and the virtual absence of State welfare facilities such as childcare, there appears to be little short-term likelihood of any significant improvement in these conditions as occur in parts of South-east Asia.

At the same time, it has been argued (with some validity) that employment in these industries provides a better alternative for the women, than do many of the informal sector activities (characterised by low and uncertain earnings) into which the majority of South Asian women workers are being pushed, in a context where neither peasant agriculture nor formal industry provide adequate employment opportunities. Apart from better earnings than usually possible in informal sector activities, work in the export factories represents a break from traditional jobs, and provides for the possibility of a growth in women's political consciousness regarding the nature of their exploitation and their rights as workers and as women; although, as noted, obstacles to the effective channeling of such consciousness into organised protest remain considerable.

On population policies

Apart from State policies in the sphere of production examined thus far, State interventions in the sphere of biological reproduction have long been a familiar component of development strategies in the Third World. For most, the preoccupation has been with over-population—propagated by governments and international aid agencies as the primary factor underlying persisting high levels of poverty and underdevelopment, thereby obscuring State failures on the production and distributional fronts. Less typical perhaps are recent thrusts in Malaysia and Singapore to boost population growth. Either way, the brunt of these policies, carried through by a mixture of persuasion and coercion, carrot and stick methods, and often with a class and even racist/ethnic bias have tended to fall on women. As Chee (Ch. 6) argues, not only do these policies reflect the State's infringement on what should surely be a woman's prerogative—control over her life and body—they also usually reflect the dominant ideology of the ruling classes, particularly with respect to the role of women in society.

In 1984, Malaysia announced a policy to raise its population from 15 to 70 million in 115 years, by encouraging women to have five children each, for providing the labour force for rapid industrialisation. Chee argues that quite apart from the mathematical miscalculations underlying this announcement (achieving the said target would in fact require a *drop* in the growth rate to 1.4 per cent) and the likely increase in unemployment and strain on available educational, health and social services it would entail, there are clear class, ethnic and gender biases in the proposed policy. Its burden would fall mainly on poor rural Malay women who can least afford to leave work for additional child-bearing, and whose access to health care too is far from adequate, although it may well help increase the percentage of Malays in the population. Singapore's attempts to increase its population are in fact noted by Chee to be explicitly class–biased—graduate women are being encouraged to have more children, and non–graduates discouraged from having more than two—on the assumption that intelligence is genetically determined, and that graduate status implies higher intelligence.[4]

[4] For an elaboration of this point see Chan and Chee (1984).

In both countries, the policies reflect and reinforce the view that women are mainly biological reproducers, mothers and homemakers, and at best peripheral workers. Indeed, the explicit use of women's bodies as reproductive machines is reflected most starkly in present–day Iran, where Afshar (Ch. 9) says women are being pressed to abandon public ambition and aspirations and concentrate on motherhood and domesticity, and to serve the country by providing sons as martyrs in its war efforts.

Forced motherhood or forced contraception can both be seen as violating the woman's right to choose whether, when and how many children she has. For rural women in poverty, the violation of this right can take many forms. For instance, South Asia today is being used as a dumping ground by First World multinationals for contraceptives such as NET-EN and Depo Provera which are banned in most western countries. With the aquiescence and cooperation of home governments, these drugs, promising long–term contraceptive 'protection', are being injected into women who are given inadequate or no information on the drugs' considerable negative side effects (Das and Sarkar, 1985), Alongside, in India (as noted) femicide (the abortion of female foetuses) is gaining in popularity. The practice, banned in government hospitals, is tolerated when done in the mushrooming private clinics, and is justified by many (including family planning officials) as an effective method of birth control in a country with a strong son preference.

It is in the Chinese context, however, that population policies (the one–child family) have produced among the grimmest consequences—the re–emergence of female infanticide on a fairly wide scale, as noted by several authors, including Kelkar (Ch. 4) and Davin (1985). Davin also speaks of the common reporting of forced abortions (sometimes carried out even in the eighth month) from areas where the campaign to limit births has met with strong opposition; of cases where the woman is simply worn down by patient, unremitting persuasion, which continues for days, weeks and even months until her reluctant consent is finally extracted by local cadres, who face a cut in salaries if their area exceeds the birth quota; and of cases of women being abused or violently beaten by husbands or in–laws for bearing daughters. The traditional preference for sons and need for more children has in fact (as noted earlier) been reinforced by the new agricultural policies which have put a premium on family labour, especially male labour. In this context, official recognition of the problem and campaigns against femicide launched by the State and the Chinese Women's Federation (of which more later) can only have limited effectiveness when the logic of official development policies is to the contrary.

On the ideology of gender

The ideology of gender—especially the assumption that women are (or should be) primarily housewives and mothers and secondarily workers—in fact permeates most policies of the modern State discussed thus far and, as seen, affects women's material situation in distinct ways—in justifying a discriminatory wage structure (including an unequal workpoint and land allotment system in present-day socialist China), a double burden of work, and an unequal access to technology, information, credit, training and productive resources.

Indeed ideology plays a crucial role in the social construction of gender and in the process of women's subordination. The family, the community, the media, the educational, legal, cultural and religious institutions, all variously reflect, reinforce, shape and create prevailing ideological norms—norms which may well conflict with and contradict one another, and usually vary in their specification and enforcement across classes and regions. In examining the relationship between the State and the ideology of gender in Asia, examples can be found of the State operating through all or some of these institutions to push forward a particular ideology for legitimising its position and policies, or to mediate between prevailing contradictory ideologies, or to set itself up in opposition to a prevailing ideology. What is striking, though, is that the content of this ideological thrust reflects a singular preoccupation with particularly two aspects—the domestication of women and control over female sexuality.

Both Amrit Srinivasan (Ch. 7) and Haleh Afshar (Ch. 9) provide examples, the former historically in the Indian context, the latter from present-day Iran, of the coming together of religion, politics and State power in domesticating women and controlling their sexuality. Srinivasan describes a process by which a community of women, the *devadasis,* were deprived of their singularly privileged social and economic position as well as ritual status in late 19th century Tamil Nadu, in the name of community reform, as a result of organised pressure from upper caste Hindu (mostly male) professionals—doctors, administrators, journalists and social workers. Strongly influenced by Christian morality and religion, they joined the missionaries in seeking a ban on the *devadasi* system by launching the 'anti-nautch' movement—holding protest demonstrations, boycotting dance functions, and publicising the system as prostitution.

The system in fact represented a clear separation of the professional and sexual from the domestic. The *devadasi,* dedicated ('married') to the temple gods and highly skilled in classical dancing—her hereditary profession—could lead a normal life in professional, sexual and child-bearing terms, but was not allowed to marry, was sexually inaccessible to all but a chosen patron—an upper caste, upper class, married Hindu male who maintained her (and her dependants) through gifts, including large land endowments (for her use but not alienation). She was the primary source of earned and ancestral property, most men of the community being dependent, and even as musicians never commanding the same power and influence. The reform campaign forced the *devadasis* to acknowledge the moral superiority of domestic values, relinquish all rights to temple service and its privileges (while the men could continue as musicians), and lose much of their land to male relatives who, under new property laws, could inherit shares in it. Indeed, as Srinivasan notes: 'The extraordinary success of the reforms was not unconnected with the fact that men in the community stood to gain by the legislation.'

Paradoxically, alongside the reform movement, a 'revivalist' movement was launched, primarily by the theosophists on grounds of preserving Indian culture and tradition but with a significant modification—they sought to preserve ('revive') the dance *form* without the *system* which gave the *devadasis* power and position, and projected the ancient temple dancer as a pure, holy and sexually chaste woman. The colonial State, Srinivasan argues, with a stake in encouraging regionalism and cultural divisions, sided with those pressing for a ban on temple dedication. By the time legislation was actually passed in 1947 however, the practice had already died, leaving space for the 'revival' of dance, but shorn of its social roots and of the privileged position accorded to the dancer.

The use of religious ideology and State power to push women into domesticity and control their sexuality is, however, revealed in its starkest form in the present-day Islamic States of Asia, especially in Iran under Khomeini. Afshar (Ch. 9) describes how women, projected as biologically and socially inferior, are not allowed the same access as men to law and justice—their evidence is unacceptable in court unless collaborated by a man, the *diyat* or blood money required to be paid to the family of a murdered woman by the murderer's relatives is half that required for a man, and women are barred from studying, teaching or practising law. Women are also strongly discouraged from seeking employment in fields other than nursing or education, forbidden to do full time work if mothers of young children (virtually all nurseries and childcare centres have been closed), forced to veil themselves in workplaces, segregated in schools, pressurised into early marriage (the minimum legal age is now 13 and marriage is seen as women's national duty), advised 'to avoid too much education . . . and to concentrate on their roles as wives and mothers', and expected to be chaste and modest in public behaviour while arousing and satisfying the passions of their husbands in private. While discriminatory educational and employment practices push women into marriage for physical survival, polygamy, temporary marriages and unilateral divorce allowed to men make the so-called protection offered by the domestic sphere illusory. Also, these enactments are enforced mercilessly by the State both directly and tacitly, by supporting fundamentalist groups who do not hesitate in resorting to violence if they deem it necessary.

The gains made by middle class women in the century prior to the Islamic Revolution—right to vote, access to education, abolition of the veil, curb on unilateral male right to divorce and child custody, etc.—have been more than negated under the new theocracy, without any noticeable gains in employment or welfare for the working class women.

Iran, no doubt, represents an extreme end of the spectrum, particularly because of the virtually total control exercised by the State over all aspects of civil life, and its ability to use repressive machinery for the promotion of an Islamic-patriarchal ideology and for curbing all dissent. But Islamisation drives across Asia have many common features. In Pakistan, the Hadood Ordinance passed in 1979 made no legal distinctions between rape and adultery, and sanctioned public flogging in both cases; the law of evidence passed in 1984 reduced the weight of women's evidence to half that of the man's; the law of *qisas* and *diyat* drafted by the Council of Islamic Ideology and passed in 1984 specifies *diyat* for bodily injury to a woman as half that for a man, and makes the testimony of Muslim women witnesses to a murder admissible for a lesser punishment than the testimony of Muslim males; and various government directives now require women government employees and college students to wear the *chador,*[5] bar women from participating in spectator sports, channelise women civil servants into only certain offices and ban those in the foreign service from being posted abroad, etc. Violent attacks by members of the clergy on educated middle-class women for not covering themselves 'adequately' have also been reported (Mumtaz and Shaheed, 1987).

In fact, even in South-east Asian countries with a predominantly Muslim population, such as Malaysia, some of these moves are in evidence, although here such thrusts often conflict with prevailing customary laws that are gender egalitarian. For instance, under *adat,* Malay women and men both enjoyed equal rights to property (including land) and divorce, and were subject to the same codes of sexual behaviour, promiscuity being condemned in both sexes (Karim, 1985), in contrast to Islamic injunctions under which the sister's share in parental property is half the brother's and permitted social behaviour is marked by double standards. In pre-colonial Malaysia, attempts at Islamisation led to differential class responses. In Perak, for instance, religious leaders, traders and the ruling classes in general favoured Islamic patrilineal law while the peasants insisted on following *adat* (Ng and Mohamed, Ch. 2). Again among matrilineal Negeri Sembilans of West Malaysia, efforts by fundamentalists to promote Islamic property laws in the 1950s, on the grounds that matrilineal inheritance *(adat perpatih)* was unfair to men, led to organised resistance by the women who even threat-

[5] A sheet that covers women's head and bodies but leaves the face visible.

ened to divorce their husbands if they persisted in supporting anti-*adat* moves, and to the ultimate dropping of the proposals. The anti-colonial movement added strength to the women's resistance which was seen as defending tradition against imperialist inroads (Stivens, 1985), in marked contrast to the situation of the *devadasis* in India who could not channel their individually expressed resentment against the reform moves into organised protest.

In present-day Malaysia, however, Islamisation is backed by an autocratic 'modern' State, and among the younger generation is observed to be used increasingly 'as a source of moral education'. Islamic movements and religious associations, led exclusively by male religious specialists who also mobilise the female members of their families, are noted to be gaining in strength, with religious knowledge and rituals having become 'a guide to everyday life' among members of both sexes in these movements, replacing customary values as the basis of social and cultural identity and organisation (Karim, 1985). There is also a drive to emphasise the roles of women as wives and mothers, encourage them to forgo employment (where traditional culture emphasised work ethics for both sexes), tailor their reproductive choices to State directives, and curb their sexual independence (which has grown with their increasing absorption in urban industry since the early 1970s).

This thrust in the Islamisation campaigns appears to be contrary to the needs of capitalist modernisation for a free and relatively independant labor force. What is significant about such campaigns, however, is their *gender selectivity* in invoking certain religious injunctions and by-passing others, or promoting particular interpretations of religious texts, whereby women are singled out as the torch-bearers and symbols (the public faces) of the campaigns, while male rights, prerogatives and freedoms go largely unchallenged.[6] In fact support for female seclusion and

[6] Also see Afshar (Ch.9) Mumtaz and Shaheed (1987), and Chhachhi (1987). This exercise in selectivity, not merely in terms of invoking certain religious injunctions and ignoring others, but also in the choice of particular interpretations of religious texts as well as of religious myths for wider propagation by a dominant group, is by no means specific to Islamisation drives or to modern day society. A pluralistic religion such as Hinduism lends itself with particular ease to this kind of usage, although, at the same time, it could be argued that it

domestication, and the barring of women from the public sphere, has often come especially from working class men to whom working class women can easily be projected as competitors in situations of high unemployment. In addition, such drives are often supported by the women themselves for reasons clearly brought out by Afshar in the context of Iran, but applicable more generally:

> The process of modernisation had, in many instances, displaced male labour by cheaper female labour without leading to alternative jobs for men. Unemployment, however, did not significantly erode the absolute control of fathers and husbands over the household; in many cases it merely intensified the subordination of women. A substantial majority ... servants, washerwomen and cleaning ladies ... often had their pay negotiated by, and paid to, their male relatives. In all cases the women continued to do all the domestic work. Hence, many lost the honour and dignity bestowed on them by their religion, without gaining any material benefits in return. As a result, the advocates of domesticity for women found a large support base among the poor and working classes, both male and female. Women expected a respite from drudgery and the men assumed that by domesticating women they would themselves be able to return to full employment and gain the dignity of paid work.

However, as Afshar notes, both these assumptions have proved false.

Quite apart from this highly 'visible' and much commented on rise of Islamic fundamentalism is the emergence of other 'fundamentalisms' (Hindu, Sikh, Sinhala, Buddhist) in multi-religious, multi-ethnic countries such as India and Sri Lanka, with significant gender fallouts as well. One such effect has been the demand for strengthening patriarchal features in laws governing marriage, divorce and inheritance which come under the purview of personal laws that vary by the religion and even geographic location of particular communities. Recent examples from India are

is precisely this plurality which can also provide scope for subsequent (less conservative) reinterpretations.

the passing of the Muslim Women's Act of 1986[7] which takes away the right of divorced Muslim women to maintenance from the husband, due to pressure from Muslim fundamentalists despite widespread protest from progressive Muslim and non-Muslim (women's and other) groups and individuals; and the demand by some Indian Sikhs (currently governed by Hindu personal law) for a separate Sikh personal law that would deprive daughters of their right to ancestral inheritance and make the custom of levirate (the widow marrying the dead husband's brother) mandatory, to ensure that any property she inherits from her husband remains within the family. The existence of multiple and gender-discriminatory personal laws is in direct violation of the secular and non-discriminatory principles enshrined in the constitutions of most countries, including India. In addition, old barbaric practices such as *sati,* banned over a century ago, are today being sought to be justified and legitimised in the name of freedom of religion by some Hindu communities and their political supporters. In fact, a growing number of *sati* cases have been reported over the past decade (Sangari and Vaid, 1982).

On violence against women

The tensions and contradictions associated with the growth of religious, ethnic, clan and caste divides, of urbanisation and modernisation, and of regional, class and social inequalities, are all increasingly being played out not only in the arena of politics and propaganda, but directly and violently in the streets and in the home. Both violence in general and violence against women in particular are clearly on the rise all over Asia.

Quite apart from the quiet violence underlying female infanticide, sex–specific abortions and discriminatory food and health care practices, is the disquieting and visible increase in all forms of violence on women, including rape, dowry murders, *sati* and witch-hunting. In fact, today dowry murders are being reported even among Muslims in Bangladesh where in the 1950s dowry itself was a rare phenomenon. Much of the violence against women, especially rape and wife–beating, goes under–and un–

[7] The full title of the Act is the Muslim Women's (Protection of Rights on Divorce) Act, 1986.

reported due to the social stigma attached to the victims and their families. Jahan (Ch. 8), on the basis of Bangladeshi newspaper reports, finds a noticeable rise in the percentage of female victims of violence—from 12.4 in 1980 to 32.7 in 1984; and attributes this to multiple causes such as the general rise of violence in the country, especially political (in the 1950s political murders were rare in Bangladesh, in the 1980s they are commonplace); the growing use of force by the police to curb protest demonstrations, especially involving students (female and male); easier access to firearms, acid and other weapons; the objectification of women in the media and increasing depiction of violence on film and TV; growing dowry demands and related violence; the spread of religious fundamentalism, strengthening the ideology of female seclusion and providing further justifications for male chastisement of women who 'transgress' into public spaces of predominantly male presence; the social and legal sanction given to husbands and relatives to physically chastise women for their behaviour; the growing landlessness and poverty forcing women to work outside the home while leaving them even more vulnerable to assualt by outsiders; and so on.

State sanction (tacit or explicit) to men to enforce State directives on female dress and behaviour, if necessary by violent means, is in fact common across the Islamic world and, in several countries, the enforcement is zealously undertaken, as by the clergy and police in Pakistan, or by groups such as the Hezbolah the so-called God-party in Iran, 'who have taken it upon themselves to attack any woman thought to be insufficiently covered. This is enforced by the provisions of the *qassas* law: an instant punishment of 74 lashes to be meted out to unveiled women' (Afshar).

Such examples lend some support to the argument made, for instance, by Chhachhi (1987) that whereas earlier the exercise of patriarchal authority rested only with *particular* men—fathers, brothers, husbands and extended family kin—*what is significant about State-sponsored religious fundamentalism is that it not only reinforces this patriarchal control, but more importantly, shifts the right of control to all men* (Chhachhi's emphasis); and 'The State . . . (thus) gives every and any man on the street the legitimate right to stop any woman who does not conform to the "traditional and proper" role assigned to her.'

At the same time, this argument misses out the crucial role that *the community* (religious, ethnic, clan, caste, etc.), and not just family and extended kin, has *always* played (and continues to play) as a mediator between the State and the individual or household, in enforcing conformity to specific norms of behaviour, action and dress, and in the specification of which the community's economically and politically influential members typically have a significant hand. Hence even when social legislation passed by the State has been progressive in a given context (in promoting, say, greater gender equality in marriage, divorce and inheritance rights)[8], this has seldom been strictly enforceable where community norms are to the contrary. Yet at least to the extent that the State in such a situation maintains a relatively secular and progressive position in policies, legislation and their implementation, it provides scope for individual women or households to escape or deviate from the community's patriarchal stranglehold. It also provides space for building organised resistance against specific anti–women practices.

However, what appears to be happening today in much of South and South-east Asia is the *convergence* of State and community–dictated patriarchal norms. In predominantly mono–religious societies such as Iran, this convergence is today starkly evident, with religious injunctions being forced on women by the dual and mutually reinforcing machinery of the State and the community. But even in multi–religious, multi–ethnic societies such as India, Malaysia and Sri Lanka, a growing State susceptibility to pulls and pressures from different communities for accepting their communal demands, including for conservative anti–women legislation, is apparent; and, alongside it, a growing identification of the State with the majority community (upper-caste Hindus in India, Muslim Malays in Malaysia, Buddhist-Sinhalese in Sri Lanka). Indeed, several Asian States which appeared to be operating relatively autonomously of religious, ethnic or caste groupings in the period immediately after independence have, especially over the past few years, assumed distinctly communal overtones, and State machinery such as the police has been found far from neutral in situations of communal tension and violence.

[8] The Special Marriages Act of 1954, the Hindu Marriage Act of 1955, and the Hindu Succession Act of 1956, passed in India, are cases in point.

What is also noteworthy at this historical juncture is that despite the considerable differences in social structures and State formations across non-socialist Asia—parliamentary democracies, Islamic theocracies, military dictatorships—there is an escalation, especially in South Asia, of strife along communal, ethnic and religious lines, and a growing communalisation of politics and civil life. What complexity of factors underlie this is a question of crucial significance today. To what extent, for instance, are basic economic and political issues being expressed in the idiom of religious, cultural and regionalistic demands?[9] What are the links between these trends and the uneven nature of capitalist development, the exacerbation of class and other inequalities, and people's rising aspirations for material gain (fanned also by modern media) in the face of increasing competition for limited opportunities and economic and physical resources? To what degree has the erosion of traditional systems of status and legitimacy for the middle classes (especially rural), with few channels for establishing an alternative basis for social identity and cohesion, or the crisis of livelihood and identity facing especially those left floating in the informal sector between village and town, field and factory, contributed to the tendency of such groups to fall back on religious, ethnic, clan, caste and regional sentiments and allegiances, and to variously exploit or be exploited on the basis of these sentiments and allegiances? In what ways has over-centralisation of State authority and associated non-participative political processes created or strengthened centrifugal tendencies towards political regionalism? What role has the geo-politics of pan-Islamisation and of neo-imperialism played? And so on. But in whatever way we look at it, or seek to analyse it, large parts of Asia, especially South Asia today, are engulfed in a crisis of major proportions—variously of economy, ecology, polity and national and group identity.

In the arising tensions and conflicts the police, even the military are being deployed with increasing frequency by the State, in the process often unleashing organised violence on the people. And these instruments of State power can thrust themselves in

[9] As Alavi (1972) notes, such expressions have long been a feature of South Asian politics.

particularly brutal ways on women: e.g. rape by army and police, including of women in custody; tacit or active collaboration between the police and dominant class/caste/ethnic groups to sexually harrass women of under-privileged communities as a means of subordinating and curbing theirs and their community's militancy; the torture of women to gain access to dissident male relatives, etc.

On resistance and struggle for change

On the positive side, however, as opposed to the weight of State machinery, there has been an emergence of grass-roots resistance, which while stemming from a range of ideological and political positions, and focussed on differing issues, together embodies a strong critique of and protest against ongoing economic and political programmes, and underlines the need for an alternative, more holistic and egalitarian approach to social and economic change.

The period since the 1970s, in particular, has seen a widespread growth in consciousness across Asia regarding women's oppression and the need to fight it. In India, for instance, women's concerns are being given recognition in diverse forums: mass-based working class, poor peasant and tribal movements that gained strength especially in the 1960s; women's associations linked to specific political parties; ecology and civil rights movements; and the many women's groups that have mushroomed in the 1980s in the larger cities, some of which have rural links as well. The issues taken up by these groups vary, and include women's independent and equal right to land and property, equal wages, adequate employment, access to credit, protection against sexual and other forms of violence in the family and outside, health protection, and curbing alcoholism, media abuse and dowry practices. Again, in Pakistan, the Women's Action Forum (WAF) formed in 1981, and today with chapters in four major cities, has initiated a cross-country campaign against gender discriminatory Islamic injunctions, legislation and State directives that disadvantage women in employment, education and the social sphere (Mumtaz and Shaheed, 1987). In Bangladesh, women's groups have been pressing, among other things, for legislation and other measures to curb dowry, violence against women, and female infanticide (Jahan). In Iran, women's secret societies have been formed to resist State repression (Afshar). Women's groups have emerged too in Sri Lanka, Malaysia, the Philippines, Thailand and elsewhere in South-east Asia, to fight against the growth of sex tourism, the exploitation of women in multinational factories, and the commoditisation of women in the mass media. Ongoing attempts to reinterpret religious texts, such as the Koran, and explore their potential for consciousness-raising are also noteworthy, although some point to the inherent limitations of such efforts, while others argue that religion needs to be analytically delinked from communalism, and its humanistic and radicalizing potential explored (e.g. Dietrich, 1986).

On this and several other issues, and especially on macro and long-term perspectives and strategies, there is no necessary agreement or convergence of understanding among women's groups within or across countries, yet there is an increasing realisation of the need for united agitation, at least on specific issues: for instance, the campaign against dowry in India brought together groups and individuals, with quite diverse political beliefs, for forming a common front.

All these represent small steps in what will clearly be an extended struggle against patriarchy. How extended, is well brought out in the context of China where even nearly four decades after the establishment of a socialist State, and the official recognition given to the woman question by the communist leadership on assuming power, many of the familiar manifestations of patriarchy in Asia persist. In present-day China the issue continues to receive attention both from the party leadership and the All China Women's Federation. Kelkar notes how the latter has been campaigning against female infanticide, discriminatory practices in education and employment, the unequal workpoint rating system (they are asking that 'equal work' be defined as 'work of comparable value' rather than as the 'same work'), the notion that childcare and housework are solely women's tasks, and patrilocality which is seen as one of the significant causes of continued son-preference and anti-female bias in the family. However, what is also apparent today is that patriarchal attitudes are not mere leftovers of feudalism but are closely linked to and being strengthened by present State policies in China. It may thus be queried whether, despite the State's conscious attempts, a significant improvement in women's welfare is possible without challenging the State's development policies themselves. This query would be relevant for other parts of Asia as well.

Some of these complexities and understandings are reflected in the post-1970s phase of women's resistance, especially in South Asia, a phase which has been marked from earlier periods by some noteworthy features. First, there is a growing, explicit recognition of the specificity of women's oppression, beyond and in addition to that stemming from class, ethnicity, race, caste, etc., and reflected in their demands for direct (and not male-mediated) control over productive resources (especially land), control over sexual and reproductive choices, greater participation in political decision-making, a curbing of and protection against violence in the home, etc. Second there is a particular concern with the cultural and ideological construction of gender, manifest in feminist critiques of existing modern media, literature and text books; in attempts at reinterpreting religious texts and myths; and in interventions in the formal and informal educational system to raise gender consciousness through the use of both modern media and traditional cultural forms. Third, there is an experimentation with alternative organisational structures that enable relatively non-hierarchical, collective and participative functioning and decision-making. Fourth, of particular significance is an emerging recognition among many that the struggle against patriarchy cannot be waged in isolation from the struggles on many other fronts, including those for secularism, democratic rights, and alternative directions in development that are environmentally sustainable, distributionally egalitarian and politically participative. Some manifestations of this recognition are the attempts by many women's groups to take up general developmental and political issues and to link up with other progressive groups to provide a wider-ranging critique of the system and a broader base for agitation. In India, for instance, several (especially left-oriented) women's groups have participated actively in campaigns relating to civil and democratic rights, environmental issues and communalism, and linked up with groups formed specifically around these concerns; in Pakistan, WAF is a significant element in the movement for the restoration of democracy; in Sri Lanka there are women's groups fighting for secularism in a society torn by ethnic strife; in Iran the underground struggle against gender discriminatory State injunctions are also linked to the wider struggle for human rights, and so on. Fifth, there is an increasing interaction between women's and other groups across Asia which has the potential for catalyzing the formation of regional pressure groups around common concerns.

However, in the course of these developments, several as yet inadequately explored questions have arisen as well. For instance, to what extent is a dialogue with the State possible? Demands by most women's and other non-governmental groups are often directed both at the State and against it. Can such groups participate in government policy-making forums or accept State funds without being coopted or controlled by the State? How can the participative and non-hierarchical character of collective functioning in small groups be maintained as organisations grow in size and locational spread? Most importantly, with the growing communalisation and repression of dissent by even democratically-elected governments, direct and violent confrontations of many such groups with the State are likely to become increasingly unavoidable—indeed are already on the increase. Yet none of the women's or other non-party groups have the strength to seriously challenge State power, except in localised pockets. Perforce, then, one needs to ask: what could be the future possibility and desirability of alliances between say left-leaning non-party groups and the left political parties? Or between such groups across Asia? And to what extent would the perspective of such a wide-based forum reflect feminist concerns?

REFERENCES

ALAVI, HAMZI: 'The State in Post-Colonial Societies: Pakistan and Bangladesh', *New Left Review*, No. 74, July-August, 1972.

BANERJEE, NIRMALA: 'Women and Industrialisation in Developing Countries', Occasional Paper No. 71, Centre for Studies in Social Sciences, Calcutta, 1985.

CHAN, CHEE KHOON & CHEE, HENG LENG: 'Singapore 1984: Breeding for Big Brother', in Chee Heng Leng and Chan Chee Khoon (eds.) *Designer Genes : IQ, Ideology and Biology*, Institute for Social Analysis (INSAN), Malaysia, 1984.

CHHACHHI, AMRITA: 'The State, Religious Fundamentalism and Violence Against Women', Public Lecture given at the Institute of Social Studies, The Hague, 1985; updated version, 1987.

DAS, S.K. & P.K. SARKAR: 'Case for Injectible Contraceptives?', *Economic and Political Weekly*, Vol. 20, No. 40, October 5, 1985.

DAVIN, DELIA: 'Gender and Population in the People's Republic of China', paper presented at the Development Studies Association Conference, U.K., 1985.

DIETRICH, GABRIELE: 'Women's Movement and Religion', *Economic and Political Weekly*, Vo. 21, No. 4, January 25, 1986.

ELSON, DIANE & RUTH PEARSON: 'The Subordination of Women and the Internationalisation of Factory Production', in Kate Young *et al.* (eds.) *Of Marriage and the Market: Subordination of Women in International Perspective*, U.K., CSE Books, 1981.

FOLBRE, NANCY: 'Household Production in the Philippines: A Neo-Classical Approach', *Economic Development and Cultural Change*, Vol. 32, No. 2, January 1984.

FOO, GILLIAN H.C. & LINDA Y.C. LIM: 'Poverty, Ideology and Women Export Factory Workers in Asia', forthcoming in Haleh Afshar and Bina Agarwal (eds.) *Women, Poverty and Ideology in Asia*, London, Macmillan, 1988.

ILO: 'Asian Women and New Jobs', in *Women at Work*, No. 1, Geneva, International Labour Organisation, 1984.

KARIM, WAZIR-JAHAN: 'The Status of Malay Women in Maiaysia: From Culture to Islam and Industrialisation', *The International Journal of Sociology of the Family*, Illinois, 1983.

MUMTAZ, KHAWAR & FARIDA SHAHEED: *Women of Pakistan: Two Steps Forward, One Step Back*? London, Zed Books, 1987.

ROSA, KUMUDINI: 'Problems Facing Organisations Working Within the Free Trade Zones', *Voice of Women*, No. 4, July 1982.

SANGARI, K. & S. VAID: 'Sati in Modern India : A Report', *Economic and Political Weekly*, Vol. 16, No. 31, August 1, 1981.

STIVENS, MAILA: 'The Fate of Women's Land Rights : Gender, Matriliny and Capitalism in Rembau, Negeri Sembilan, Malaysia', in Haleh Afshar (ed.) *Women, Work and Ideology in the Third World*, London and New York, Tavistock Publications, 1985.

TRIKHA, SUSHIL K.: 'A Study of Women's Employment in the Kandla Free Trade Zone', mimeo, Indian Council for Research on International Economic Relations, New Delhi, 1985.

Voice of Women: 'Women in Free Trade Zones', No. 4, July 1982.

BLUEPRINT FOR UNDERNOURISHMENT

The Mahaweli River Development Scheme in Sri Lanka

Joke Schrijvers

INTRODUCTION

Hunger is not only a matter of acute famine or protein-deficiency, but also of chronic undernutrition. The total number of undernourished is now estimated at between 450 million and 1.3 billion people (*UN World Food Council,* 1984:4), of whom around 55 million per year die as a result of hunger, a number equal to the total number of victims of World War II. Daily, some 40,000 children are among these victims.

The majority of undernourished people, ironically, live in the rural areas where food is produced. The new settlements in the Mahaweli River Development Scheme in Sri Lanka, a large-scale irrigation project to increase the country's rice production, are no exception. Here, in the largest development project in Sri Lanka, the number of chronically undernourished people is more than five times as high as the average for the whole country (Siriwardena, 1981:56).

It is increasingly acknowledged that political factors of a national and international nature play an important role in the distribution of the world food supply, i.e. in the access to the food available by the citizens of each country (*UN World Food Council,* 1984:11). The most vulnerable people are those who have no land or insufficient land to produce adequate food, or who have an insufficient cash income to buy food. Female-headed households are mentioned as a high-risk category, together with the families of landless labourers, marginal peasants and poor fisherfolk. Moreover, we read that 'Women, whether in urban or rural areas, represent a disproportionally heavy share of the undernourished' (*UN World Food Council,* 1984:6).

Deficiencies of food do not chiefly affect rural people who live in remote areas that cannot be reached by development efforts. On the contrary, rural settlement schemes and rice development schemes in the most diverse regions have themselves been the cause of nutritional problems, for instance in Kenya (Hanger & Moris, 1973); in Gambia (Dey, 1981); in Papua New Guinea (Cox, 1984); and in Sri Lanka (Postel & Schrijvers, 1980:113). These reports all point to the deteriorating position of women in connection with food deficiencies. The example of the Mahaweli Scheme is therefore not at all exceptional.

The above facts suggest that increasing undernutrition is due to macro-economic and political relations on the one hand, and to changes in the position of women on the other. Is there indeed a link between undernutrition, relations of production and gender relations? And if so, what does this tell us about planning?

This paper first discusses the use of sex-specific data in view of access to food. This is then related to changes in the relations of production between women and men. In addition, the case of the Mahaweli River Development Scheme in Sri Lanka, where undernutrition has become an acute problem, is presented.

REPRODUCTION, PRODUCTION, UNDERNUTRITION

Access to food

A quick review of the literature reveals that in statistics about malnutrition, undernutrition and death, rarely is a distinction made between boys and girls, men and women. As a rule, in the field of health and nutrition women are mentioned as a separate category only in their role as mothers. A Dutch authority on health care in Third World countries, for instance, noting that one half of people born alive in these countries die before the fifth year as a result of nutritional deficiencies, states that 'many of these deaths would have been prevented if the Mother (capital in the original) could have spent more attention on the new baby' (van Amelsvoort 1979 : 27; *transl.* J.S.). Mothers could do this if their own health condition were better. By spacing births, the health conditions of both mother and child are influenced positively, and, moreover, 'the woman can make herself more productive in agriculture and trade; has more time for bringing up her children and for her own development' (van Amelsvoort 1979 : 27; *transl.* J.S.).

It seems to be internationally accepted that the issue of malnutrition and death as a result, particularly of babies and infants, is generally connected with the health condition of women as mothers:

> Maternal malnutrition not only represents a drain on the woman herself but also significantly increases the risk that the baby will have a low birthweight, which limits the infant's chance of survival and its potential for healthy growth and development (WHO, 1980:9).

Experts from the The Third World also emphasise the importance of the health condition of mothers. A special issue on food in the *Economic Review* of Sri Lanka, for instance, contains the following statement:

> About a million children in Sri Lanka are said to be suffering from various degrees of protein-calorie malnutrition .... In a large number of these, the nutritional deficiencies can be traced to pregnant mothers and thereafter to lactating mothers (*Economic Review,* 1976b:7).

Programmes for improving the health of mothers, i.e. of all women between 15 and 45, would require knowledge about the existing situation. In other words, sex-specific data and figures must be a precondition for making such programmes really effective.

An expert of Indonesian origin, Kusin, makes a very explicit connection between the position of women and undernutrition. Not only do pregnant and nursing mothers have an extra need for high-quality food, which is scarce for everybody, but of the food available they get the least, quantitatively as well as qualitatively. According to her, the relations between the sexes are responsible for the fact that women and infants become victims of undernourishment: 'Socio-culturally, men always enjoy preferential treatment: they get the best food and the biggest share' (Kusin

1982: 351; *transl.* J.S.). Further research will need to prove whether the generalisation 'always' is correct. What is important here is the indication that the distribution of the available food is not only determined by the international and national power relations, but also by the power relations between the sexes at the level of the household: those having the highest status and power get more food, quantitatively as well as qualitatively. Kusin argues that these power relations within the family are often supported and legitimated by food taboos (with regard to meat, fish and eggs) concerning women, particularly during vulnerable periods like pregnancy and lactation. Other sources also point at the effects of such food taboos (see e.g. WHO, 1980:9; Postel and Schrijvers, 1980:46).

The conclusion seems to be justified, then, that the concept of the 'household', or the 'household group', which is often used as the smallest unit of analysis, obscures problems of this nature (*cf.* Thomas-Lycklama à Nijeholt 1980b:76). The concept refers to a mutually dependent but homogeneous group which satisfies material and immaterial human needs. The underlying assumption of harmonious relations hides the fact that households consist of individuals who have *unequal power* (men, women and children).

The inadequacy of considering the household group as a homogeneous unit is not only evident from food taboos, but also from other expressions of the unequal power of men and women. In many countries it is for instance customary for women to eat last, only after serving husbands, other male members of the household, and children. 'And if, very rarely, we get fish, only the head is left for me . . .', a village woman from Sri Lanka explained laughingly to me. Another woman in Sri Lanka, who had just given birth and was afraid of not having enough milk told me (not laughingly but in tears):

> I bought *lula* (a variety of fish) from the money I earned myself, because it is good for breastmilk. When I had just prepared it my brother entered. He smelt the fish and wanted me to dish up food. When I told him that it was *my* fish and that I needed it myself to have enough milk for the baby he got terribly angry. He grabbed the pot and threw all the fish to the dogs . . . .

This gives some indications of *why* in poor circumstances women, even more than men, are in danger of becoming the victims of undernourishment.

Production of food

Of equal importance as the reproductive tasks of women in connection with the daily meal are their *productive* roles: who are the ones actually working for a livelihood and how do these facts relate to the issue of poverty and undernutrition?

At a rough estimate, in more than one-third of the rural households, a woman is, in fact, the main or the only, breadwinner, and this number is still rising (Buvinic 1978; Blumberg 1981:41). The implications of this, in particular with regard to policy, are discussed by Postel:

> Estimations vary from 25 to 40 per cent of all households in the world with extremes in parts of Latin America, and high frequencies for the landless and the urban poor. . . . We also have to bear in mind that within the category of female breadwinners strong fluctuations occur; any woman can at any moment come to belong to it or drop out of it. Therefore, there is a high chance for women to have to provide for their own livelihood at least part of their lives, a chance of about one to two (Postel 1983:554; *transl.* J.S.).

What are the impediments for women to earn a livelihood for themselves, their children and other dependents? Statistics about registered male and female labour highlight that on an average, women's wages are 25 per cent lower than men's; in some countries more than 50 per cent (Boesveld 1985). These figures are particularly alarming in that, being breadwinners, the position of women in the labour market is literally of life importance, to themselves, their (future) children and all others who depend on their income. However, only a minority of women earn their livelihood with registered wage labour. Poor women in cities try to earn their daily meals in the informal sector, doing home labour, working in retail trades, or in prostitution. In the rural areas they work long hours in agriculture. This labour is however hardly reflected in statistics, as it counts as unpaid family labour, or consists of subsistence or seasonal day-wage labour.

According to estimates of the ESCAP and the ECA, women in

Asia and Africa do 60-80 per cent of the agricultural work. The ECA gives a figure of 40 for Latin America (UN 1978:5).[1] These figures do not reflect the many female activities falling completely beyond the money economy, which are necessary to transform agricultural produce into edible food: conserving, storing and processing; providing water and fuel; preparing meals. In the agricultural season, working days of 14 to 16 hours are not unusual (Palmer 1977:99; Rogers 1980:155-166). My own observation in the North Central Province of Sri Lanka confirm these figures; about 80 per cent of the cultivation on the swiddens is done by women, while men take a greater part in paddy cultivation. This means that at least half of the total work in agriculture is by the women. In the agricultural season, working days of 16 hours for women are the norm.

This overburdening is increasing rather than decreasing (*cf.* Palmer 1977: 100-102). The 'modernization' of agriculture has meant that the best agricultural land has been reserved for cash crops. The production of these cash crops falls under the control of men who are considered the breadwinners by governments and development experts. Women remain responsible for producing the daily meals in the subsistence sector, which is being marginalized to the most extreme 'periphery'. Boulding calls women who work in subsistence agriculture 'the fifth world'. (quoted in Blumberg, 1981:31;). Whether paid or un(der)paid, these women also have to participate in the production of cash crops that are sold on the market by men. The poorer the household, the more crucial is the labour of women, as producers of their own food and as cheap labourers. As already shown, the poorer the people, the higher the chance that women have to earn their own and their children's livelihood at the margins of society, without any contribution from men.

Poverty and undernourishment are directly connected to the relations of production between men and women. Women are increasingly cut off from the main means of production whereas they are the ones responsible for the survival of their children and other dependent family members. In spite of this (and during

[1] ESCAP: Economic and Social Commission for Asia and the Pacific
ECA: Economic Commission for Africa
ECLA: Economic Commission for Latin America

the past ten years it has been brought to the attention of policy makers and development experts from various sides and in diverse ways), the model of the 'male breadwinner-and-his-housewife' continues to be exported to the countries of the Third World (see e.g. Rogers, 1980; Harris 1981; *Advies Vrouwen en Ontwikkelingslanden,* 1980). The ideal of the nineteenth century European family is implemented with the support of the national elite in countries dependent on 'development aid' (Postel 1983: 551).

The African scholar Muntemba (1982:46) convincingly argues that researchers and policy-makers cannot afford any longer to put aside the women's question, particularly in the light of the world hunger issue. Analysing the history of Zambia she shows how, since the colonial period, the capacity of women to provide for their children, other members of the household and themselves has declined. The commercialization of agriculture, encouraged by the (colonial) government has removed both the land and the labour power of women from the subsistence sector in which food is grown for the family. Locally, this has resulted in food shortages: in the north-western province of Zambia the yield of cassava and groundnuts (typical women's crops) has sharply declined. The income of the cash crops is controlled by men, who do not spend the money on the necessities of life. Women are thus forced to sell an ever greater part of the poor yield of their food crops in order to survive in the money economy. And so the vicious circle closes, in which the producers of the daily food are the ones who suffer most from hunger.

The question, therefore, is: What then? Muntemba's answer is that alternative development strategies first of all have to be directed at women: 'It is imperative to consider women not because they are women but because, as we hope we have shown, they are central to food strategies' (Muntemba 1982:48). Women's control of land, of the productive forces, of their labour and the product of that labour, according to Muntemba, must be viewed as the most urgent priority. In short, her plea is for a food strategy directed at women's *autonomy*. But such a strategy from above is not enough, she says. Peasant women have to participate in the political machinery to implement these priorities, and they 'must be conscientized to challenge the sexual division of labour which subjects their labour to men'

(Muntemba, 1982:48).

This is a far-reaching recommendation: the implementation would transform women into a rather militant key target group of development planning. It would do away with the 'soft' programmes to erase malnutrition through 'nutritional education' for mothers, and introduce a completely new development strategy primarily dealing with the production and reproduction of women. And this at a time when we are still trying to overcome the agitation raised by the requests of Third World and western women for some special attention to women in development policy.

Poverty and undernourishment are related to both relations of production and gender. An example of the practical consequences of this theoretical insight is given by the Mahaweli River Development Scheme. Similar blueprints for large-scale irrigation schemes exist the world over.

THE MAHAWELI RIVER DEVELOPMENT SCHEME

Chronic undernutrition

The Mahaweli River Development Scheme is situated in the North Central and North Western parts of the dry zone of Sri Lanka. It is the largest and most costly development project in this country, and also the largest *river basin scheme* in South Asia. According to the plans, extensive parts of the dry zone have to be irrigated with water from the Mahaweli, Sri Lanka's major river. It implies the (re)settlement of thousands of farmers' families who have to run their farms according to instructions from the government.

Since the planning of this project at the end of the '60s, increased food production has been emphasized as the main target with the aim of Sri Lanka becoming self-sufficient, at least in rice. However, ten years since the first construction was started in the so-called H-area,[2] it is precisely this region which is recorded as having the highest percentage of chronic undernourishment in the whole of Sri Lanka: 38:5 per cent as against

[2] I carried out research in Sri Lanka, in 1977-1978, in the H-area of theMahaweli Scheme and in a *purana* (traditional) village in the North Central Province.

the national average of 6.6 per cent (Siriwardena, 1981:56).

In recent years, the nutrition condition of pre-school children in general has seriously deteriorated in Sri Lanka. The Sri Lankan economist, Jayantha, relates this to the abolition of food subsidies, a measure conditioned by the International Monetary Fund for obtaining foreign loans to finance the 'public investment programme' that was started aftér the change of government in 1977. The food subsidies were replaced by food stamps for the poor. Before that

> the free rice and commodities were collected by the mother, and thereby prepared for the entire household including the young children. The food stamp scheme means that this food is no longer available in kind. Food stamps may be used for the purchase of food, but they may just as well be resold on the black market, and the proceeds used to purchase alcohol, tobacco or whatever. As the father collects the food stamps, this is what generally happens. The needy family therefore does not get the same sort of nutritional quota it received in the food subsidy era. This has been further exacerbated by the rapid price inflation since 1979 (Jayantha, 1983:23).

But why is chronic undernutrition highest in the region most influenced by planned development?

Rice crop, macro and micro

Self-sufficiency in rice for Sri Lanka would have lessened the dependence on costly food imports—a target of the highest importance in view of the country's negative balance of payments. Other goals included creating employment, and self-sufficiency in energy (by the generation of electricity by means of the canalized water) which would terminate the country's dependence on the increasingly costly import of oil.

In spite of the high expectations, self-sufficiency in rice has not yet been reached. In 1982, rice still had to be imported at a cost of Rs. 925 million (*Sri Lanka Socio-Economic Data*, 1983). The cost of the implementation of the total project after 1977 was estimated at between Rs.25,000 million—Rs.30,000 million (i.e. US $ 2,907-3,488 million) and had to be fully covered by foreign loans (Ponnambalam, 1981: 156). These loans, mainly from the International Monetary Fund and the World Bank, were provided with conditions. The stipulated measures entailed a 100 per cent devaluation of the rupee; 40 per cent inflation; 80 per cent price increases for the necessities of life, and abolition of food subsidies. According to the original plans, the implementation of the total project would take thirty years, spread over three stages. The costs of the second and third stages would be covered by the output of the first stage. The government's decision in 1977 to speed up the implementation to only six years created, among other things, the need for four times the amount of foreign capital originally estimated, and thus a highly increased dependence on foreign powers.

A rapidly worsening nutrition condition was one of the negative consequences. The record rice crop of 1978 in the Mahaweli H-area did not improve the food condition of the farmers' families. The agricultural credits provided to the farmers in that year were six times higher than in 1976, and only 20 per cent were repaid. These loans were not used for productive aims, but for buying food.[3]

Since 1977, rice has more than doubled in price. Many therefore have been forced to replace daily rice regularly with commercial white bread, or wheat flour *roti*, the home-made bread. Those who have least access to cash income, for instance the small farmers, find it increasingly difficult to make ends meet. This applies to a high degree to new settlers in the Mahaweli Scheme. Interviews with inhabitants of a hamlet in the H-area in 1978, showed that women felt the quality of their lives to have deteriorated since they came to live in the colony a few years before. Even if their families had been landless before, the idea of now belonging to the landowning class was of little comfort: the two and a half acres of land allocated to each head of family for the majority of settlers has not yielded enough to live on so far. According to other research in the same area, 97 per cent of the settlers could not produce enough to cover the necessary agricultural inputs plus the families' needs for consumption; 75 per cent did not even earn enough for their consumption (Siriwardena, 1981:54).

Debts and undernourishment, therefore, have been the result for many. The women attributed the nutritional shortcomings in the first place to the fact that they were unable to grow their own

[3] Personal communication from S.S.A.L. Siriwardena.

food crops in the settlement. The land had been allocated for producing cash crops, and the half-acre compound around the house was hardly big enough for a latrine and some fruit trees. According to all, the diet had severely worsened since living in the colony. Mothers added that their pre-school children were continuously ill: 'We don't have money, we cannot grow food for our families, the water is polluted by agricultural chemicals, the babies and myself are all the time ill and there is not even a doctor here.' The women did not understand how the *loku mahatturu*, the big gentlemen, had been induced to plan the colony like this. 'We get crazy here', some said; 'there is nobody here' (i.e. no relatives); 'we do not live here as human beings but as wild animals'. They could not cope with the problems of loneliness and poverty, and even less with the feelings of shame and loss of dignity. How had the 'big gentlemen' planned all this, then?

Project plan

The history of Sri Lanka's colonisation schemes goes back to the times of the ancient kings, some 2000 years ago. Even then the water of the Mahaweli was used to irrigate part of the dry zone for the production of wet rice. During this century, a large-scale colonisation policy was implemented with renewed efforts, first by the British colonial government, and later by the successive governments of Sri Lanka. This policy was regarded as a means both to increase production and to cope with the increasing dissatisfaction of the landless poor: 'By giving peasants a small piece of land two needs were met: increased rice production and political control (Dunham 1982:56). It is against this background that the planning of the Mahaweli project has to be viewed. What is new is the tremendous size and cost of the enterprise.

According to a Master Plan of 1968 (based on a survey by the UNDP/FAO), Mahaweli water would be used for irrigation and energy purposes by the construction of a huge dam. Through a tunnel, water reservoirs (tanks) and irrigation channels, part of the river which rises in the rainy wet zone was directed towards the dry zone in the North Central and Western parts of Sri Lanka.

The plan envisaged that the Mahaweli water would irrigate 645,000 acres (i.e. 39 per cent of Sri Lanka's total land area;

Mendis 1973: *vii*). To undertake the new rice production, 1.5 million people would be settled in the newly opened-up area. The productive unit was the small, nuclear family, headed by the farmer who was provided with 2.5 acres of irrigable paddy land and a half-acre homestead. The farmer was expected to develop this as a commercial enterprise, growing rice and other cash crops under the direction of the government. To support and to check the farmer, both technical provisions and an extensive administrative apparatus were established (one official to 18 settlers; see Siriwardena 1983a) in which agricultural extension, credit facilities, marketing and the formation of community development societies were included.

About 60-70 per cent of the colonists are original inhabitants of the area who, as a result of the re-organisation were first driven from their land but later given priority in the allocation of land plots. These original inhabitants were cultivators before, so how did they survive in this dry zone before the Mahaweli project was implemented?

The original situation

From early times, the population of the dry zone had to cope with a highly precarious climate, making agriculture an uncertain means of existence. People survived through a combination of two types of agriculture with different technologies and social organisation: slash and burn or swidden (*chenna*) cultivation in which technology is simple and there is little need for strictly organised cooperation; and paddy cultivation with the aid of rain-fed reservoirs characterised by sophisticated technology and a high degree of cooperation. Outside the project area, these two forms of cultivation continue to be practiced jointly in the dry zone.

In a situation of irregular and insufficient rainfall, paddy cultivation undertaken with the aid of rainwater is a precarious business, especially in villages where the tank has a very small catchment area. In about three in five seasons the rice crop is a failure due to lack of rainfall (Brow, 1978:98). In contrast *kurakkan* (finger millet)—the principal foodcrop of *chenna*—is much more adaptable to fluctuations of rainfall, it can be stored for long periods (upto ten years), and because of its high nutritional value is most useful as a reserve against famine (Ohrling, 1977:110-111). In addition, *chenna* allowed for the cultivation of a variety of crops. Hence, the traditional diet of the villagers practicing both types of cultivation was varied—based on *kurakkan* and rice, various other grains and pulses, vegetables and wild leaves cooked with coconut, spices and chillies, fruit, tank and salt fish, game and milk.

The sexual division of labour is also different between *chenna* and paddy. In *chenna* cultivation, apart from the initial clearing of jungle and the watching at night which is done by the men, and the reaping of millet exclusively by the women,[4] all other activities can be carried out by either sex. In practice, however, women usually play the greater part, cultivating not only millet but various other grains, pulses and vegetables. This is partly due to the fact that when rainfall is sufficient, the preparation of the paddy fields requires the man's full-time attention during the same period (Kloos, 1981:5). From September to February and again from April to June, the women's work on the *chenna* entails the cutting and burning of old branches and twigs, the removal of the small stubs and the collection of firewood; they sow, plant, weed, keep watch during the day, and harvest. In contrast, tasks in paddy cultivation, with the exception of harvesting and transplanting (which is a modern method), are dominated by men. Children help during the peak seasons in both cases.

Also, in both cases, the production of edible food requires much additional work after harvesting: threshing, winnowing, drying, parboiling, pounding, grinding and finally cooking, for which water and firewood have to be fetched. Those tasks are also the women's responsibility and are done manually, with the exception of threshing, for which buffaloes are used.

Nowadays, the *chennas* are primarily used for the cultivation of cash crops like chilly, cowpea, soya, green gram, mustard and gingelly. This is encouraged by agricultural extension, and it is also one of the ways to survive in today's money economy. However, for their own use, the women continue to grow food crops as well, such as millet, highland rice, maize, cassava and

[4] Millet (*kurakkan;* finger-millet) is cultivated by women exclusively; a man reaping millet would be considered ridiculous.

vegetables. The millet is kept by the women as a foodstock and 'savings-bank': every time they are in urgent need of money they sell small quantities. Moreover, to supplement their diet they collect wild fruits, plants and leaves—important sources of vitamins, minerals and protein.

However, increasing poverty, with the accompanying sales of paddy land, have forced more and more women and men to earn additional income as casual labourers for the local elite. And although the *chennas* are out in the forest and shrub-land which is Crownland (therefore, not private property), those who work as casual labourers often have no time left to cultivate a *chenna* of their own; they have to buy all their food. It is this category of people that shows signs of increasing undernourishment. But, although the nutritional value of their diet (and to a lesser degree of the diet of the small farmers) has declined rapidly during the last decades, their situation is less alarming than that of the settlers in the Mahaweli Scheme. There, as shown, about one-third of the population is suffering from chronic undernutrition, whereas for the districts directly bordering the H-area of the Mahaweli Scheme the figures are between 2.6 per cent (Kurunegala), 4.0 per cent (Puttalam), and 4.3 per cent (Vavuniya; see Sirwardena, 1981:56). The figure for Anuradhapura District, immediately east of the project area, is not given, but there is no reason to assume that it would vary significantly.[5]

Relations of production in the Mahaweli Scheme

The above facts clearly establish why the vast majority of the pioneers in the new settlement of the Mahaweli H-area were dissatisfied with their existence. The circumstances were completely different from those expected. Both men and women shared this opinion, and both affirmed that women had to bear the heaviest burden of the new existence. They had to take care of the daily meal, the household and the children who were frequently ill, while basic facilities such as schools and medical care were still lacking, at least for the first few years after settlement. Moreover, all women who did not have to look after a baby themselves worked as hard in the paddy fields as the men.

5 The *purana* village where I carried out research is situated in Anuradhapura District.

Contrary to the official project ideology, which emphasises equality of position and opportunity for all, it was perfectly clear that important economic differences were emerging. Effective cultivation depends on good quality land, sufficient water, realistic advice, credit facilities and good relations. Differential access to these resources had, within a few years led to an economic differentiation that will most likely become a structural one. Although the lease, mortgage or sale of allocated land is not officially allowed, leasing and mortgaging are normal practices. Those farmers who fail to become entrepreneurs have their land illegally controlled by the new elite, and subsequently hire themselves out to them as casual labourers. 'Thus not only the allotments but even the labour power of the settlers are used for cultivation of the land by a minority who could afford to do so' (Siriwardena, 1981: 54). Together with the 'squatters', the illegal inhabitants of the project area (i.e. former peasants to whom no land was allocated, and newcomers looking for work), and the future landless belonging to the next generation of settler families, the failing farmers form the labour supply needed by the successful entrepreneurs.

This class formation, together with growing inequality between the sexes, finds its basis in the project plans and implementation. First of all, unequal property relations were created between women and men, contrary to the traditional Sinhalese inheritance rules which prescribe that sons and daughters inherit equal shares of paddy land, cattle and other properties. Special legislation for the Mahaweli Project ensures that only one heir be appointed—to counteract fragmentation of land. As paddy cultivation is traditionally considered the responsibility of men, one of the sons is usually appointed heir. To avoid or postpone quarrels between sons, the wife's name is often mentioned as heir, until after the landowner is sure about which one of the sons will be the most suitable successor. This habit of naming the wife first does not have any consequences for the women regarding land rights: the owner has the right to change the name himself any time and if the marriage is not officially registered (as is often the case), the wife can never be the legal heir (*cf.* Farmer, 1957: 290).

Men are the new owners of the land; indeed, the *first* allocations of land in the Mahaweli Scheme predominantly favoured male colonists, although this preference was nowhere laid down officially in the regulations or selection criteria. In the settlement where I carried out in-depth research, it appeared that in 96 of the 112 household groups (82 per cent) the plots of land were allocated to a male. Of the 16 females who had been allocated land only two lived in the project area; they were a widow and a separated woman, who had settled with their children, and both managed their own farms (see also Lund, 1978:45).

Given the traditional division of labour between the sexes, according to which men are responsible for paddy cultivation, and the age-old ideal of the male head of family, it is not surprising that, in practice, males were favoured in the selection of new landowners. This was strengthened by the formulation of the criteria for selection in the various reports by foreign experts. The western ideology, described above as the 'male-bread-winner-cum-housewife', is reflected clearly by these criteria. Looking for instance at the feasibility study of 1972 drafted by a French firm on the settlement policy for the second stage of the project (this is the H-area), the ideal pioneer (called the 'paradigmatic settler') comes clearly to the fore as a young man gifted with entrepreneurial qualities. Experience has taught us, the report says, 'that good farming (with, as a result, high production) does not as a rule go with the selection of settlers according to the criteria of landlessness and big families, used in older colonisation schemes. 'Such a selection contributed to the crowding of colonisation schemes with a very large number of mediocre farmers' (*Sogreah Report,* 1972:157). Not only are the landless put aside in this recommendation, but women, too seem to have little chance of getting a piece of land. The *ideal settler* is

> . . .one who is not inhibited by a long practice of submissive behaviour towards officials and who is capable of dealing with them on equal terms ... one with initiative, enthusiasm and a pioneer spirit ... who is an experienced farmer ... able to participate in the management of his community .... He should live in the project area *with his family* (*Sogreah Report,* 1972: 157-160; italics J.S.).

That land has been allocated to female settlers (in about 12-18 per cent of the cases)[6] in spite of this planning may be explained as a continuation of the traditional rights of women to land (*cf.* Rogers, 1980: 149). However, my research data show that a woman only applied for land if there was a minimal chance for male members of her family to obtain a plot (Schrijvers, forthcoming). Whatever the causes, a majority of women in the scheme are cut off from the main means of production: land. Moreover, only a minority of those who own land in the project area appear to live in the colony themselves. They thus have no control over it whatsoever.

Ownership and control of land is an important criterion for determining the relations of production. *Control of one's own labour and the products thereof* is a second criterion. Just like other projects financed by the World Bank and similar organisations, the Mahaweli project is based upon the small nuclear family in which the man is head, breadwinner and owner of the allocated land. Only those farmers who can function as small entrepreneurs are successful in this framework. They control the unpaid labour of their wives and children. This enables them to accumulate the necessary capital without investment in hired labour or machines. The women do not have a place in the project as independent producers; they do not control the produce of their labour; and in practice they do not have access to the various services of agricultural extension, credit, marketing and community development, all directed at male breadwinners. According to the new ideology that goes with this mode of production, it is modern for a man to have a housewife 'who does not work'. Those who can afford it financially, replace the unpaid labour of women with hired labour if there is sufficient labour supply, or with farm machinery. This raises the status of the head of the family. As one of the farmers explained to me: 'Because we don't have enough labourers here, we have to do the work with women.' A little embarrassed by his explanation, he hastened to add that as soon as it was possible his wife would occupy herself with the home and children only. Whether his ideal will ever be attained is questionable. After some years,

[6] My own research data show 18 per cent of female land-ownership in one settlement of the H-area. S.S.A.L. Siriwardena found 12 per cent female land-ownership (personal communication).

structural differences emerge between the few 'who make it' and the majority who fail as small entrepreneurs. This majority remains poor, or becomes even poorer. And women in the project area cannot any longer ease poverty by growing food themselves. There are no *chenna* anymore, the compounds are too small. Outside agriculture there is no employment, and as far as there is a demand for female agricultural labour it is highly seasonal and underpaid: a woman's pay as a day-labourer is only half to two-thirds that of a male. The ideology of the male breadwinner helps to rationalise the differences here also: 'Women work less hard than men; they only do it for a few extra earnings, and they have to cook for their husbands and children first, haven't they?' Such views are so dominant that they seem to blur observed reality. Even when confronted with contrasting facts during discussions, male farmers found it difficult to acknowledge that female agricultural labourers worked as many hours as males, and very often did exactly the same work. Although women in general expressed the same views, they had less trouble than men in seeing these contradictions.

The ideology of the housewife

The ideology of the breadwinner-cum-housewife is proclaimed, too, by all those who are responsible for the implementation of the planned policy at the micro-level. During the research, when I expressed concern to locally employed officials about the conditions of the settlers, and also discussed the marginal position of women, they showed much goodwill but appeared to be rather ignorant of the traditional contribution of women in agriculture. This urbanized bureaucracy voiced a theory in which the real historical process had been reversed: 'Our village women here in Sri Lanka are not yet as modern as you western women; they still have to get used to coming out of their homes, not to mention doing cultivation themselves.' An important export product of 'development' policy had apparently found a ready market! This ideology however, hides the fact that only the wives of the most successful producers—a small elite—are housewives in reality. All the other women are doing the double work of housewives and agricultural labourers: unpaid by their husbands, and underpaid by other men. This 'family labour' of women is increasing, because the economic conditions are worsening (Vidanapathirana, 1983:25).

The process of *housewifisation* (Maria Mies 1982: 180), so directly connected with planned production, was further stimulated by the Mahaweli Authority (the body in charge of the project implementation) by the establishment, in 1981, of a 'Home Development Centre'. Here the women settlers are supposed to learn 'in short courses' how to become better farm housewives. The training programme contains 'health, nutrition, sanitation, poultry, home-gardening and needlework' (with special emphasis on macrame). All this '. . .to learn the basic technical concepts required for normal healthy growth and living. The Home Development Centre meets this end.' (Mahaweli Authority of Sri Lanka, 1981:3; see also Mahaweli Authority of Sri Lanka, 1983.) The concern for the health, nutrition and hygiene of the inhabitants of the Mahaweli Scheme is increasing, since a survey of the Ministry of Plan Implementation in 1980 revealed alarming figures on undernutrition in the Mahaweli H-area. Consequently, to improve the health condition of children, eight day-care centres were established under the auspices of UNICEF, where children between the ages of two and five could benefit from free health care, Thriposha (a soya product rich in protein), and training in hygiene. However, research has made clear that the children taken to these centres all belonged to the higher income families, those of traders and more affluent farmers. An important reason for this was the fact that the children were expected to bring a meal from home and to be dressed properly. The poorer mothers did not have the means for this, and had, moreover, no opportunity in between all their other duties to bring and fetch their children together with a good homemade lunch. Siriwardena concludes therefore:

> The day-care centres . . . have reached only those already in control of economic and social power in the settlement village. The fundamental problem appears to lie in the diagnosis which focusses on the lack of material needs, while what appears crucial is that the undernourished are undernourished because they are prevented from achieving the power to secure the things that could nourish them (Siriwardena, 1983b: 29).

CONCLUSION

The facts presented in this paper show that sex-specific data as well as information regarding the power relations between the sexes are needed to understand the problem of undernourishment. This is all the more urgent for taking action against malnutrition. It is important to emphasise that the undernourished do not suffer from a mere lack of material things and training, but primarily from the *power to secure the things that could nourish them*. Indeed, within this category of people women have the most marginal position, and this itself is a factor *causing* undernutrition.

The chronic undernutrition in the Mahaweli H-area is a direct result of planning that cuts women off from their productive resources. It is of primary importance that women who have to provide the daily food to children and other members of the family have the means themselves to obtain sufficient food. This would imply power within the household group, in the reproductive sphere, but also power with regard to the means of production. In the present situation, women cannot be sure that the income from male breadwinners, if any, will be spent on daily food. Research shows that only 35 per cent of the net income of the male farmer (after debts were paid off) benefited the rest of the household.[7] The concept of household as the smallest unit of analysis obscures intra-household inequalities which lead to undernutrition.

The example of the Mahaweli Scheme illustrates why a better training of mothers in health, nutrition, hygiene and family planning, is deficient as a means of fighting undernourishment. Mothers do not primarily need training, but power for autonomous access to food. It is precisely this autonomy that is systematically undermined by 'development' planning such as the Mahaweli Scheme.

REFERENCES

ADVIES VROUWEN IN ONTWIKKELINGSLANDEN: *Nationale Adviesraad voor Ontwikkelingssamenwerking,* 's-Gravenhage: Ministerie van Buitenlandse Zaken, 1980.

AMELSVOORT, V. VAN: *Gezondheidszorg Derde Wereld.* Leiden: Stafleu's

[7] Personal communication from S.S.A.L. Siriwardena.

Wetenschappelike Utigeversmaatschappij B.V., 1979.

BLUMBERG, RAY LESSER: 'Females, Farming and Food: Rural Development and Women's Participation in Agricultural Production Systems' in Barbara Lewis (ed.), *Invisible Farmers: Women and the Crisis in Agriculture.* pp. 24-103, Washington: Office of Women in Development, 1981.

BOESVELD, MARY: Vrouwenwereld: Een Beeld in Cijfers' in: Els Postel-Coster (red.), *Ongekende Wegen: Macht en Onmacht Van Vrouwen in Sri Lanka, Egypte en West-Afrika.* Leiden: D.S.W.O. Press, 1985.

BROERTJES, PIETER: De Paradox van Het Honger Probleem: 'De westerse landen moeten minder voedsel produceren' (interview with Prof. Dr.J. de Hoogh), *De Volkskrant,* Oct. 1983.

BROW, JAMES: *Vedda Villages of Anuradhapura: The Historical Anthropology of a Community in Sri Lanka,* Seattle: University of Washington Press, 1978.

BUVINIC, MAYRA, NADIA H. YOUSSEF & BARBARA VON ELM: *Women-headed Households: The Ignored Factor in Development Planning,* Report submitted to the Women in Development Office, AID, Washington D.C., 1978.

COX, ELISABETH: 'Women Oppressed and Women Organized in Planned Rural Settlement Schemes: The Gavien Settlement Scheme in Papua New Guinea. The Hague: Institute of Social Studies (M.A. thesis), 1984.

COX, PAUL: 'Who Controls the World Food System?' University of Wisconsin, Food/Climate Research Institute, 1974.

DEY, JENNY: 'Gambian Women: Unequal Partners in Rice Development Projects?' *Journal of Development Studies,* Vol. II: 109-122, 1981.

DULLEMEN, MAARTEN VAN: Voedsel is Handelswaar, Net Als Olie, interview with Susan George: Veodsel Als Wappen, in *De Groene Amsterdammer,* October 1982.

DUNHAM, DAVID: 'Politics and Land Settlement Schemes: The Case of Sri Lanka, in *Development and Change,* vol. 13: 43-61. London and Beverly Hills: Sage, 1982.

FARMER, B.H.: '*Pioneer Peasant Colonization: A Study in Asian Agrarian Problems,* Oxford: Oxford University Press, 1957.

HANGER, JANE & JON MORIS: 'Women and the Household Economy', in Robert Chambers and Jon Moris (eds.), *MWEA: An Irrigated Rice Settlement in Kenya,* Munchen: Weltforum Verlag, 1973, pp. 209-244.

HARRIS, OLIVIA: 'Households as Natural Units' in Kate Young *et al.,* (eds.), *Of Marriage and the Market : Women's Subordination in International Perspective,* London: CSE Books, 1981, pp. 47-68.

HEALTH AND THE STATUS OF WOMEN: Geneva, World Health Organization, Division of Family Health, 1980.

JAYANTHA, DILESH: 'Some Recent Trends in the Nutritional Status of Sri Lankan Pre-Schoolers (1975/76 to 1980/82)'. *Economic Review,* vol. 9, no.2, May 1983, Colombo: People's Bank Research Department, 1983.

KUSIN, J.A.: Voedingsproblematiek In Ontwikkelingslanden: Wat Doen Wij Er Ann? Landbouwkunding Tijdschrift/pt. 94, nr. 9: 349-353, 1983 Voeding in Ontwikkelingslanden, Enkele Dimensies Van Het Voedingsprobleem, in *Voeding, the Netherlands Journal of Nutrition,* jrg. 44, no. 6: 206-212, 1982-83.

LUND, RAGNHILD: 'A Survey on Women's Working and Living Conditions in a

Mahaveli Settlement Area With Special Emphasis on Household Budgets and Household Surplus.' Colombo: People's Bank Research Department, 1978.

MAHAVELI AUTHORITY OF SRI LANKA: *The Home Development Centre at Nochchiyagama, H5: Current Developments and Tentative Plans,* and *Home Development Centre: Objectives and Courses Offered,* Colombo: The Community Services and Project Development Section of the Sri Lanka Mahaveli Authority, 1981, 1983.

MIES, MARIA: *The Lace Makers of Narsapur: Indian Housewives Produce for the World Market.* London: Zed Press, 1982.

MONTAGU, ASHLEY: *The Natural Superiority of Women.* New York: Macmillan Publishing Co. Inc, 1978.

MUNTEMBA, SHIMWAANI: 'Women As Food Producers and Suppliers in the Twentieth Century. The Case of Zambia, in *Development Dialogue,* a *Journal of International Development Cooperation,* no. 1-2: 29-51. Uppsala: Dag Hammarskjold Foundation, 1982.

NUTRITION (cover story): *Economic Review,* vol. 1, no. 12. Colombo: People's Bank Research Department, 1976.

PALMER, INGRID: 'Rural Women and the Basic-Needs Approach to Development,' *International Labour Review,* vol. 115, no. 1, 1977.

PONNAMBALAM, SATCHI: *Dependent Capitalism in Crisis: The Sri Lankan Economy 1948-1980.* London: Zed Press, 1980.

POSTEL-COSTER, ELS: 'Misverstanden Rond De Kostwinner in Het ontwikkelingsbeleid,' *Internationale Spectator,* 549-555, September 1983.

POSTEL, ELS & JOKE SCHRIJVERS (eds.): 'A Woman's Mind is Longer Than a Kitchenspoon', Report on Women in Sri Lanka. Colombo/Leiden: Research Project' Women and Development, 1980.

ROGERS, BARBARA: *The Domestication of Women: Discrimination in Developing Societies,* London: Kogan Page, 1980.

SCHRIJVERS, JOKE: '*Manipulated Motherhood.* The Marginalisation of Peasant Women in the North Central Province of Sri Lanka,' in *Development and Change,* vol. 14: 185-209. London/Beverly Hills/New Delhi: Sage, 1983.

'Cultuur Als camouflage: Westerse Weerstanden Tegen Vrouwen Als Ontwikkelingsrelevant Onderwerp', in *Internationale Spectator,* 556-563, September 1983.

i.p. 'Planned Domestication: Women Settlers in the Mahaveli River Development Project, Sri Lanka.' Leiden: Research Centre Women and Development, 1983.

SIRIWARDENA, S.S.A.L.: 'Emerging Income Inequalities and Forms of Hidden Tenancy in the Mahaveli H Area.' Colombo: People's Bank Research Department, 1981.

'Smallholders in a Large Scale Irrigation Settlement in Sri Lanka: Some Experiences in the Mahaveli Irrigation Settlement Scheme.' Paper presented at the International Seminar on Incorporation and Rural Development, Colombo, 11th January, 1983.

'Rural Poor and Child Care Services in a Modern Irrigation Settlement' *Economic Review,* vol. 9, July/August, Colombo: People's Bank, 1983.

SOGREAH: '*Mahaveli Ganga Development Project 1, Feasibility Study of State II.* (Vol. VII:) *Settlement Planning and Development,'* Mahaveli Development

Board. Colombo, Sri Lanka — Sogreah, Grenoble, France, 1972.

SRI LANKA SOCIO-ECONOMIC DATA: Colombo, Statistics Department, Central Bank of Ceylon, 1983.

STATISTICS ON CHILDREN IN UNICEF COUNTRIES: 1984, Unicef, May 1984.

THE WORLD FOOD AND HUNGER PROBLEM: 'Changing Perspectives and Possibilities, 1974-1984.' United Nations World Food Council. WFC/6/1984.

THOMAS-LYCKLAMA A NIJEHOLT, GEERTJE: 'The Household, a Woman's Cage? A Policy Perspective.' in C. Presvelou and S. Spijkers-Zwart (eds.), *The Household, Women and Agricultural Development.* Wageningen: H. Veenman en Zonen B.V., 1980.

UNITED NATIONS: 'Effective Mobilization of Women in Development.' Report of the Secretary General, UN/A/33/238, 1978.

VIDANAPATHIRANA, UPALI: 'Some Issues in the Economics of Peasant Farming in the New Settlements: A Study of Two Villages in the Galnewa Area, in *Economic Review,* vol. 9, no. 6, September, Colombo: People's Bank, 1983.

PRIMARY BUT SUBORDINATED
Changing Class and Gender Relations in Rural Malaysia

Cecilia Ng and Maznah Mohamed

Introduction

This paper discusses the impact of agricultural development policies on class and gender relations in rural Malaysia. It is shown that capitalist penetration has resulted in the emergence of new forms of these relations, leading to the increased exploitation of rural women. Not only has woman's labour intensified, but her dual involvement in production and reproduction has ensured the survival of the peasant household while freeing (predominantly) male labour to the capitalist sector. At the same time this has also provided for the maintenance and reproduction of labour at no cost to capital.[1]

While the production-reproduction debate is still unresolved, we nonetheless adopt the concept of reproduction from Harris and Young (1981), as incorporating three aspects: social reproduction, reproduction of labour, and human or biological reproduction. Social reproduction is defined as the process by which the conditions which maintain a particular social system are recreated and perpetuated; the reproduction of labour means the care and socialisation of children and the maintenance of adult individuals who will fit into the social structure of society; human or biological reproduction includes not only bearing children, but also reproducing the relationships of marriage, kinship, fertility and sexuality. That male dominance is predicated

[1] This is also noted by Deere (1979) in the context of Latin America.

upon the control of female reproduction is one of the major themes underlying gender subordination (Beneria, 1979). We understand patriarchy as a system whereby social relations enable men to control women's productive and reproductive labour (Hartman, 1981). It has a material base in the economic realm (such as unequal gender control over the means of production) and expresses itself in the gender division of labour, be it in production or reproduction.

The nature of peripheral capitalist development in Malaysia has affected the existing gender division of labour in production whereby women are 'pushed' into the backward agricultural sector, while the men are provided with opportunities in the capitalist or State sector, where cash income is more accessible. Where rural women do engage in urban wage-work, gender inequalities in the labour market reinforce their subordination. In addition, rural women continue to bear the prime responsibility of reproduction. Thus the concept of the gender division of labour is used in our analysis to understand gender subordination, being defined as 'the system of allocation of agents to positions within the labour process on the basis of sex, and a system of exclusion of certain categories of agents from certain positions within social organisation on the basis of sex, and lastly a system of reinforcement of the social construction of gender' (Young, 1978:125).

Further, State intervention in the form of agricultural reforms and policies, with an emphasis on increased productivity, places landless and female-headed households at a disadvantage, as their agricultural contribution is often overlooked by the State. This problem is compounded by their lack of control over the means of production and their limited access to other productive resources. They are thus forced to sell their labour-power to ensure their own reproduction.

With the above framework in mind, this paper intends to examine the economic aspects of State agricultural policies in historical perspective, and their impact on the social and gender division of labour through the discussion of two case studies.[2]

[2] While unequal class and gender relations also operate at the political and ideological level, such discussion, while important, is beyond the scope of this paper. For further discussion see Ng Choon Sim (1985).

THE HISTORICAL SETTING

The pre-colonial era

The basic social unit of production in pre-colonial Malaya was the family, situated in clusters near rivers or in the interior, linked by jungle paths to the rivers. The division of labour by gender and age seemed to have been an important criterion for work and role differentiation in that society. While women bore the main responsibility for reproductive activities, they also contributed equally with the men to subsistence and petty commodity production, although peasant women specialised in certain tasks such as mat and handloom weaving. The economic contribution of women was highly appreciated and recognised in Malay peasant society. This was reflected in the customary *(adat)* law relating to land tenure. Land was freely available, and people enjoyed usufructury rights, that is, the right to use but not to own land in the modern sense. Here, women, as much as men, had the right to cultivate and possess land.

There were, however, at least two main sets of *adat* governing inheritance — the patrilineal *adat temenggung* and the matrilineal *adat perpatih.*[3] Under *adat temenggung* male and female children have equal inheritance rights to their parents' property, while under the *perpatih* tradition, all the inheritance would go to the female heirs, since ancestral property is vested in the female line. Upon divorce, women received an equal share of whatever property, including land, was acquired during marriage (Haji Mohtar bin H. Md. Dom, 1979).

The equality and high status accorded by *adat* to women in the sphere of production was tempered, however, by the more patriarchal interpretations of *fara'id,* the Islamic law of inheritance, under which the inheritance of female children is half that of the male children. If the wife survives her husband, she receives one-fourth of her husband's property if there are no children, and one-eighth if there are. On the other hand, a widower receives

[3] *Adat perpatih,* the matrilineal social organisation brought by the Minangkabau people of Sumatra, is presently practised in Negeri Sembilan, especially in Naning, Rembau and Sungai Ujong. The majority of the Malay population practise *adat temenggung,* a bilateral kinship system which confers equal landholding rights to men and women. Descent in terms of inheritance is, however, determined through the males.

one-half of his deceased wife's property (Ahmad, 1975).

However, it is important to note that peasant women's high status was largely limited to the economic sphere; in other aspects of gender relations, particularly at the political and ideological level, women were generally subordinate, suggesting that gender subordination existed even in pre-colonial Malay society.

The colonial era

The introduction of land and labour policies in the late nineteenth century significantly altered the lives of the men and women in the Malay Peninsula. For instance, the implementation of a new Torrens land tenure system in the 1880s eliminated usufructury rights, establishing an 'indisputable right of ownership to registered land through the issue of title certificates' (Jomo, 1977:147). All unused or uncultivated land became, *de facto,* State property. The institutionalisation of private property relations in land added a new factor to the existing tension between the *fara'id* and *adat* laws of inheritance. For example, it implied that inherited property could no longer automatically be divided equally between sons and daughters as could previously be done under *adat temenggung*. If no prior arrangements were made, land automatically became subject to *fara'id* law, in which the female received half of the male share of inherited property. While there have been no case studies undertaken, it seems that peasant women were affected more adversely than peasant men as, for example in terms of decreasing control and access to land and other productive resources. This is reflected in petitions written by or on behalf of women demanding their rights to land.

The introduction of cash cropping, especially rubber, was also to have far-reaching consequences on the status of rural women. The rapid adoption of rubber cultivation by the Malay peasantry meant the increasing penetration of capitalist forces into the economy. In the early stages of this new cash crop cultivation women seem to have remained in subsistence production, while peasant men had direct access to cash income, which became more important with the increasing commoditization of the economy.[4] The relative economic equality which men and

[4] Field research by Cecilia Ng in a village in Pahang revealed that many of the older women did not know how to tap rubber as they were forbidden to do so by their fathers or husbands.

women shared in pre-colonial times was gradually eroded by male dominance in the cash economy. The importance of money income cannot be underestimated, and this money was obtained mainly by men who worked as rubber smallholders, as wage labour in the capitalist estates, or as petty bureaucrats in the colonial sector, while women were apparently confined to the subsistence economy and to reproductive activities.[5]

The post-colonial era

The conditions of gender subordination did not substantially change during the post-colonial era; in fact, the marginalisation of peasant women became even more formalized with the active involvement of the State in rural production.

Malaysia's post-colonial agricultural policies were aimed chiefly at improving the agricultural productivity of the rural smallholding sector. Massive inputs, in terms of financial and technical aid, were made into such schemes as the Muda and Krian *padi* (paddy) irrigation projects which were largely funded by international aid. While this intervention was successful in increasing productivity, its long-term distributive effects were not taken into consideration. One of the most important failures of Malaysia's agricultural modernisation programme, or its 'green revolution', was the widening of the poor-rich gap (Cleaver, 1972; Pearse, 1980; Sundaram and Shaari, 1980; De Koninck, Gibbons and Hassan, 1980). The effects on peasant women have yet to be systematically documented.

The practical impact of Malaysia's agricultural policies on the position of women can best be discerned from the role that several agricultural development agencies played in the realisation of such policies. The setting up of various agencies to take care of agricultural programmes and specific crop production, like FELDA for land development, RISDA for rubber smallholders and MADA for *padi,*[6] were all responsible for promoting

[5] There were, of course, women who were expert traders, as can still be seen in Kelantan and Trengganu today.

[6] FELDA is the acronym for Federal Land Development Authority, RISDA for Rubber Industries Smallholders Development Authority, and MADA for the Muda Agricultural Development Authority.

a rural development ideology that was generally supportive of the more enterprising and landed peasants, while neglecting the role of women as full-time rural workers. The role of women in rural production has only been recognized insofar as they have indirectly contributed as wives to their peasant husbands (Afifudin and Norazizah, 1973).

The relegation of women's role to a secondary reproductive one has been further reinforced with the setting up of separate women's organisations within these rural agencies, in order to complement the main, or rather the male, organisation. For example, the Community Development Division of the Ministry of Agriculture specifically set up the Family Development Programme to create in the rural communities, 'ideal homes and families' (Ministry of Agriculture and Rural Development 1975:3). This programme is aimed at training women to be better housewives and mothers, to gain skills for increasing the family income and to be better equipped in home management. RISDA has also set up a separate women's organisation at the village level or the PWPK, while the PPPK (Village Level Rubber Smallholders Association) is *assumed* to be the main village body that takes care of the important functions of dealing directly with the produce and the producers. Within land development schemes that are administered by FELDA, there are also separate women's associations for 'wives of settlers' (Talib, 1984).

The misperception and non-recognition of women's vital contribution to agriculture is not only disadvantageous to women belonging to female-headed households, it also denies them their rightful access to the various kinds of benefits that come with government investments in rural development. For example, the natural tendency of government extension workers, who are almost always male, to interact with the male household members puts female heads of households in a disadvantageous position. Again, female farmers are normally dependent on their male relatives for taking care of official matters like land transfer and applying for technical and financial aid.

Other aspects of gender inequality have also been accentuated with agricultural modernisation, as described in the section below, based on two case studies — one in a *padi* community in Krian and the other in a mixed (rubber and *padi*) agricultural community in Kubang Pasu, Kedah.

VILLAGE CASE STUDIES

Production relations in Semanggol

The village of Semanggol in Krian District, Perak, is located in the south-eastern corner of the Krian *padi* irrigation scheme. Built in 1906, and considered one of the oldest irrigation schemes in Malaysia, it was brought under the Krian-Sungai Manik Integrated Agricultural Development Project (IADP) in 1979, and sponsored partly by the World Bank. The entire scheme covers 75,615 acres and serves a total of 24,496 families (Lim, 1976; Selvadurai, 1972).

The area under study covers 180 households with a total population of 910 people, of which 51 per cent are female and 49 per cent male. Of the sample households, 53 per cent are nuclear in structure and 31 per cent are female-headed. The female heads are either divorcees, widows, or women whose husbands are working in the capitalist or public sector and living away (mostly temporarily) from the village proper.

(a) Land relations and rural differentiation. The empirical data reveal that there exist socio-economic differences among the villages in Semanggol based on their access to land and the type of employment — and hence income — they obtain. Social differentiation has divided the villagers into three main socio-economic classes, namely the poor *(susah),* the moderate (*sederhana),* and the comfortable *(senang).* These groups also correspond roughly to local perceptions of where they are placed on the socio-economic ladder, (Syed Husin, 1975; Wong, 1983).

The *susah* households which form 64 per cent of total households consist of poor peasants who either own no land or insufficient land for household reproduction. Consequently, they either have to rent in extra land or are forced to undertake wage labour to supplement their inadequate farm income. In Semanggol, the men go out of the village for wage work while the women are usually seasonal rural workers, or if they are young, factory workers. There is also a substantial number of female-headed households in this category. These women take on the extra burden of rural wage work, family farm and reproductive work in the absence of the men.

The *sederhana* households, which constitute 28 per cent of the sample, have sufficient labour and land for their own reproduction, many of them devoting their time and energy to farm production. At the same time these owner-operators also have stable wage jobs in the capitalist or State sector or other semi-skilled occupations with steady returns. As such, it is access to alternative non-agrarian employment that has economically stabilized the *sederhana* households, and accorded them a higher status in the community.

Relative to the village economy, the *senang* households, eight per cent of the sample, are much better off than the *sederhana* and *susah*. This social class consists of rich peasants, shopkeepers and middle-level government salaried employees who can, and do, accumulate from their returns in agricultural production, profits from trade, and wages from the State. Most of the men do not work on the land; they either hire in labour, get the household women to do unpaid work on the land or supervise other female labour.

Table 1

GENDER OWNERSHIP OF PADI LAND (ACRES) BY CLASS, SEMANGGOL

Household	0	0.1-3	3.1-6	6.1-9	>9.1	*Total*	*Total Acr**	*Average Acr*
Susah								
Male	55	27	10	—	—	92	65.1	1.9
Female	73	27	7	1	—	108	75.7	2.1
Sederhana								
Male	22	12	11	—	—	45	72.4	3.1
Female	41	4	4	1	—	50	32.7	3.6
M & F	—	—	—	1	—	1	6.5	6.5
Senang								
Male	4	5	2	2	2	15	55.3	5
Female	14	1	—	—	—	15	1.3	1.3
Total	209	76	34	5	2	326	309	3.3

Total female ownership : 112.95 acres (36%)
Total male ownership : 196.05 acres (64%)
Total : 309.00 acres
*Acr : Acreage

Table 2

GENDER OWNERSHIP OF RUBBER LAND (ACRES) BY CLASS, SEMANGGOL

Household	0	0.1-3	3.1-6	6.1-9	>9.1	*Total*	*Total Acr**	*Average Acr*
Susah								
Male	83	4	1	—	—	88	11.3	2.4
Female	105	2	—	1	—	108	7	2.6
Sederhana								
Male	41	2	2	—	—	45	12.7	3.4
Female	49	1	—	—	—	50	0.5	0.5
Senang								
Male	11	—	4	—	—	15	15.5	4.1
Female	15	—	—	—	—	15	—	—
Total	304	6	10	1	—	321	51	2.6

Total male ownership : 39.5 acres (84%)
Total female ownership : 7.5 acres (16%)
Total : 47 acres
*Acr : Acreage

In terms of the ownership of *padi* and rubber land, Tables 1 and 2 indicate that land ownership is unequal not only across classes but also between sexes. More women than men across the three socio-economic classes do not own any land at all. Female ownership accounts for 36 per cent of the total *padi* land owned and 16 per cent of the total rubber land owned. For those who own land in the *susah* class, an almost equal number of men and women own an average of two acres. Most of the women who own land are widows who have inherited from their husbands. Land inheritance is noted to work in favour of the men who obtain bigger parcels of land compared to the women, this being true across all three socio-economic classes (Table 3).

The same pattern of gender inequalities in land ownership is repeated in the *sederhana* and *senang* households. In fact it becomes progressively unequal — ten females, as against 25 males, own land in the *sederhana* class, while for the *senang* class, only one woman had access to land, through inheritance. The men in the *sederhana* and *senang* classes, because of their access to cash income, are in a better position to acquire more land. As

Table 3

ACCESS TO LAND (ACRES) BY GENDER AND CLASS*

Class	*ALL*	*AVE ACR*	*CL*	*AVE ACR*	*BL*	*AVE ACR*	*RL*	*AVE ACR*	*SL*	*AVE ACR*	*ILS*	*AVE ACR*
Susah												
Male	17	1.95	—	—	8	3.23	48	2.09	1	.1	—	—
Female	23	1.32	—	—	6	2.38	10	2.11	—	—	10	3.93
Sederhana												
Male	12	3.09	—	—	13	4.2	27	2.8	—	—	—	—
Female	4	2.45	—	—	1	3.3	2	2.6	—	—	5	5.28
Senang												
Male	16	2.75	—	—	9	6.92	5	6.82	—	—	—	—
Female	1	1.3	—	—	—	—	—	—	—	—	—	—

* : data where available

Information on the variables below relates to numbers of persons.

AVE ACR : Average Acreage

ALL : Ancestral Inherited Land
CL : Cleared Land by Oneself
ILS : Inherited Land from Spouse
RL : Rented Land
SL : Squat Land
BL : Bought Land

Table 3 shows, only one *sederhana* woman could afford to accumulate land, as compared to 13 *sederhana* and nine *senang* men. The fact that it is the men who have more access to, and control of, the means of production, forms one of the material bases for rural women's subordination. Their lack of land ownership means that they are less independent economically, even though they might put in more labour on their husbands' land.

(b) The division of labour by gender in padi production. Our data in Krian, covering 35 selected households, does not manifest a clear or rigid division of labour by gender, except in certain production activities (Tables 4,5 and 6). While in general women across the three classes put in more labour days than men in the total *padi* production cycle, there do exist certain clear gender variations as well as types and patterns of labour arrangements, whether family, cooperative or wage labour.

We would like to highlight three sets of complementary tasks undertaken by male and female labour, tasks rather independent of one another. The first set relates to land preparation whereby the men use a kind of scythe *(tajak)* to slash the underlying weeds and overgrown grass, while the women use a rake *(sisir)* to draw the decomposed weeds into clumps *(melonggok)* which are then pulled to the bunds. In the area under study the men put in 77 per cent of the total labour in *menajak,* and the women 75 per cent of total labour in *sisir* and *melonggok.* Except for the *sederhana* households, which used only family labour, male wage labour was hired in the *susah* and *senang* households, although the conditions for hire differ between the two classes. In the first place it is usually the non-availability of male labour which forces the *susah* households, especially female-headed ones, to hire in labour, while the *senang* households can easily afford to hire in male labour, thus putting their own male family labour to more profitable use. At the same time, the general scarcity of male labour forces some of the women from the three classes to undertake the traditionally 'male' task of *tajak.*

The second set of activities involves plucking the seedlings from the nursery *(tapak redih)* and transplanting them in the main field. The seedlings are normally pulled by the men on the afternoon before transplanting and then strewn in bunches at strategic points all over the field. The next morning the women

TOTAL LABOUR UTILISATION BY OPERATION (PERSON-DAYS) OF SUSAH HOUSEHOLDS DURING MAIN PLANTING SEASON, IN SEMANGGOL 1983

No: households : 22

Operation	*Male Labour*			*Female Labour*			*Total Labour*		
	Female	*Cooperative*	*Wage*	*Family*	*Cooperative*	*Wage*	*Total*	*% M*	*% F*
Preparation of first nursery (*Rakit*)	21.5	0	0	28	0	0	49.5	43.4	56.5
Preparation of second nursery (*Tapak redih*)	24	0	0	24.5	0	0	48.5	49.5	50.5
First transplant	26	0	0	44	0	0	70	37	63
First fertiliser	21.5	0	0	19.5	0	0	41	52	48
Scythe (*tajak/racun*)	163.5	2	51.5	40.5	0	0	257.5	84	16
Clear land (*sisir*)	54	0	0	189	0	0	243	22	78
Repair bund	25	0	0	27	0	0	52	48	52
Pull seedlings	25.5	0	0	12.5	0	0	38	67	33
Second transplant	98.5	7	35.5	240	57	50.5	488.5	29	71
Weeding	7	0	0	28	0	0	35	20	80
Spray pesticide	1	0	0	10	0	0	1	100	0
Second fertiliser	8.5	0	0	29.5	0	0	38	22	78
Reaping	5	0	1	298.5	22	118	544.5	19	81
Threshing	192.5	0	58.5	19	0	0	270	93	7
Total	773.5	9	146.5	1000	79	168.5	2176.5	42.7	57.3

Total acreage operated : 53.65 acres

Average acreage operated : 2.33 acres.

Table 5

TOTAL LABOUR UTILISATION BY OPERATION (PERSON-DAYS) OF SEDERHANA HOUSEHOLDS DURING MAIN PLANTING SEASON, IN SEMANGGOL, 1983

No : households : 9

Operation	*Male Labour*			*Female Labour*			*Total Labour*		
	Family	*Cooperative*	*Wage*	*Family*	*Cooperative*	*Wage*	*Total*	*% M*	*% F*
Preparation of first nursery	10.5	0	0	13.5	0	0	24	44	56
Preparation of second nursery	8.5	0	0	10	0	0	18.5	46	54
First transplant	8.5	0	0	15.5	0	0	24	35	65
First fertiliser	8.5	0	0	9.5	0	0	79.5	82	18
Scythe	64	0	1.5	14	0	0	79.5	82	18
Clear land	12	0	0	49	0	0	61	20	80
Repair bund	7.5	0	0	6	0	0	13.5	55.5	44.5
Pull seedlings	15	0	0	15.5	0	0	30.5	49	51
Second transplant	70.5	1.5	0	166.5	8.5	0	247	29	71
Weeding	4	0	0	9	0	0	13	31	69
Spray pesticide	.5	0	0	0	0	0	.5	100	0
Second fertiliser	8	0	0	5.5	0	0	13.5	59	41
Reaping	19	1.5	0	239.5	20	9.5	289.5	7	93
Threshing	78	8.5	16	7	.5	0	110	93	7
Total	313.5	11.5	17.5	560.5	29	9.5	941.5	36.4	63.6

Total acreage operated : 24.6 acres

Average acreage operated : 2.73 acres

Table 6

TOTAL LABOUR UTILISATION BY OPERATION (PERSON-DAYS) OF SENANG HOUSEHOLDS DURING MAIN PLANTING SEASON, IN SEMANGGOL, 1983

No : households : 4

Operation	*Male Labour*			*Female Labour*			*Total Labour*		
	Family	*Cooperative*	*Wage*	*Family*	*Cooperative*	*Wage*	*Total*	*% M*	*% F*
Preparation of first nursery	3.5	0	0	4.5	0	0	8	44	56
Preparation of second nursery	4	0	.5	4	0	0	8.5	53	47
First transplant	5	0	0	8	0	0	13	38	62
First fertiliser	0	0	0	2	0	0	2	0	100
Scythe	30.5	0	10	21	0	0	61.5	66	34
Clear land	15.5	0	0	31	0	0	46.5	33	67
Repair bund	4.5	0	0	4	0	0	8.5	53	47
Pull seedlings	6.5	0	0	3	0	0	9.5	68	32
Second transplant	14.5	4	6.5	17.5	8	16.5	67	37	63
Weeding	1	0	0	3	0	0	4	25	75
Spray pesticide	0	0	0	0	0	0	0	0	0
Second fertiliser	2	0	0	3.5	0	0	5.5	36	64
Reaping	0	0	0	61	5.5	32.5	99	0	100
Threshing	63	0	7.5	0	0	0	70.5	100	0
Total	150	4	24.5	162.5	13.5	49	403.5	44.2	55.8

Total acreage operated : 10.35 acres

Average acreage operated : 2.58 acres

begin planting, the first planting usually being conducted on a cooperative and reciprocal labour basis (*berderau*). However, because the men are increasingly drawn to non-agricultural wage work with better remuneration, women have increasingly become responsible for planting (63 to 71 per cent of total labour time), and even the pulling of seeds, be it as hired or cooperative labour. *Berderau* gangs can also be mixed male/female units; but, as mentioned earlier, the withdrawal of male labour to the capitalist sector has meant an increasingly female-dominated *berderau* combination. The women, however, say that *berderau* is on the decline being replaced by wage labour; the latter lays the foundation for the erosion of prevailing labour exchange arrangements, signalling changes in the relations of production across both class and gender lines.

Third, reaping (*kerat)* and threshing (*pukul)* of the matured *padi* are generally undertaken by males and females respectively, accounting for 91 per cent and 95 per cent of total labour input. Again, the female labour used in threshing belongs to the female-headed *susah* households which cannot afford to hire in male labour. The sale of the produce is handled by men in a totally male-dominated marketing network. The gunny sacks of threshed *padi* are usually left by the roadside and young peasant men on motor-bikes transport them to the middlemen's shop at rates ranging from 50 cents to as much as two dollars per sack.

To sum up, our study shows that the division of labour in *padi* production does not, per se, give rise to gender or economic inequality. These tasks have historically been rendered as complementary tasks, of a technical nature, with no single operation harbouring a value higher than the other. The concept of cooperation (*kerjasama)* is best understood in this context. Male and female labour both are highly valued in the production of this important food crop.

Over time, however, the division of labour has changed, due to the impact of external forces, namely the expansion of rural wage labour, the introduction of mechanisation, and the intensification of wage labour in the non-farming sector. Subsequently the position of rural women has also been variously affected.

In Semanggol, wages paid for the second transplant, regardless of gender, are five dollars for the morning session and four dollars for the evening session or ninety dollars per *relong* (roughly 1.3 acres). Likewise, reaping wages are paid equally for male and female labour at five dollars and four dollars for the morning and evening, respectively. Reaping and threshing have historically been paid in the ratio of two parts to ten of the produce (*sepuluh-dua),* whether the labour is male or female. With the advent of wage labour in harvesting, it is interesting to note that while the women are paid a fixed sum per morning or evening session, the men who thresh insist that they be paid in kind *plus* the proportionate benefits of subsidy. Inevitably, unless the harvest is spoiled, they would receive more, relative to the women.[7] To a certain extent the scarcity of male wage labour has given the men a better bargaining position and a little more control over their own labour. Maznah's study in Kedah (1984) also points out that men and women are paid different wages for different tasks, with men obtaining the more lucrative wage jobs. For example, she points out that while the daily wage rate for planting and reaping per *relong* (one Kedah *relong* is equal to 0.7 acres) is six dollars per person, a male — dominated task, such as threshing enjoys a wage rate of ten to fifteen dollars per day.

The introduction of mechanization has also undermined the position of rural women. In the Muda areas it has been revealed that with mechanisation, women's ability to earn cash income becomes limited as female labour in planting and harvesting is eliminated (De Koninck, 1981; Wong, 1984). Men, especially from the richer households, can now take control of machines (e.g. tractors, combine harvesters, motorcycles) which command higher returns. For example, driving a tractor pays between eighteen and thirty dollars a day (Maznah, 1984). Consequently poor, and especially single, women and poor men are the worst affected, as they are unable to afford such high-cost technology.

[7] In Semanggol it takes eight to nine women to reap one *relong* of *padi* land in one morning. They are paid five dollars each, making a total of forty to fifty dollars per *relong* for reaping. Threshing is paid in kind, consisting of ten per cent of the harvest plus ten per cent of the subsidy. Assuming that one *relong* of land yields 20 gunny sacks, and one sack weighs an average of 65 kilos, the sum received for threshing would be: 2 sacks (10 per cent) × 65 kilos = 130 kilos. After deducting 16.4 kilos (2.4 kilos for the sacks and 14 kilos for wetness), the total sum received would be $ 74.44 (113.6 kilos × $ 49 padi price plus 113.6 kilos × $ 16.54 subsidy price). Thus the total sum received for threshing per *relong* is about seventy-five dollars, while the female-dominated task of reaping is paid forty or fifty dollars per *relong*.

A new avenue of work, with the coming in of the combine harvester, is the packing and carrying of *padi* from the field to the transportation vehicle. This task, which is mainly handled by men, pays about thirty dollars for 100 bags of *padi*.

The intensification of mechanised production in the rural areas, together with increasing labour shortage, has also rationalized rural restructuring policies that are aimed at creating integrated land schemes where production is centrally managed and labour is hired. Such schemes benefit bigger landowners, while at the same time reducing the opportunity for wage employment due to mechanisation. Limited work availability will also push wage rates to a more competitive level, and is likely to discriminate against women. While men from landless households can seek non-agricultural employment outside the village, poor women who are tied to their reproductive responsibilities will find it harder to earn income, in the absence of easily available agricultural wage employment within their village boundaries.

In Krian, however, many of the *padi* operations are still handled manually; the impact of mechanisation is therefore minimal, although in other similar ways, the division of labour is being transformed.[8] The impact of non-farm wage labour is especially far-reaching. When the men have steady jobs or contract work away from the village, women's participation in *padi* production is greater, transforming the existing division of labour by gender in farm production. This occurs in four inter-related ways.

First there is a further gender polarisation in some tasks such as transplanting and reaping which become overwhelmingly female. The lower wages paid in these tasks, compared to those paid to men in off-farm employment, tend to lower the overall value of women's work. Second, women tend to remain in the more backward, agricultural subsistence sector, while the men enter the so-called capitalist or State sectors with low but relatively better income-earning opportunities. This also leads to an increase in

[8] When Semanggol was re-visited in January 1985, combine-harvesters had started to come in as the roads had been widened. Not all households used this new technology; the *susah* ones in particular could not afford to pay the costs. A study of the impact of this mechanisation process is important but beyond the scope of this paper.

the incidence of female-headed households, where female members undertake the responsibility of agricultural and household subsistence production, including selling their labour-power to obtain more income, while their husbands are out of the village.

Third, women from different socio-economic households are differentially affected. While rural women in general put in more labour than the men, women from the *senang* class tend to put in less work compared to the *sederhana* and *susah* categories. Thus women from the *susah* and *sederhana* households are increasingly involved in this backward sector with heavier work responsibilities, as the division of labour becomes transformed. The women also have to bear the cost of reproduction while their men work in the urban wage sector. On the one hand, men from the *susah* and *sederhana* classes are dependent on the agricultural sector and ultimately on the women for subsistence and reproduction; on the other hand, women are relegated to lower-paying jobs in agricultural work. Ultimately, it is the *susah* women who are doubly subordinated both in terms of their responsibility in reproduction and in their limited access, or even non-access, to the more remunerative male-dominated agricultural and non-agricultural tasks. It is only with the advent of these new wage relations, and particularly rural and urban wage labour, that the division of labour makes gender subordination possible. In other words, the conditions are now being created for the establishment of a gender division of labour in *padi* production, breaking down previous complementary tasks and cooperative relations as further discussed below.

Fourth, production relations are slowly changing, with wage-labour, predominantly consisting of women from. *susah* households, replacing or displacing *berderau*. Where *berderau* lingers on during planting and harvesting time, it is mainly practised by the *susah* households. Many factors account for the emerging importance of seasonal wage labour: (*i*) the intensification of commodity production creates the basis for the dominance of cash relations in almost every aspect of peasant economy; (*ii*) the development of peasant differentiation means that a certain group can appropriate the labour of others who are forced to sell their labour power for survival; the latter group are usually owners of small plots of land or are tenants trapped in a situation of increasing costs of production; (*iii*) with an aging population, older men and women withdraw from the labour force while the younger ones prefer to work in non-farm occupations or to migrate out of the village. The concentration and intensity of labour required within a short period, especially with double-cropping, do not allow for much breathing space for the older peasants who work from dawn to dusk. They prefer to work slowly, but surely, on their own plots of land, and if they can afford it, to hire in labour.

Production relations in Kampung Penia

The village of Kampung Penia is situated in the Kubang Pasu district of the state of Kedah, and consists of 36 households. The village does not constitute a unified and complete social unit since public, political and social-based activities are not confined to the village; they are carried out in close interaction with several adjacent villages. Rubber smallholding and *padi* planting form the main economic activity of the village. From Table 7, we see that only 44 per cent of all the respondents interviewed are fully involved in agricultural production. Of these, 50 per cent are women; the rest, particularly the males, have jobs outside of agriculture, such as in construction. Here wages are paid on a daily basis, and work is intermittent. The people often revert to work in the *padi* fields during the busy harvesting season. About 16 per cent of the respondents are involved in seasonal agricultural work, of whom 76 per cent are women. In Table 7, a category for those not involved in productive activities is also included. They are mainly the disabled, the old, or women who are involved in reproductive activities at home. In Kampung Penia, only about 25 per cent of the villagers own *padi* land and 19 per cent own rubber land. Other than this there is little apparent disparity among villagers in their living conditions. This study is based on field observation and a survey of the 36 households, with 108 male and female respondents, 17 years or more in age.

(a) Access to means of production in padi. From Table 8, we see that the difference in land ownership between men and women in the village is minimal; 14 women and 13 men own *padi* land. The average size of land owned by women is 2.5 *relong* (one *relong* is

Table 7

DISTRIBUTION OF MALE AND FEMALE RESPONDENTS BY INVOLVEMENT IN PRODUCTION—KAMPUNG PENIA

Production Status	*Male*		*Female*			
	No	*%*	*No*	*%*	*Total*	*%*
Agricultural production	24	50	24	50	48	44
Seasonal agricultural production	4	23.5	13	76.5	17	16
Non-agricultural employment	4	66.7	2	33.3	6	6
Waged non-agricultural employment*	8	100.0	0	0	8	7
Not involved in productive work	6	20.7	23	79.3	29	27
Total	46		62		108	100

* Refers to contractual jobs that normally pay wages at a daily rate.

Table 8

DISTRIBUTION OF RESPONDENTS BY MAIN TENURIAL STATUS IN PADI PRODUCTION—KAMPUNG PENIA

Tenurial Status	*Male*			*Female*			
	No	*Row %*	*Col %*	*No*	*Row %*	*Col %*	*Total No.*
Owner-operator	11	58	85	8	42	57	19
Owner non-operator	2	33	15	6	77	43	8
Total owners	13		100	14		100	
Tenant operator	9	100		0	0		9
Family operator	4	13		26	87		30
Agricultural labourer	0	0		4	100		4

equal to 0.7 ares in Kedah) and that owned by men is 2.4 *relong*. However only about 57 per cent of the female landowners operate their own land as compared to 85 per cent of male landowners. Other characteristics of female landowners that differentiate them from males are factors such as age and the manner of inheritance. From the survey, it is found that 21 per cent of female landowners, as compared to seven per cent of males, are above 70 years of age. The older women normally pass the land to other family members to work on.

There are more aged female landowners because 35 per cent of all those women who own land in the village inherited the land from their late husbands. This suggested that their control over the land came later in their lives, by when they were too old to work the land. Another interesting point to note is that about half these female landowners are heads of households.

The difference in control exercised over the land by male and female landowners suggests that ownership does not necessarily imply social and economic power for women. Demographic features, like age, confer late ownership of land upon women and make them less able to participate in production. Women who survive their spouses are also heads of households. This is not particularly advantageous either for the status of the women or for the economic maintenance of their households. They are actually very much dependent on the help of male relatives and mechanisation for the tasks of ploughing and harvesting. However, rural male outmigration and uneven mechanisation have left such households in a greater state of dependence.

Women's access to, and control over, rented land is even more limited. In the village only households with male heads rent in *padi* land; female household heads do not do so. This is probably because they are not able to command adequate family labour for producing the high yields necessary for paying the high land rents.

Men and women are also involved in *padi* production as family operators and agricultural labourers. Females constitute 87 per cent of the family operators and 100 per cent of the agricultural labourers. The work of female family operators is unremunerated, and intermittent in nature. One of the reasons for this is their responsibility for reproductive tasks at home. Similarly, agricultural wage work, which is often done on a daily or piece rate basis, is also relegated to women because the work allows them to combine it with their reproductive roles. Since wage rates in agricultural production are low compared with other non-agricultural wage jobs like construction, none of the male members of the female agricultural labourers' household work in agriculture. Women of these households, which are all landless, are, however, compelled to work in the low paid agricultural wage sector, because this does not require them to leave their homes and villages.

(b) Access to means of production in rubber. In Kampung Penia, rubber smallholding is a more important source of income than *padi. Padi* is only planted during one season whereas rubber tapping is carried out through the year. Forty-eight respondents are fully involved in rubber production and of them, half are female. As compared to males, females comprise 25 per cent of owner non-operators, 82 per cent of family operators and 100 per cent of all those working as agricultural labourers (Table 9). As in *padi* production, none of the female respondents is a tenant operator.

Table 9

DISTRIBUTION OF RESPONDENTS BY MAIN TENURIAL STATUS IN RUBBER PRODUCTION—KAMPUNG PENIA

	Male			*Female*			*Total*
Tenurial Status	*No*	*Row %*	*Col %*	*No*	*Row %*	*Col %*	*No.*
Owner-operator	9	75	70	3	25	38	12
Owner non-operator	4	44	30	5	56	62	9
Total owners	13		100	8		100	
Tenant operator	9	100		0	0		9
Family operator	4	18		18	82		22
Agricultural labourer	0	0		5	100		5

As in *padi,* there exists little disparity between male and female land ownership size. Women's control of their land is somewhat precarious : 44 per cent of female landowners are legally entitled to the land inherited from their husbands, but the land is still in their deceased husband's name. Female landowners who are non-operators have given their male relatives the right to tap or have it share-cropped out, either because they are too old to work the land themselves or because they cannot get enough family help for full time production.

Households that can afford to rent in rubber land are those with male heads. As in *padi*, it is the maximisation of the land's productivity that is crucial, and households headed by females find this objective difficult to achieve. Although women are fully involved in tapping they find it harder to be involved in such maintenance tasks as the occasional clearing of the land, the application of fertilisers and pesticides, the replanting of trees and keeping up with information on new techniques for the improvement of tree yield, and related activities.

(c) Poverty and female land operators. Productivity on the female-owned rubber land is low. The majority of females who operate their land only collect scrap rubber, which means that they do not process the latex into sheet rubber. In scrap rubber production all they have to do is to tap the trees and collect the coagulated pieces of rubber in the collecting cup the next day. These pieces of rubber can either be dried and sold, or sold in wet form. Unlike scrap rubber production, sheet rubber processing is a more elaborate and time-consuming process, that requires that the latex be collected on the day the trees are tapped. The latex then has to be brought to the village processing centre where it is coagulated, processed and rolled into sheets. They then have to be dried before selling.

The earnings from scrap rubber differ considerably from those of sheet rubber. One household which taps about three *relong* of trees in a day is able to yield about 10 sheets of rubber. This will earn the household about sixty-six dollars per week if tapping is done for five days. In contrast, another household which produces scrap rubber is only able to earn eighteen dollars a week from the same land area.[9] Female operated land is thus less lucrative, even when compared with earnings obtained from sharecropped land. Earnings from sharecropped land are divided by half while earnings from scrap rubber production are less than half

[9] The price of scrap rubber in its dried form is about 60 cents per kilo and in its wet form, 50 cents per kilo. For sheet rubber, the average price is $ 1.32 per kilo (grade B rubber). A sheet of dried rubber weighs approximately one kilo.

those earned from sheet rubber production.[10]

This productivity gap between male and female owned operated rubber land does not end at the basic production level; it extends into the sphere of exchange. Households that are landed and produce sheet rubber sell them through RISDA. In Kampung Penia, only the most productive landowners use this facility. Poorer households, which include those that only produce scrap rubber, cannot sell their produce through RISDA. For those who do not produce sheet rubber and are too poor to wait for the weekly sale, their rubber is sometimes sold to the nearest dealer as soon as it is processed. In this way, cash can be obtained immediately and sometimes even credit can be acquired through the dealers. Those who collect scrap rubber also sell their produce through rubber dealers.

The problem of women land operators is compounded if they are situated far from markets. Women normally sell to the nearest rubber dealer, usually within walking distance of the village, even though the price offered by the dealer is low. However, those who have transport prefer to sell their produce to other dealers in town for a higher price. In this respect, households without male adults are at a disadvantage, as they have to depend on a male relative to help transport rubber to the further market or, when this is not possible (as is often the case), to sell at a lower price.

Thus women's access to their productive resources brings less monetary benefit than that of male landowners; at both the production and exchange levels, they are the losers. The prevailing problem of the shortage of male labour for land cultivation is further exacerbated by the State's neglect of low productivity producers, largely the landless households and female land operators. On the one hand, female-headed households are increasing, on the other, the State essentially revolves around a male-biased conception of rural household structures.

Many of the RISDA officials prefer to deal with male household heads, to the exclusion of females. In Kampung Penia, the registration exercise for the PPPK is focussed on recruiting male members, on the assumption that they will automatically repre-

[10] All the households that are involved in sharecropping produce sheet rubber. This is to be expected, as income from sharecropping is very much dependent on the maximisation of the yield from rubber trees.

sent the interests of their households. This creates a problem for women, especially if they are also landowners and heads of households, as they have to depend on male relatives to liase with male RISDA officials. The PPPK, being a body through which most State aid is chanelled, is thus not easily accessible to most female land operators. Through RISDA's grant-in-aid scheme, production subsidies for replanting, as well as for new variety high-yielding seedlings and technical education for the proper maintenance of trees, are only accessible to those who own rubber land and, at the same time, can be fully and actively involved in production. In this respect, not only will landless peasants but also female landowners and operators be denied such benefits.[11]

Subsequently, female land operators' inability to maximise production on their land is often construed as the neglect of their land. However, this problem is hardly even recognised at the official level. There is thus no special provision for aiding women land operators.

The low productivity of female operated land and the State's neglect of it creates a vicious circle, further underdeveloping the capacity of female land operators. As noted, since women smallholders have limited ability to utilise the State's assistance schemes, the yield from their land remains low. Moreover, women smallholders (who produce and sell scrap rubber) together with landless peasants are automatically cut off from mainstream participation in such State-sponsored activity. Due to this they are also dissociated from gaining access to other benefits, disseminated through the PPPK, for the improvement of their trees and land.

THE ROLE OF THE STATE

The domestication of women

The pervasive influence that the State has on all aspects of rural development ensures that women too are brought within the

[11] Even those who are involved in sharecropping will tend to lose out on similar benefits. Some landowners are not willing to put in too many resources into their sharecropped land since the income from it will still be shared by half, even if the owners have to invest more in it to keep up its productivity.

purview of some development schemes. However, the emphasis on and concern for rural women are expressed for the wrong reasons. Instead of being dealt with as farmers, they are dealt with as farmers' wives. Thus, development schemes that reach men and women are separate and distinguishable. Development programmes for rural women have actually heightened sexist consciousness between rural men and women.

Through State intervention rural women are undergoing a 'housewifisation' process, as can be seen through the various home-oriented improvement programmes that emphasise a woman's place in the home. One such is the World Bank funded Karyaneka project launched in 1979 to enable rural women to earn an income. The idea was to train village women to make handicrafts that would then be marketed locally and abroad. One of the aims of the project is to provide supplementary income to the rural community in general, and to ease the problem of rural-urban migration by providing additional income to unemployed agricultural workers (Ahmad, 1981:1). At the village level though, only women seem to be integrated in it.

The proposed organisational structure of Karyaneka seems to have been modelled on the modern, hierarchical factory system. The management, based in Kuala Lumpur, will run the day-to-day administration, marketing, financing, training and promotion, while the production unit will consist of groups, individuals, and family units in the village (Ahmad, 1982 : 18-20); that is, production will be dispersed, while management and control will be centralised. Such a disparity in locations will undoubtedly create problems related to communication, worker control, worker productivity and growth in the long run. Needless to say, the structure does not give workers the opportunity to confront management directly, or to have a say in decisions on various matters related to production and their own welfare, except through their proposed local level organisations, whose functions are merely to coordinate and supervise (Ahmad, 1982: 55-62). Since management may not be able to directly control and regulate production, it will have to depend on locally based leaders. Given such a role, we would expect the male leaders to have an important status there, and for them to emerge as the new elites in the village.

At present, in Kampung Penia, the leader of the local JKKK

(Village Development and Security Committee) seems to exert a considerable amount of control over the Karyaneka Village Committee. The local level male leaders control almost all aspects of the female-run Karyaneka project: they receive the materials (e.g. thread, cotton and cloth) distributed by the State and redistribute them indiscriminately to the female workers. Women working in the handicrafts centre also receive little co-operation from the male villagers; this is because the men are slightly envious, and perhaps unhappy, that this income-earning opportunity is only given to women. For example one factor underlying the slow work progress has been the issuing of a generator for the electric motor, for running the embroidery machines. Since the generator is manually started and requires some physical strength to pull the throttle, women are usually dependent on some male help. Their appeals for help, however, have constantly been turned down by the village males, thus impeding their work. Such problems have lowered the morale of the women, and being mostly young and unmarried, they become easy victims of male domination.

Another example of how their docility has been exploited is in the area of remuneration. Since the terms of production and employment were not fixed, the women had no say in what they would like to produce, nor how the payments were going to be made. For example, the women of one village were not paid anything for five months even after they started producing embroidered items.

One incorrect assumption of the Karyaneka Committee has been that the project would merely provide additional or supplementary income to rural households; but given the rising rural unemployment, such a project may well become the main income-earning source for a lot of the young women in the village today. The issue of wage payment and monetary reward thus is crucial.

With Karyaneka's proposed expansion plan, more and more rural women will gradually be integrated into it. Labour provided by these women will be expected to be cheaper than urban labour as the standard of living is lower in the village. Furthermore, if wage rates are based on the assumption that the income is purely supplementary, it will be even lower than the adjusted rates. The involvement of the State through Karyaneka has certainly not helped in any substantial improvement in living standards of the rural poor, and of women. Rather, it has eased the way for a reconstitution of rural women's roles from that of peasants to wage labourers within domestic confines. (Lochhead and Ramachandran, 1983: 19-38). This makes the exploitation of women as both productive and reproductive workers, even easier.

CONCLUSIONS

The above discussion on the role of the State and the changing rural production structure points to the emergent social relations between men and women. It is in this context that rural women's labour has been reconstituted according to the specific class and gender system of the different historical periods. While pre-colonial social and legal systems recognised women's rights to land and production, patriarchal structures, in the form of religious impositions, challenged and contested such rights. The colonial State introduced new dimensions of gender inequality: it paved the way for the development of a peripheral capitalist economy in which rural production became increasingly monetised with the cultivation of cash crops. However, pre-existing gender notions in which women were seen as less mobile than men and as needing male protection, ensured that it was the male who took initial advantage of cash cropping, particularly rubber cultivation. Women, in contrast, concentrated on subsistence production which did not fetch a cash income.

During the post-colonial era the direct intervention of the State played a vital role in redefining and consolidating women's secondary position in development. The objective of uplifting the economy of the rural small-holding sector necessitated massive State investment in rural production. Together with economic inputs a parallel social programme was introduced to develop the farmers' minds and hearts. Since some of the 'backward' attitudes of the peasant were construed to be among the root causes of poverty, extension education became an important social resource for rural development and modernisation. While male farmers received organisational, management and technical education, women participated in separate programmes which assumed that they did not directly contribute to farm work, or if they did, only as a supplement. The effect of this was that a new ideology was imposed on rural communities. This era seems to have marked the domestication process of rural women, in which they are being recognised as farm housewives or 'home-makers', and are therefore only valued as such. An extension of this domestication policy is in the area of State-supported income-generation schemes. Village handicraft projects like Karyaneka are massive investments and operate on the basis of gender differentiation. Additionally, the non-recognition of females as peasants is an important conditioning factor in exacerbating poverty among rural producers.

The two village studies in this paper illustrate some of the above developments in post-colonial Malaysia, vis-a-vis the position of rural women. The conclusions from both case studies indicate that the division of labour in *padi* and rubber production is being heightened by a patriarchal State and the nature of the capital accumulation process in the periphery. With the expansion of wage labour in both the agricultural and non-agricultural sectors, and the introduction of mechanization, the basis for a gender division of labour is being established making for gender inequality in the *padi* production process. In both case studies, women, especially those from the poorer peasant and female-headed households, are relegated to a secondary and subordinate position in production. Their reproductive roles are being increasingly emphasised and being used to justify this relegation, as in the case of lower paid wage work and the imposition of the putting-out system.

SELECT BIBLIOGRAPHY

AFIFUDIN, OMAR & NOR AZIZAH AZIZ: *A Brief Socio-Economic Study on Rural Farm Housewives in the Muda Scheme,* MADA, 1973.

AGARWAL, BINA: 'Rural Women and High Yielding Variety Rice Technology', *Economic and Political Weekly,* Vol. XIX, No. 13, 1984.

AHMAD, IBRAHIM: *Islamic Law in Malaya,* Kuala Lumpur, Malaysian Sociological Research Institute, 1975.

AHMAD, PARVEEN: *Development Plans: Karyaneka 1982,* Kuala Lumpur, Karyaneka, 1982.

BENERIA, LOURDES: 'Reproduction, Production and the Sexual Division of

Labour', *Cambridge Journal of Economics,* Vol. 3, No. 3, 1979.

CLEAVER, H.: 'The Contradictions of the Green Revolution', New York, *Monthly Review,* 24.2. 1972.

DE KONINCK, R.D.S. GIBBONS & IBRAHIM HASSAN: *Agricultural Modernization, Poverty and Inequality: The Distributional Impact of the Green Revolution in Regions of Malaysia and Indonesia,* Farnborough, Saxon Home, 1980.

DEERE, CARMEN DIANE: 'Rural Women's Subsistence Production in the Capitalist Periphery', in Robin Cohen *et al.* (eds.) 'Peasants and Proletarians,' New York, *Monthly Review,* 1979.

HAJI MOHTAR BIN HJ. MD. DOM: *Malaysian Customary Laws and Usage,* Selangor, Federal Publications, 1979.

HARRIS, OLIVIA & KATE YOUNG: 'Engendered Structures: Some Problems in the Analysis of Reproduction', in Joel Kahn and Josep Llobera (eds.) *The Anthropology of Pre-Capitalist Societies,* London, Macmillan, 1981.

HARTMANN, HEIDI: 'The Unhappy Marriage of Marxism and Feminism: Towards a More Progressive Union', in Lydia Sargent (ed.) *The Unhappy Marriage of Marxism and Feminism,* Pluto Press, London, 1981.

HILL, R.D.: *Rice in Malaya: A Study in Historical Geography,* Oxford University Press, Kuala Lumpur, 1977.

JOMO K.S.: *Class Formation in Malaysia: Capital, the State and Uneven Development,* Ph.D. Thesis, Harvard University, 1977.

JOMO, K.S. & ISHAK SHARI: 'Capital Accumulation and Technological Change in Malaysian Rice Farming', Paper presented at the Conference on the Peasantry and Development in the Asean Region, Bangi, Selangor, 1980.

LIM TECK, GHEE: *Origins of a Colonial Economy: Land and Agriculture in Perak 1874_1897,* Universiti Sains Malaysia, Penang, 1976.

LOCKHEAD, JAMES & RAMACHANDRAN: *Income Generating Activities for Women: A Case Study of Malaysia,* KANITA Project, Penang, 1983.

Malaysia: National Agricultural Policy, Government Printers, Kuala Lumpur, 1984.

MAZNAH, MOHAMED: 'Gender' Class and the Sexual Division of Labour in a Rural Community in Kedah' *Kajian Malaysia,* Vol. 11, No. 2, December, 1984.

MIES, MARIA: 'Dynamics of Sexual Division of Labour and Capital Accumulation—Women Lace Makers of Narsapur', *Economic and Political Weekly,* March, 1981.

MINISTRY OF AGRICULTURE & RURAL DEVELOPMENT:Community Development Division: KEMAS, Kuala Lumpur, Malaysia, 1975.

NG, CHOON SIM, CECILIA: 'Production and Reproduction in a Padi Farming Community in Krian', *Illmu Masyarakat* (Journal of the Malaysian Social Science Association), 5, 1984.

——: *The Organization of Gender Relations in a Rural Malay Community,* Ph.D. Thesis, University of Malaya, Kuala Lumpur, 1985.

PEARSE, ANDREW: *Seeds of Plenty, Seeds of Want: Social and Economic Implications of the Green Revolution,* Oxford University Press, London, 1980.

SELVADURAI, S.: *Krian Padi Survey,* Kementerian Pertanian dan Perikanan, Kuala Lumpur, 1972.

SYED HUSIN, ALI: *Malay Peasant Society and Leadership,* Oxford University Press, Kuala Lumpur, 1975.

TALIB, ROKIAH: 'Women's Participation in FELDA Schemes', Paper presented at UWA Seminar on Women and Employment, 16-17 April, Kuala Lumpur, 1984.

WONG, DIANE: *The Social Organisation of Peasant Reproduction: A Village in Kedah,* Ph.D. Thesis, Bielefeld, 1983.

YOUNG, KATE: 'Modes of Appropriation and the Sexual Division of Labour: A Case Study from Oaxaca, Mexico', in Annete Kuhn and Wolpe (eds.) *Feminism and Materialism,* Routledge and Kegan Paul, London, 1978.

NEITHER SUSTENANCE NOR SUSTAINABILITY

Agricultural Strategies, Ecological Degradation and Indian Women in Poverty

Bina Agarwal

Introduction

After three and a half decades of State-directed development, India continues to be characterised by high levels of poverty and economic inequality. Over the past two decades in particular, the pursuit of primarily growth-oriented policies, without due consideration of distributional aspects and structural reform, has resulted in its own contradictions: agricultural stagnation in several parts of the country, and the rapid degradation of the natural resource base which will ultimately constrain long-term agricultural growth rates; a continuing large population under poverty; and a deteriorating physical, social and political environment. More than ever before there is a need to ask: Development for whom? Development in terms of what? And, most important, development how?

A crucial aspect in examining India's development strategies in the light of these questions is their implications for women. So far, typically, it has been assumed that the household is a unit of convergent interests, wherein the benefits and burdens of existing policies will be shared equally by all its members. Growing evidence to the contrary points to the fallacy of this assumption; it highlights the need to examine the intra-household implications of specific strategies, and indicates that the challenge for alternative strategies cannot be posed adequately without taking note of the gender dimension.

This paper seeks to examine the direct and indirect implications for women, especially of poor rural households, of India's post-independence agricultural development and natural resource use policies. In particular it will look at the effect of two aspects: (i) the promotion from the mid-1960s onwards of the so-called green revolution strategy embodied in a specific technological mix, viz. the high-yielding variety package of practices, with little attention paid to structural agrarian reform; and (ii) the lack of an integrated and ecologically sound approach to the use of natural resources, embodied, in particular, in the destruction of forests, reflecting (among other things) an inadequate recognition of the complementarity on the one hand between long-term agricultural productivity and preservation of the natural resource base, and on the other, between food and fuel.

The implications of both these aspects for rural women relate closely to the pre-existing patterns of class and gender relations in the rural community and the changes, if any, in these relations resulting from State policies. The underlying premise of this paper is that in addition to the effect of development strategies on women as members of a socio-economic class, there would be differential effects by gender within each class.[1]

The paper is divided into four parts. The first will briefly examine the indicators of the existing disproportionate burden of poverty that women bear, and on which agricultural development strategies then impinge. The possible linkages between women's contribution to household earnings, dowry patterns and extent of intra-household discrimination against females will also be discussed. In part II the implications of the green revolution strategy on women in poverty will be examined; part III looks at the factors underlying deforestation and overall ecological deterioration and their implications for rural women; and part IV contains concluding comments.

I. THE BURDEN OF POVERTY—WOMEN'S UNEQUAL LOAD[2]

Gender differences in the impact of agricultural modernisation

[1] The discussion in the paper focuses essentially on class and gender although it is recognized that other aspects of social inequality, such as caste, are also important in the Indian context.

[2] A much more detailed discussion of the issues and studies mentioned in this section is to be found in Agarwal (1986a).

within any socio-economic class may be expected to stem primarily from initial differences between women and men in (a) the extent and nature of their involvement in agricultural field work; (b) the extent and nature of their involvement in non-field work, including cattle-rearing, fetching fuel, water and fodder, domestic work and childcare, etc; (c) the extent of their control over and the patterns of distribution of household earnings and consumption items; and (d) the extent of their direct access to productive resources, especially land.

These initial differences would themselves stem from historical, social and cultural factors which, in addition to the economic, govern the norms vis-a-vis the sexual division of labour, both within the home and outside, in any community. These norms are manifest within the home in women being primarily, and often solely, responsible for housework and childcare, and outside the home in their being confined to certain agricultural tasks and physical spaces, and socially barred from others. Technological changes impinging on such initial differences in labour are likely to lead to different implications for women and men in their access to employment in agricultural and non-agricultural work, and in their overall work burden. Further, to the extent that there are inequalities in the control over and distribution of household earnings and expenditure between women and men, any income/consumption impact of agricultural modernisation may be expected to vary by gender.

Also, methodologically, if we admit the possibility of a systematic sex-bias in the intra-household distribution of income/consumption, then existing poverty estimates would need revision. The current practice is to first identify poor households (by specified criteria) and then calculate the numbers involved, the assumption being that *all* members of poor households are poor, and further that they are all *equally* poor. However, with intra-household distributional differences we could have poor women among households with an average income/consumption level above the poverty line, and non-poor men in households below the poverty line. Estimates of inequality among the poor may need to be revised significantly as well, as would poverty alleviation strategies. Let us now consider the evidence.

Unequal access to food and health care

By one estimate, in 1977-78, 56 per cent of poor rural households (that is, those who obtain over 50 per cent of their income from agricultural wage work), were agricultural labour households, most of the rest being marginal and small cultivators (Bardhan, 1981). Women of such landless or near landless rural households typically hire themselves out to work for others, and are often the main or even sole income earners of their families. Although studies on exact time allocations by gender in rural India are few, existing ones indicate that women of this class work long hours, often longer than men, when all work including domestic work is counted (Jain and Chand, 1982, Khan, *et al.* 1983); or expend more energy in the tasks they do even when the work time put in is the same (Batliwala, 1983). Time-allocation studies from other parts of Asia provide strong supportive evidence.[3] Women's primary responsibility for cooking, fetching water and gathering fuel and fodder, presents particular hardships when ecological degradation of forests and common lands reduces the availability of essential non-monetised resources. Also, the nature of women's work in the fields exposes them to specific health hazards (UNDP, 1980; Mencher and Saradamoni, 1982).

At the same time, wages, even for the same agricultural tasks, are almost always lower for women than men. Despite this, women's contribution to family income in agricultural labour households often exceeds men's as found, for instance, in a six-village study (in Kerala, Tamil Nadu and West Bengal) of landless households where both women and men were wage earners (Mencher and Saradamoni, 1982).

However, taking on a large, and often disproportionately large share of the household's workload, or making a significant contribution to household earnings, does not ensure women a greater or even equal access to crucial needs such as food or health care. The distribution of these within the household generally favours males over females. This is apparent both in

[3] See for instance, Nag, *et al.* (1978), and Acharya and Bennett (1981) for Nepal; White (1976) for Indonesia; Quizon and Evenson (1978) and King (1976) for the Philippines. In all these studies, women are noted to work longer hours than men, taking all tasks into account. Also see Agarwal (1985a) for a more detailed review of most of these studies.

direct assessments of food intake relative to requirement, and in indirect indicators such as male/female differentials in malnutrition, morbidity and mortality. On comparing estimates of the daily energy expended by women and men in rural Karnataka with estimates of their respective caloric intake, Batliwala (1983) finds that the women have an intake deficit of 100 calories, and the men a surplus of 800 calories. Gulati (1978) notes that in a typical agricultural labour household in Kerala, on working days the woman's caloric intake fell short of the recommendations made by the Indian Council of Medical Research by 20 per cent, while the man's fell short by 11 per cent; on unemployed days the respective shortfalls were 50 per cent for the woman and 26 per cent for the man. Again, in a survey in Western Uttar Pradesh, Mathur *et al.* (1961) found the protein and caloric intake of females to be far below that of males among all socio-economic groups. Of course, these studies are only indicative, as none is based on a systematic measurement of food intake levels. But more careful and detailed direct measurements in Bangladesh by Chen *et al.* (1981) clearly indicate the sex bias, as does Schofield's (1979) extensive survey of several hundred village studies across the Third World.

Indirect indicators provide strong supportive evidence. Sen and Sengupta (1983), on studying two West Bengal villages, found a systematic sex bias in child nutrition reflected in the higher prevalence of malnourishment and the lower growth dynamics among girls, relative to boys, of under five years of age (Table 1). Similar findings are noted by Taylor and Faruque (1983) in a ten-village study in Ludhiana, Punjab—a state where female children are also noted to be breast-fed for a shorter time and given less supplementary milk and solid food (Levinson, 1974). Sex bias in food distribution is not confined to poor households, although it appears to be sharper under poverty conditions (Sen and Sengupta, 1983). Discrimination against females also tends to be more in times of economic distress, as during floods, etc. (Sen, 1981).

Women and female children are, again, typically worse off than men and male children in terms of susceptibility to illness and health care received, as noted in rural health surveys in Maharashtra and Gujarat, West Bengal, Punjab and Uttar

Table 1

PERCENTAGE OF UNDERNOURISHMENT OF CHILDREN BELOW THE AGE OF FIVE BY SEX

	West Bengal				
	Degree of malnourishment*				
	Below 1	*Below 2*	*Below 3*	*Below 4*	*Undernourishment index*
Sahajahanpur boys	94	71	39	6	53
Sahajahanpur girls	92	73	44	9	55
Kuchli boys	79	52	19	7	39
Kuchli girls	90	75	48	8	55

		Punjab			
		Marasmus	*Undernourished*	*Sub-total*	*Normal*
Boys	(1108)	1.7	13.4	15.1	84.9
Girls	(924)	2.5	22.7	25.2	74.8

Sources: West Bengal: Sen and Sengupta (1983: 856);
Punjab: Taylor and Faruque (1983: 150).

Notes: *Below 1 = slightly undernourished
Below 2 = moderately undernourished
Below 3 = severely undernourished
Below 4 = disastrously undernourished
Figures in brackets give the sample size.

Pradesh.[4] Also, typically, a greater percentage of females than males receive no treatment for illnesses, or are treated with traditional medicines. Women's ailments are usually ignored in the initial stages; medical aid is sought only when the disease becomes chronic or serious. The same pattern of sex differentials is revealed in hospital admission data (Kynch and Sen, 1983; Ghosh, 1985), child mortality figures (Agarwal, 1986a), life expectancy rates (gender differentials in rates increased con-

[4] See Dandekar's (1975) health survey of six rural communities in Maharashtra in 1957; Chakraborty *et al.*'s (1978) survey in Singur (West Bengal); Taylor and Faruque (1983) on the Narangwal health research-action programme and Gordon *et al.*'s (1965) survey, both in Punjab; and Khan *et al.*'s (1983) study in Uttar Pradesh.

sistently between 1921 and 1970, although the gap has been decreasing since; see Table 2), and in overall sex ratios which continue to be adverse to women in all states except Kerala (see Table 3). Given these biases, any further deterioration in the household's economic situation, with State policies, is likely to have a disproportionately adverse effect on the nutrition and health of women and female children; and any improvement at the household level cannot be assumed to bring about an automatic betterment for them.

In this context, women's independent access to employment and cash income also becomes an important issue. In poor rural households cash controlled by women is usually spent by them on family needs, that by men more on personal needs (Mencher and Saradamoni, 1982; Gulati 1978). Not surprisingly, therefore, the daily nutritional shortfalls of children (especially if female) are found to be related more closely to the mother's employment than the father's (Gulati, 1978; Kumar, 1978).

Further, the incidence of poverty fluctuates by agricultural seasons. During the lean season the family is most vulnerable to indebtedness and bondage. This affects women more than men because their employment is much more seasonal in nature, being concentrated in specific operations,[5] and nearly always casual and short-term rather than annual or long-term. During the slack period, therefore, women have a lesser possibility of employment and hence of food-at-work, which increases their risk of undernourishment and starvation. It is noteworthy that in Gulati's (1978) case study, the woman agricultural labourer in Kerala was much more undernourished than the man on days when both were unemployed. Children are similarly at greater risk in lean seasons given the noted association of women's access to independent income with the family's expenditure on basic necessities such as food.

Of note, too, is an observable regional pattern in intra-family gender discrimination in access to food and health care, the differentials being sharpest in the north-western states (such as Punjab and Haryana) and least in the south, with the eastern states falling in-between. This is revealed in state-level differ-

[5] See Agarwal (1984) for an analysis of Andhra Pradesh and Tamil Nadu, which clearly establishes this.

Table 2

LIFE EXPECTANCY AT BIRTH BY SEX FOR ALL INDIA
(1901-10 to 1976-80)

Period	Life expectancy at birth (years)		
	Males	*Females*	*Differences**
1901–1910	22.6	23.3	0.7
1911–1920	19.4	20.9	1.5
1921–1930	26.9	26.6	−0.3
1931–1940	32.1	31.4	−0.7
1941–1950	32.4	31.7	−0.8
1951–1960	41.9	40.6	−1.3
1961–1970	46.4	44.7	−1.7
1970-75 +	50.5	49.0	−1.5
1976-80 +	52.5	52.1	−0.4

Source: Sample Registration System (SRS) 1979-80, Office of the Registrar General, Government of India.

Notes: *Female minus male life expectancy.
+ Based on SRS data; rest based on Census data.

Table 3

SEX RATIO (FEMALES PER 1000 MALES): INDIA

All India		State-wise	
Year	*Sex ratio*	*State*	*Sex ratio (1981)*
1901	972	Kerala	1032
1911	964	Orissa	981
1921	955	Tamil Nadu	977
1931	950	Andhra Pradesh	975
1941	945	Karnataka	963
1951	946	Bihar	946
1961	941	Gujarat	942
1971	930	Madhya Pradesh	941
1981	933	Maharashtra	937
		Rajasthan	919
		West Bengal	911
		Assam	901
		Jammu & Kashmir	892
		Uttar Pradesh	885
		Punjab	879
		Haryana	870

Source: Census of India (1981a: 4, 5), Series 1, paper 2 of 1983.

ences in overall sex ratios which are distinctly lower in the north-west relative to the south (Table 1), in juvenile sex ratios (JSR: that is, sex ratio of children under 10) as mapped by Miller (1981), and in child mortality rates and health care.

Why females are discriminated against: some pointers

An examination of the noted cross-regional differences also helps throw some light on the question of why females are discriminated against. A variety of interlinked historical, cultural and economic factors underlie these differences. Historically, female infanticide was practised widely in the northern and western (Gujarat upwards) belts, especially in the states of Rajasthan, Punjab and Haryana, with very few and scattered instances noted elsewhere. It was most common among the upper castes and is attributed to factors such as hypergamy, heavy dowry expenditures, prevention of excessive land fragmentation, etc. (Panigrahi, 1972; Miller, 1981). Culturally, among the important factors is differences in marriage patterns. In the south, the greater frequency of marriages between close relatives, especially cross-cousins, within or close to the natal village, facilitates social contact and reciprocity between the bride's and groom's families; in the north, on the other hand, especially the north-west, women are typically married to total strangers at considerable distances from their parental homes,[6] with strict social taboos among many communities against parents accepting hospitality from their married daughters. Hence, most north Indian parents can expect no material support from their daughters after marriage.

What are of particular interest in the present context, however, are the specifically economic factors, especially the earning capacity of females relative to males, and relative female/male marriage costs (as indicated by the incidence of and expenditure on dowry or brideprice[7]) which would affect the relative economic valuation placed on males and females in the family.

[6] Revealed by my cross-regional mapping of these marriage patterns on the basis of available ethnographic evidence.

[7] In broad terms, dowry relates to marriage gifts and payments from the bride's family to the bride, groom or the groom's family; and brideprice to marriage payments from the groom and/or his family to the bride's family.

The arguments underlying the interrelationships of these factors with intra-household gender discrimination are complex, based on diverse supportive evidence, and have been spelt out in detail by me in another paper.[8] Here it would suffice to summarise the broad conclusions. An examination of cross-regional variations in juvenile sex ratios (indicative of gender disparities in child survival), in female labour participation (FLP: proportion of female workers in specified female population), and female marriage costs, suggests the following.

1. Regions of high female labour participation and low gender disparities in labour participation are associated with: (a) low gender disparities in child survival (less female-adverse JSRs); (b) low female marriage costs (low dowry incidence).
2. Regions of low female marriage costs are associated with low gender disparities in child survival.

In other words, FLP and female marriage costs (or gender disparities therein) act both independently and interactively on the extent of discrimination against female children in the family.

In general, the northern states are characterised by lower FLP rates (and higher gender disparities in participation), a higher incidence of dowry, greater intra-household discrimination against female children, and lower female (to male) survival chances than the southern states. It is still controversial, however, why FLP itself varies across regions, and explanations based primarily on ecological variations in cropping patterns and associated demand for female labour are found to be only partially valid.[9] Clearly, among other things, cross-regional differences in cultural norms relating to female seclusion and control over female sexuality, in attitudes to manual work along caste

[8] See Agarwal (1986a). In particular, I have drawn upon Miller (1981) and Rosenzweig and Schultz (1982).

[9] For instance, Bardhan (1984) argues that the north-south difference in discrimination against females relates to the greater demand for female labour generated under rice cultivation which characterizes much of southern and eastern India, than under wheat cultvation which characterizes the north. However, the rice/wheat dichotomy proves inadequate as an explanation in that while female labour participation is generally lower in the traditionally wheat-growing belt of the north-west relative to the rice-growing south, there are also considerable variations between rice regions in women's involvement in agriculture, with women's participation in the eastern states being low and close to that in the wheat-growing north-west.

lines, in the incidence of low caste and tribal populations and in cultivation techniques, all impinge on this as well. Similarly, underlying inter-regional variations in dowry would be a complex set of factors of which FLP is one, but others such as the importance of hypergamy, and the incidence of close-kin marriages[10] which reduce the importance of dowry in marriage alliances, would also play a significant part.

Among the poor, since FLP is typically higher and dowry incidence lower than among the well-to-do households, we would expect anti-female bias to be lower. But if underemployment among poor women is high, so that their *realised* contribution to the household income is low, or any increase in their employment is not sustained long enough for it to have an impact on attitudes towards girl children, or the work is not economically or physically 'visible', or cultural factors in the region make for strong son preference and high dowry among all classes, then despite more women entering the labour force there could be a stronger bias against girls under poverty conditions, as indeed has been noted in several studies.[11] The question of the 'visibility' of women's work is especially important as it does not appear enough that women and girls do productive tasks, but also that the work is *socially recognised* as valuable. Agricultural fieldwork, which is physically more visible than home-based work, and work which brings in earnings, which is economically more visible than say the 'free' collection of fuelwood, fodder and water, appears to be given (by no means justifiably) a higher social valuation. For instance, in the Sen and Sengupta (1984) study, where higher gender discrimination was found among the landless, the boys of poor households were more involved in earning activities, girls in collecting (cowdung, paddy after harvest, etc.), although the total time spent in both activities did

[10] As noted, this is the preferred pattern in the south.

[11] For instance, Sen and Sengupta (1983); Rosenzweig and Schultz (1982), and Miller (1981). Rosenzweig and Schultz's household-level survey for all-India showed that gender differentials in child survival were more among the landless than the landed, although the district-level analysis revealed otherwise; and Miller (1981) found from her mapping of ethnographic evidence that gender differentials were greater among the unpropertied, but only in the north, not the south.

not differ much between the sexes. Also, in the village where discrimination against girls was sharper, the differentials in girl/boy involvement in earning activities was greater. Again, the association of shifts from brideprice to dowry with women's withdrawal from fieldwork, following an economic improvement in small peasant households (as noted, for instance, in Karnataka by Epstein, 1973), would be attributable not to a decline in women's input in productive work *per se*, but a decline in socially-valued 'visible' work in favour of work that is socially undervalued and rendered 'invisible'.

In other words, while there would be a lesser tendency towards discrimination against females among the poor, this tendency would be modified and even reversed in a situation where there is a high and sustained unemployment among women, where the productive work done is not visible, especially economically, or where gender differentials in earnings are high. This tendency would also vary in degree, inter-regionally, since the ideology justifying female neglect would to some extent tend to permeate all classes in the region, as for instance in the north-west. In either case the arguments for increasing the employment opportunities for women in poor households and of reducing gender differentials in earnings remain strong.

The next section will examine how women's employment opportunities and gender differentials in earnings, as well as dowry patterns are being affected cross-regionally by the State's agricultural policies, and what implications this could have on intra-household gender discrimination.

state intervention

An additional issue of relevance and concern is the disproportionate burden of poverty suffered by female-headed households (FHHs) which are noted to be much more poverty-prone than male-headed households. Female heads are usually the widowed, separated or divorced, with much less access to and control over land, greater dependency on wage labour for employment, a higher incidence of involuntary unemployment, lower levels of education and literacy and, on an average, older (many more also being over 60), than male heads of household (Visaria and Visaria, 1983). FHHs form a higher percentage of the lower income deciles — often being among the poorest of the poor. About 10 per cent of households in India are so classified by the census although this is noted to be an underestimate.[12] Added to all this is the vulnerability of women in poor rural households to sexual exploitation by landowners and employers outside the home and to violence within the home.

It is against this background that the implications of specific State strategies need to be assessed.

II. AGRICULTURAL GROWTH AND WOMEN IN POVERTY

Are present patterns of agricultural growth and development likely to exacerbate or diminish the burden of women in poor rural households? The answer would depend partly on changes in the overall incidence of rural poverty in recent years in India and its association with agricultural growth which affects both women and men, and partly on the gender specificities of particular effects.

Agricultural growth and poverty incidence

By the National Sample Survey (NSS) data, the percentage of people in absolute poverty in 1973-74 was 47.8 : the figure being highest in the eastern states and lowest in the north-western. The relationship between absolute poverty and agricultural growth has been the subject of considerable controversy in India. The debate has centred around the existence or otherwise of a time trend in absolute poverty, and on whether growth in agricultural production has led to a decline in poverty through the 'trickle down' effect or to an increase, or to a neutral effect. Taking an overview of the studies (reviewed in detail elsewhere[13]) the broad picture that emerges is that agricultural growth has led to no significant reduction in the incidence of absolute rural poverty. At best it may have helped through its output-increasing effect to stem further increases in poverty incidence in certain areas. And even this may not be a lasting effect insofar as the increases in agricultural production have been accompanied by other less

[12] For a discussion on biases in existing census data on female-headed households see Agarwal (1985b, 1986a).

[13] See Agarwal (1986a). The studies reviewed include Ahluwalia (1978); Griffin and Ghosh (1979): Saith (1981); Gaiha (1981); Mundle (1983); ILO (1977); and Bardhan (1981).

favourable changes in the agrarian economy, discussed later. Also, recent work suggests that whatever may be happening vis-a-vis the incidence of poverty at the aggregate level, a significant minority has been further impoverished, and inequalities among the poor have been increasing (Gaiha, 1984).

One of the significant factors underlying this is the nature of the agricultural development strategy adopted by the government in the mid-1960s, in a situation where the agrarian structure was characterised by sharp inequalities in land ownership and control and in production relations.[14] The period also marked a shift in emphasis away from the earlier focus on land reform[15] to a technological package for promoting agricultural output.[16] The green revolution 'story' is by now well known but a brief recapitulation of some salient features is relevant here. The success of this package has been primarily in the wheat-growing areas of the north-west and in limited pockets of the principally rice-growing areas, among farmers who have been able to invest privately in irrigation in terms of tubewells and procure the necessary inputs. The 'package' needs cash expenditure on seeds, fertilisers, etc, so that only farmers with adequate personal resources or access to institutional credit can take advantage of it. For the better-off farmers who have been able to adopt the new practices, the associated high profitability has been an inducement to resume leased-out land for personal cultivation

[14] In 1970-71, 78 per cent of all rural households either owned no land or less than 2 ha., accounting for 25 per cent of the cultivated area; while three per cent of them owned nearly 30 per cent of the area. In terms of operational holdings the distribution was even more skewed with 25-35 per cent operating no land in various regions (Singh, 1981, based on National Sample Survey data). Also between 1951 and 1971 the proportion of agricultural labourers to the total population of cultivators and labourers is noted to have risen from about 28 per cent to about 35 per cent (Patnaik, 1986).

[15] Land reform as conceived at the beginning of the 1950s was radical in terms of the government's statement of intent, but as implemented it benefitted essentially the rich peasantry (Joshi, 1974; also see Frankel, 1978, for some interesting insights into the political economy underlying the failure of implementation).

[16] This package may be seen to have two components : bio-chemical inputs such as high-yielding variety seeds and chemical fertilisers used with an assured water supply (whether provided by pumps/tubewells or other means) — the HYV-irrigation package; and mechanical equipment (other than irrigation-related) such as tractors, combine harvesters, threshers, etc.

through tenant eviction, as observed in both the wheat and rice areas.[17] The overall area under tenancy has fallen from 20 per cent in 1953-54 to 11 per cent in 1970-71, with cash tenancy increasing too, indicating a tightening of the land-lease market (Singh, 1981; Dasgupta, 1977). All this has meant that the new technology has benefitted certain classes of farmers more than others, and impoverished many of the small and marginal. It has sharpened regional imbalances in agricultural development as well, with growth being concentrated primarily in the north-western states (especially Punjab and Haryana) and in selected parts of the rest of the country. These imbalances reflect not only the soil-climatic advantages of certain geographic regions over others but also technical and institutional ones. Technically, for instance, HYV wheat is a much less risk-prone crop than HYV rice, giving the mainly wheat-growing areas of the north-west an advantage. Again in terms of the spread of cooperatives and commercial credit institutions, extension networks, rural electrification, surface irrigation, and especially the agrarian structure, the north-west is in a more favourable position relative to the east.

Also, as noted, the green revolution strategy had depended strongly on the availability of irrigation, especially through tubewells. However, tubewells are now causing a serious drop in groundwater levels even in parts of Punjab and Uttar Pradesh (Dhawan, 1983). In semi-arid parts of Karnataka the water table is noted to have fallen permanently to a level that is now accessible only to rich farmers via deep tubewells, leaving the marginal farmers with barren land.[18] Again with poor management of canal irrigation a good deal of land is lost due to water-logging and soil salinity. Ironically, therefore, by both types of irrigation the new gain in total agricultural production is low and falling. In other words, the present strategy for increasing agricultural output which neglects crucial aspects of natural resource management, may be self-defeating in the long run.

Further, the adoption of labour-saving machinery has reduced the employment increasing potential of the biological part of the

[17] See Bhalla (1977) on Haryana, and Bardhan and Rudra (1978) on West Bengal.

[18] Presentation made by Jayanto Bandyopadhyay at a workshop on drought and desertification, India International Centre, May 17-18, 1986.

package. And while there has been a noteworthy increase in foodgrain output, there has also been a rise in administered prices of foodgrains (of which agricultural labourers and marginal farmers are net buyers). This would be attributable at least in part to the rise in the political bargaining power of the rich farmers (following the prosperity associated with the new agricultural strategy), with wages typically lagging behind prices (also see Bardhan, 1981: Saith, 1981; Byres, 1981).

In addition, there is noted to be an increase in the incidence of landlessness, in terms of the percentage operating no land. In one study for all-India between 1968 and 1970, landlessness increased from 25 per cent to 35 per cent among the same set of households; and for a fair proportion of the rural cultivating households that were poor in 1968 and became poorer in 1970, the proportionate contribution of and hence dependence on wage income (agricultural and non-agricultural) to total income, increased several fold (Gaiha, 1983).

The growing dependence of the rural population on agricultural wage work is indicated too by the sharp increase in the number of agricultural labourers over 1964-65 and 1974-75, that is the period over which the new agricultural technology gained a foothold in India (an increase which cannot be explained only by population increases).[19] Over this period, as indicated by the Rural Labour Enquiries (RLEs) of these two years, the proportion of agricultural labour households to all rural households increased from 21.7 per cent to 25.3 per cent, and in 1977-78 the figure based on NSS data was 30 per cent (Bardhan, 1981). In other words, the available evidence points to an increase in the dependence of rural households on agricultural wage income either as the sole or primary source of income. (Such households are noted by Gaiha (1981) to have the highest risk of poverty.) At the same time, the average annual days of agricultural wage

[19] Among possible reasons for this would be the eviction of small tenants; the displacement of village artisans (who now seek agricultural wage employment) due to competition from factory products (as noted by Bhalla, 1977); the marginalisation of small and marginal farmers who were unable to take advantage of the new technology and who are now seeking supplementary income; the reduced productivity of traditional irrigation devices used by small farmers, as the installation of tubewells by large farmers lowers the water tables, etc. (see also Bardhan, 1981, on this).

employment available per agricultural labourer have declined at the all-India level as has the annual wage income (from farm and non-farm work) of all earning members of agricultural labour households in all states (with one exception), including the highest growth states of Punjab and Haryana (Bardhan, 1981; Agarwal, 1986a).

Gender-specific effects

Women are affected by these changes as members of poor households and additionally because of gender-specific implications. As already noted, women's access to employment and income and male/female differentials in this access are significant factors impinging on both their economic and social situation. The data reveal that the dependence of rural women on agricultural wage work is higher, and is increasing faster than that for men. According to census figures, in 1961, 25.6 per cent of rural women workers were classified as agricultural labourers relative to 16.2 per cent of men. In 1981 the figures for women and men had increased to 49.6 per cent and 24.3 per cent respectively.[20] This means a doubling over two decades of the dependence of rural women workers on agricultural wage work as their main source of earnings. Also in 1981, 55.3 per cent of rural male workers and only 36.9 per cent of rural female workers were cultivators, highlighting women's lack of independent access to land. Further, according to the RLEs, the increase in the number of female agricultural labourers in agricultural labour households was substantially greater than that of male agricultural labourers during 1964-65 and 1974-75; this increase was highest in the eastern states which also have the highest incidence of absolute rural poverty.

What has been the change in the income of these women agricultural labourers during the period of agricultural modernisation? Elsewhere, I have analysed in detail the sex-wise employment and real wage rate effects that have been associated with the introduction of the new agricultural technology, and also tried to separate the differential employment effects of the bio-

[20] The 1981 figures related to 'main workers' classification. However, the figures obtained from the five per cent sample census results, which relate to main plus marginal workers, give percentages very close to the above.

Table 4

ANNUAL REAL EARNINGS FROM AGRICULTURAL WAGE WORK OF AGRICULTURAL LABOURERS IN AGRICULTURAL LABOUR HOUSEHOLDS(Rs.)

Region/State	*Annual real earnings per person*				*Differential: ratio of male to female earnings*		*Percentage rural population in poverty*	
	Women		*Men*					
	1964-65	1974-75	1964-65	1974-75	1964-65	1974-75	1964-65	1973-74
North-Western								
Haryana	250.8 (Haryana and Punjab)	213.3	600.7 (Haryana and Punjab)	406.8	2.39 (Haryana and Punjab)	1.91	26.5 (Haryana and Punjab)	23.0 (Haryana and Punjab)
Punjab		239.5		618.1*		2.58*		
Rajasthan	166.8	150.2	369.6	310.7	2.22	2.07	31.8	29.8
Uttar Pradesh	94.9	133.2*	207.9	277.4*	2.19	2.08	53.7	47.3
Western and Central								
Gujarat	285.6	168.0	408.7	278.1	1.43	1.66*	49.8	35.6
Maharashtra	140.9	114.3	351.3	241.2	2.49	2.11	59.1	49.8
Madhya Pradesh	126.4	114.1	235.3	162.9	1.86	1.43	42.1	52.3
Eastern								
Bihar	152.4	119.7	275.2	229.5	1.81	1.92*	54.3	58.4
Orissa	146.8	73.1	297.9	155.7	2.03	2.13*	61.9	58.0
West Bengal	293.8	167.1	486.9	294.3	1.66	1.76*	64.0	66.0
Southern								
Andhra Pradesh	88.4	104.8*	246.8	198.2	2.79	1.89	41.5	39.8
Karnataka	151.7	134.2	275.9	246.4	1.82	1.84*	55.1	46.9
Kerala	180.8	159.4	365.0	286.5	2.02	1.80	60.7	49.3
Tamil Nadu	124.1	93.4	269.7	183.9	2.17	1.97	57.4	48.3
All India	141.6	121.9	310.3	243.3	2.19	2.00	50.4	47.6

Sources: (1) Government of India (1981:140, 143, 206, 212), Tables 3.3(a). 1M, 3.3(a). 1W, 3.6(a). 1M 3.6(a). 1W.
(2) Government of India (1979:102, 103, 162), Tables 3.1(a). 1 and 3.4.
(3) Ahluwalia (1978) for the poverty indices.

Notes: †Money earnings have been deflated by the Agricultural Consumer Price Index with 1964-65 = 100.

chemical and mechanisation components of the new technology (see Agarwal, 1984, 1986a). Here it may be noted (see Table 4) that the annual real earnings from all agricultural wage work of male and female agricultural labourers belonging to agricultural labour households, over the period 1964-65 and 1974-75, declined for both men and women at the all-India level, and almost all states. (A very similar pattern was observed vis-a-vis annual real earnings from *all* wage work — agricultural and non-agricultural.)

When we examine the *differentials* in male and female earnings from agricultural wage work, we find that while at the all-India level the differentials declined, at the state-level an interesting picture emerges. In 6 out of the 15 states listed in the table, there has been an increase in male-female earnings differentials. This includes both the agriculturally backward eastern states of Bihar and Orissa and also West Bengal, and the high growth, high technology-adopting state of Punjab. The increase is especially high in Punjab where the differential is also the largest among all the states in 1974-75. Much of the southern region and especially Andhra Pradesh shows a decline in differential (the increase in Karnataka being slight). The degree of differential is also generally lower in the southern states relative to the north-western in 1974-75.

Underlying the regional variations in the changes in earning differentials there are likely to be a complex set of factors, including differences in the demand for female labour created by HYVs in the predominantly wheat-growing states relative to the mainly rice-growing ones. In absolute terms, in all the states, the differentials are substantial in both survey years, with women's earnings being about half or less of men's earnings, in most cases. Further, if we consider *total* wage earnings (from agricultural *and* non-agricultural wage work) of agricultural labourers, the male-female differences are higher than for agricultural wage work alone. Taking these results along with the noted regional differences in the incidence of intra-household sex-discrimination, the FLP rates, and the practice of dowry, some noteworthy pointers emerge.

The north-western states, especially Punjab and Haryana, as noted, rank amongst the highest in terms of the increase in agricultural productivity and the adoption of the new agricultural technology. Punjab and Haryana also have the two lowest levels of absolute poverty in India (Table 4). Rajasthan, again, has a low incidence of absolute poverty and relatively high agricultural growth rates, although its adoption of the new technology is still limited. However, it is precisely the north-western region where discrimination against females is most noted both historically and in the recent period. Historically, female infanticide was widespread in this region, as was sati[21] among the upper castes in Rajasthan. In recent years it is from Punjab that the demand for sex-determination tests on unborn babies and the abortion of female foetuses has been most commonly reported (Deshpande, 1982, and *Manushi*, 1982). While sex-selective abortions are associated with relatively well-off families who can afford private clinics, the ideology underlying sex selectiveness and discrimination against females permeates and affects all classes, even if in varying degree. The same is true of the practice of dowry. In general, a daughter's birth is seen here as an unwelcome event and son preference among all classes is strong. In other words, while the overall incidence of poverty may be lower in the north-western states, among the poorer households we could expect a sharper anti-female bias in this region than elsewhere.

Now if we were to take the view that the growth process associated with the new agricultural technology has unleashed forces which, over time, will have a negative effect on the poor, then we would expect an increase in the overall incidence of poverty, or at least a worsening of the economic position of a significant section of the poor. Either way it would have a greater negative effect on women and female children because of the noted intra-household inequalities. Also, the degree of discrimination against females could strengthen in this region given that (a) employment opportunities for female agricultural labour have not been increasing relative to supply; rather male labour appears to be substituting for female labour (Dasgupta, 1977); and (b) gender differentials in earnings have increased in relation to agricultural wage work and *all* wage work in the Punjab.

Even if we were to take the more optimistic view of some 'trickle down' effect of agricultural growth on poverty (although, as noted, much of the existing literature on long-term trends does not support this view), we could still have a worsening of the

[21] The practice of burning the widow on the husband's funeral pyre.

economic situation of a significant section of the poor. This is because the overall incidence of poverty can decline even while inequality among the poor increases and some sections of the poor become further impoverished.[22] Further, for households that may benefit in any such 'trickle down', women and female children are likely to benefit less than men and male children. There is also a chance that they may be as badly off as before in that an improvement in the household's economic position could be accompanied by an aspiration for the social status of the better-off. This could cause some of the now 'not poor' households to confine women to home-bound work (without necessarily reducing their total workload) and adopting customs such as dowry where they were not practised before.[23] In the Punjab in fact (as also in Himachal Pradesh) Sharma (1980) notes that in the village she studied there has, in recent years, been a total shift from brideprice to dowry amongst all but the lowest castes, and not only among those where women have withdrawn from outdoor labour. Also, the amounts paid in dowry, even among agricultural labourers, are noted to have increased several fold in this state (Horowitz and Kishwar, 1983). Underlying these trends would be factors such as the unequal gender effects of changing employment and earning opportunities with technological change, the homogenisation of cultural values and practices brought about by modern media, rising consumerism, etc. These trends are likely to further strengthen the view that women and female children are economic liabilities, with consequent negative implications for the survival of female children over time.

The eastern states, especially Orissa and Bihar, in contrast to the north-western states, have been characterised by agricultural stagnation, and the highest incidence of absolute poverty in the country. Regional imbalances in agricultural growth have led to high male out-migration from this agriculturally stagnant east to the north-west, leaving behind *de facto* female-headed house-

[22] As found by Gaiha (1981, 1984) for the period 1968-69 and 1970-71 at the all-India level.

[23] This was in fact noted by Epstein (1973) in her study of social change in two Karnataka villages visited by her in 1955 and again in 1970. In one, dowry had replaced brideprice altogether, and in the other partially. One of the factors to which she attributes this shift is the withdrawal of women from fieldwork due to prestige considerations, among peasant families whose economic position has improved.

holds dependent mainly or solely on the woman's income. The earlier-noted sizeably higher increase in women agricultural labourers in the eastern states relative to other states between 1961-1981, would reflect partly an increase in female-headed households, and partly the overall higher poverty incidence in these states. Hence women and female children here are affected both by the sex-bias in access to food etc. (although this bias appears to be less than in the north-west at least as reflected in the sex ratios) and by the indirect effect of high poverty and uneven development. Also, given the rise in male/female differentials in wage earnings in this region, and a relatively greater decline in the average days of employment for women than men in Bihar and West Bengal, the existing sex-based discrimination could strengthen over time in this part of the country.

The southern states fall somewhere in between the east and north-west in the adoption of the new technology, and in the incidence of absolute poverty. They have an advantage over the eastern and north-western states in terms of a lower intra-household discrimination against women and female children. Also, the noted trend towards a reduction of male/female differentials in agricultural wage earnings in states such as Tamil Nadu, Andhra Pradesh and Kerala, if sustained, could well help weaken the existing sex bias. However, the threat from any future mechanisation in operations such as transplanting, weeding, etc. is higher for female labour in most of the southern states, since these operations employ primarily female labour here, and are also the operations in which women are basically concentrated.

Additional aspects of concern are the increase in the incidence of dowry even among households in south India as noted by Epstein (1973) in Karnataka, and Gulati (1984) in Kerala; and the emergence of female infanticide among some groups such as the Kallars of Tamil Nadu due to the growing burden of dowry payments (Venkatramani, 1986).

III. WOMEN AND ECOLOGICAL DEGRADATION[24]

Apart from the implications of agricultural modernisation

[24] For a comprehensive discussion on the class and gender implications of the growing depletion and destruction of our entire natural resource base (soils,

policies on rural women in poverty as examined so far, are closely-related ones stemming from State policy towards forest land, village common land and the environment in general. Except very recently, in limited ways, both in analysis and policy there has been an inadequate recognition of the complementarity between agricultural production and the natural resource base, especially forests, on the one hand, and between fuel and food in people's lives on the other.[25] The specific implications for women have been particularly neglected.

These implications arise from two types of linkages. The first is the adverse effect of deforestation on agricultural output, particularly in the hills and other vulnerable ecological zones. Appropriate tree cover protects the subsoil and prevents soil erosion; trees act as a sponge for absorbing rain water and so replenish groundwater sources for irrigation, and when planted along field boundaries, serve as a wind-break and protect the crops. The disappearance of forests produces a tendency for rain water to be released in floods during the wet seasons, followed by drought in other seasons.[26] These and other ill-effects adversely affect agricultural productivity, especially in the hills, where women are frequently the primary cultivators.

The second relates to the forest being a crucial source of fuel, fodder and water. In the hills and desert areas of northern India, an estimated 67 and 65 per cent, respectively, of total domestic energy comes from firewood, although the average for northern India as a whole is 42 per cent and for southern India, 31 per cent (NCAER, 1981: ITES. 1981). Where inadequately available, firewood is supplemented by animal and crop wastes. Over 90 per cent of domestic energy is used for cooking and water heating in both regions. Most households depend on gathering and not purchasing firewood and other domestic fuels — hence local availability and personal ownership of trees, land and cattle can make

waters, forests), and its causes, especially in terms of State policies, see Agarwal (1987).

25 For a detailed discussion on the fuelwood crisis in India, other parts of Asia, as well as Africa, see Agarwal (1986b).

26 In the forested zones of Indonesia, Malaysia and the Philippines, the green revolution is assessed to be losing its momentum because farmers can no longer find regular supplies of irrigation water for multiple rice farming (Myres, 1978).

a significant difference to the degree and level of fuel use. Landed rural households can obtain firewood (often through hired labour) from trees located on their own land, residues from their crops, and dung from the cattle they own. The landless, however, have to depend for firewood and supplementary fuel on forest and common land or obtain it from other people's land in return for labour contributions. Hence, as noted in a study of semi-arid areas in five Indian states, common property resources (CPRs) which are of marginal importance as fuel sources for the larger farmers, provide 66-84 per cent (varying by region) of the domestic fuel and 91-100 per cent of firewood consumed by small farmers and landless households (Table 5).

Not surprisingly, therefore, differences in domestic fuel consumption between the large farmer households and the small and landless, are marked. Other studies, too, note a close positive relationship between access to fuel and average land holding size or average household income (ASTRA, 1981; NCAER, 1981; ITES, 1981). Hence, the greater the concentration of land and cattle ownership the greater the likely inequalities in access to fuel.

With increasing deforestation and the degradation and declining availability of common land, these differences are strengthening. Over the past three decades, the area under CPRs in many semi-arid regions has declined by 23-56 per cent, attributed partly to the privatisation of the land in favour of large landed households, via illegal encroachments as well as through redistribution by the government (ostensibly to the poor but effectively to the better-off), and partly to government auctioning of CPRs to private contractors. This has forced the landless and near-landless to depend on declining tracts of commons (Jodha, 1986).

The burden of this falls primarily on women and female children, whose time and energy in gathering firewood has increased substantially (Table 6). In parts of Bihar where, upto a few years ago, women of poor rural households could get wood for self-consumption or sale within a distance of one or two kms. they now have to trek 8-10 kms. daily. In some villages of Gujarat, even a daily search of four to five hours can no longer yield enough, and dependence on tree roots, weeds and shrubs is increasing. These do not provide continuous heat, thus also increasing women's cooking time. Given the already heavy work-

Table 5

DOMESTIC FUEL CONSUMPTION BY HOUSEHOLD ECONOMIC POSITION AND SOURCE OF FUEL IN RURAL INDIA

District/State	*Household's economic position*	*Weekly fuel consumption per household*	*CPRs*	*Per cent fuel from own sources*		
				Firewood	*Dung*	*Crop residues*
Mahbubnagar	Poor (13)	119	84	—	9	8
(Andhra Pradesh)	Others (7)	190	13	26	41	20
Akola	Poor (13)	104	79	—	3	18
(Maharashtra)	Others (7)	185	13	20	24	43
Sholapur	Poor (13)	119	72	2	12	14
(Maharashtra)	Others (7)	205	10	18	34	38
Sabarkantha	Poor (20)	184	66	—	25	9
(Gujarat)	Others (10)	213	8	18	28	46
Raisen	Poor (20)	185	74	9	11	6
(Madhya Pradesh)	Others (10)	219	32	24	29	15

Source: Jodha (1986:1173).

Notes: 'Poor' includes agricultural labourer and small farmer (with <2 ha of dry land equivalent) households; 'Others' includes only large farmer households (i.e. the top 20% of landowners in the village).

Figures in brackets give sample size.

CPRs: Common Property Resources, i.e. resources jointly owned by the whole village such as village forest, community pasture, wastelands, river banks and beds, ponds, tanks etc.

ing day of most rural women, especially in the poorer households, any additional time and energy spent on such chores becomes an overwhelming burden.

Further, the new agricultural technology has reduced the availability of crop and animal wastes to the poor in complex ways. The combine harvesters adopted by many large farmers in Punjab and Haryana displace labour and leave virtually no crop residues; under manual harvesting, employment is higher and payment to labour is often made with grain, alongwith straw and stalks. Also with the spread of irrigation and HYVs it is now more profitable to use cattle dung as manure, leaving less for the labourers to forage for fuel. By one estimate, between 1963-64 and 1973-74 the dung burnt as fuel declined even while dung output in general and that used as manure in particular increased (Desai, 1980). Further, the noted drop in the water table with unchecked tubewell spread, especially in semi-arid regions, has reduced CPR productivity and associated availability of fodder, fuel, etc.

Where adequate fuel is not obtainable despite the additional effort, there can be changes in consumption patterns. Inadequacies of fuel are driving villagers in several regions of South Asia to shift to foods that require less fuel or can be eaten raw but are less nutritious, or to eat partially cooked food (which could be toxic), or cold leftovers (with the ever present danger of them rotting in a tropical climate), or to miss some meals altogether and go hungry (Hugart, 1979; Howes and Jabbar, 1986). A trade-off between the time spent in gathering fuel and that spent on cooking is also noted to adversely affect the nutritional quality of the meal (Skar, 1982). As one observer put it: Lack of fuel can be as much a cause of malnutrition as lack of food (Poulsen, 1978:13).

While the adverse nutritional effects impinge on the whole household, women bear an additional burden because of the noted biases in the distribution of food in the family, and are, moreover, unlikely to get the extra food necessary to make up for the additional energy expended on fuel collection.

Deforestation also affects the availability of forest products other than firewood, such as fruit, fodder, turpentine, resin, bamboo, certain flowers and pods which provide oils, liquor and cattle feed, etc. By one estimate 30 million people in India

Table 6

TIME TAKEN AND DISTANCE TRAVELLED FOR FIREWOOD COLLECTION BY REGION

Region	*Year of data*	*Firewood collection** *Time taken*	*Distance travelled*	*Data source*
Chamoli (hills)				
(a) Dwing	1982	5 hr/day†	over 5 km	Swaminathan (1984)
(b) Pakhi	1982	4 hr/day	over 3 km	Swaminathan (1984)
Gujarat (plains)				
(a) Forested	1980	Once every 4 days	n.a.	Nagbrahman and Sambrani (1983)
(b) Depleted	1980	Once every 2 days	4-5 km	Nagbrahman and Sambrani (1983)
(c) Severely depleted	1980	4-5 hr/day	n.a.	Nagbrahman and Sambrani (1983)
Madhya Pradesh (plains)	1980	1-2 times/week	5 km	Chand and Bezboruah (1980)
Kumaon (hills)	1982	3 days/week	5-7 km	Folger and Dewan (1983)
Karnataka (plains)	n.a.	1 hr/day	5.4 km/trip	Batliwala (1983)
Garhwal (hills)	n.a.	5 hr/day	10 km	Agarwal (1983)
Bihar (plains)	c. 1972	n.a.	1-2 km/day	Bhaduri and Sarin (1980)
	1980	n.a.	8-10 km/day	
Rajasthan (plains)	1986 (winter)	5 hr/day	4 km	Personal observation

Notes: *Collected primarily or solely by women and children

†Average computed from information given in the study

n.a. = Information not available

(mostly tribals and forest dwellers) depend on such minor forest products for some part of their livelihood, and it is they who are getting increasingly marginalised (Kulkarni, 1982). An estimated 2-3 million rural people (mostly women) in India, for instance, depend on the sale of wood to urban areas for their livelihood (Agarwal and Deshingkar, 1983).

Further, deforestation reduces groundwater recharge, contributing to falling water tables and drying streams, thus compounding the difficulty women face in getting drinking water, especially in the dry season. In some areas, such shortages are linked crucially to life and death questions; in the hills of Uttar Pradesh, for example, there have been several cases during the past three years of young women committing suicide because of the growing hardships in their lives, with ecological degradation. Their inability to obtain adequate quantities of water, fodder and fuel leads to tensions with their mothers-in-law (in whose youth forests were plentiful), and soil erosion has made it much more difficult for the women to produce enough grain for subsistence in a region of high male out-migration. In one year, seven such cases of suicide were observed — four in a single village where shortages were especially acute (Bahuguna, 1984).

What has caused the crisis? Contrary to the popular belief that it is the gathering of wood for fuel that is responsible for deforestation and fuelwood shortages, existing evidence points to past and ongoing State policies and schemes as the significant cause. Historically, under British rule, vast tracts of forest in the Garhwal and Kumaon hills and elsewhere, were cleared to supply wood for railways and shipbuilding, through Indian and European contractors. Often no supervision was exercised on the activities of the contractors, leading to enormous wastage. Large areas of forest land were also given to private individuals for establishing tea and coffee plantations and the clearing of land for agricultural purposes was encouraged for land revenue gains.[27]

The cutting of forests for commercial use has continued in the post-colonial period to provide building logs, industrial raw materials, especially for paper manufacturing, fuel to small-scale and cottage industries, etc. Forest land has also been lost due to

[27] On these historical aspects see Guha (1983).

mining, stone quarrying, agriculture, and large river valley projects. The National Remote Sensing Agency data revealed that between 1972-75 and 1980-81, the area under forest declined from 55.5 m ha (16.9 per cent of land) to 46.4 m ha (or 14.1 per cent of land) — an annual decrease of 1.3 m ha. A good deal of felling continues illegally. What is noteworthy is that the use of wood for almost all purposes, other than as a domestic fuel in the rural areas, requires the cutting down of trees. In contrast, both micro and macro studies indicate that firewood is typically gathered (especially by the rural poor) in the form of twigs and small branches which causes no deforestation (NCAER, 1981; Ravindranath *et al.*, 1978). Rural shortages of fuelwood are also accentuated by the cutting down of trees to satisfy urban demand: it is estimated that to meet Delhi's firewood needs, at least 6 ha of forest must be clear-felled *daily* in Madhya Pradesh (700 kms. away) from where much of Delhi's firewood is obtained (Agarwal, 1983).

State attempts in recent years to 'protect' forests and to encourage tree-planting on public and private land has, however, done little to alleviate the problem. To begin with, in many areas, the protection of forests by the forest department has in effect meant barring the local people from their traditional rights to forest produce, and the smallest transgressions are severely punished. Further, existing forests in many areas are being replaced by monocultural commercial tree plantations. In Jharkhand (Bihar), for instance, the natural sal forest was being cut by the forest department to plant teak for commercial use. Here, resistance by the local residents took the form of cutting down the government-planted teak to prevent the further felling of sal (Makhijani, 1979). In West Bengal, eucalyptus is noted to have been planted on land where tribals earlier grew paddy (*Indian Express*, 1983); in Uttar Pradesh, shisham and sal trees were cut to plant eucalyptus (Dogra, 1984); in Madhya Pradesh, 40,000 ha of deciduous forest were to have been clear-felled to plant tropical pine, as a raw material for the paper industry. Due to strong resistance by the tribals and a public controversy, the scheme was shelved (Guha, 1983). Such examples abound.

Government schemes to undertake tree-planting for the use of the community have, in most cases, failed to take off because of the little effort made to involve the local population (the implementation is typically 'top down') or to provide them with an assurance that they will benefit from a scheme under which land used by them for other purposes, has been taken over for the scheme (see Agarwal, 1986b, for examples). At the same time, high inequalities in the distribution of land and wealth in the village circumvent co-operation among the villagers for village self-help woodlot schemes.

In fact, in Karnataka, Gujarat and Uttar Pradesh several thousand hectares have been shifted from crops (including staple foodcrops such as *ragi* in Karnataka) to commercial tree species, which bring in several times the profit per acre, that crop cultivation brings.[28] This has had a negative effect on employment, and also reduced crop output and the availability of crop wastes — all to the detriment of the rural poor, especially women. Eucalyptus is neither a satisfactory source of fuel (it burns too quickly), nor of fodder, and it is noted to be highly groundwater-depleting.[29] Yet the spread of farm forestry is being hailed by many as the success story of social forestry in India. Additionally, several thousand hectares of degraded forest land have been leased out in Karnataka, and are proposed to be leased out in several other states for afforestation to provide pulp for private paper manufacturers (*India Today*, 1984; CSE Report, 1985). Undeniably, at the national level the thrust and implementation of forest policy in India remains oriented to commercial needs, while, as the fuelwood crisis deepens, it will be women of the poorest households who will be affected most adversely.

Not surprisingly, such State policies have brought resistance from the local people, ranging from non-cooperation in the so-called community schemes to direct confrontation with the State including violent clashes between the people and the police, in recent years. In rare instances, such resistance has taken the form of successful community mobilisation for tree protection and planting as in the Chipko Andolan in the hills of Uttar Pradesh, where 95 per cent of the forest land is owned by the government and managed by the forest department. The Movement was

[28] For the effect of these shifts on employment etc. in Karnataka see Bandyopadhyay (1981).

[29] See Shiva & Bandyopadhyay (1984). On this last point there is still a considerable ongoing debate.

sparked off in 1972-73 when the villagers (including women), mobilised by the local labour cooperative, resorted to Chipko (meaning to cling to or embrace the trees), challenging the employees of the sports good company which had been allotted a vast tract of ash forest, to axe them first. Since then people in the region have sought to end the contractor system of forest exploitation, have demanded a ban on green-felling and excessive resin tapping, and agitated for minimum wages for forest labourers. In several instances, peaceful protest demonstrations by Chipko activists have led to the cancellation of tree auctions. Women are at the forefront of the campaign which is now focussed both on tree protection and reforestation. The Movement has also highlighted male-female differences in interest and concern for ecological preservation. In 1980, a government scheme to cut down a large tract of oak forest in Chamoli district to establish a potato seed farm and other village infrastructure, was strongly and successfully opposed by the local women who resorted to Chipko to save the trees. The scheme was supported by the men (especially those of the village council) who saw in it the potential for profit; the women, however, argued that with the forest would also be destroyed their main source of fuel, fodder and water, while the men would fritter away the cash on tobacco and alcohol. One of the women's slogans is: 'Planning without fodder, fuel and water is one-eyed planning'. A campaign to fight male alcoholism has also been launched, and they are asking: 'Why aren't we members of the village councils?'

At the same time, one cannot ignore the specificities of the Chipko area, inhabited by hill communities which are not characterised by sharp class and caste inequalities, and where women have always played a significant role in the agrarian economy, without being subject to the rigid norms of seclusion typically prevalent in the plains of the north-west. Recent, localised examples from other parts of India again relate to relatively egalitarian, typically tribal, communities. It is a moot question whether in the more rigidly hierarchical socio-economic contexts prevailing in most of India, widespread community mobilisation would be as readily possible.

IV. CONCLUDING COMMENTS

In examining the implications of State strategies vis-a-vis

agriculture and ecology for women of poor rural households, we noted that the effects are closely related to pre-existing inequalities in class and gender relations (and to the regional variations therein). For both agriculture and natural resource use, policies have favoured the relatively privileged sections of the population and increased the burden of poverty for a significant section of the underprivileged. Given existing intra-household gender inequalities in the division of labour and in access to food, health care, cash income and productive resources, women of such households have typically been left worse off than the men. And because of the primary responsibility that women have for fuel, fodder and water collection, deforestation and overall erosion of the natural resource base has affected them adversely in an immediate way.

Further, there are noted to be long-term negative associations between women's (absolute and relative) contribution to family earnings, dowry payments, and the extent of anti-female bias in food and health care within the home. Hence, any negative effect of agricultural growth strategies on the income-earning opportunities of poor rural women, both in absolute terms and relative to men, is likely to adversely affect not only theirs and their children's immediate sustenance, but could also, in the long term, strengthen inequalities in gender relations and the extent of intra-household discrimination faced by female children. In this context, the observed rise in gender differentials in earnings among agricultural labour families in certain states, in addition to the overall decline in the absolute earnings of the women, is a particular cause for concern.

There would clearly need to be major shifts in State policies away from existing preoccupations with short-term growth, towards options which enable a more egalitarian and ecologically sustainable development, if a dent on the burden of poverty in general, and on female poverty in particular is to be made. That the present State (given its specific class alliances) would or could undertake such changes on its own initiative is doubtful. The point of hope, however, lies in the growth of consciousness among rural women in recent years, of the need to organise and unite for fighting against oppression, both outside the home and within it. A development of particular interest is the growing recognition, within several left mass organisations of the rural poor (both related to and outside the political party context), of the need to wage a struggle against women's oppression, in addition to their ongoing mobilisation against class and caste oppression. Women's specific concerns—both economic, such as their independent need for employment, income and land rights, and other, such as the violence they face from husbands, employers and landlords — are finding a voice, usually via women's committees within these organisations.

Some examples of such struggles launched in the 1970s via non-party political organisations are the assertion by landless women of their independent right to land in the Bodhgaya Movement in Bihar; the agitation by tribal women against low and unequal wages, inadequate employment, wife-beating and rape, through the Shramik Sangathan (toilers' organisation) in Maharashtra; the struggle by poor women for higher wages and land, and against wife-beating in Andhra Pradesh via the Comprehensive Rural Operation Service Society (CROSS); the revolt of low caste poor rural women via Mahila Sangams (women's groups) against exploitation by upper caste landlords in some parts of Andhra Pradesh; women's noted resistance against alcoholism through the Chipko Andolan, and so on.

There is a growth too of solely women's organisations, such as the Self Employed Women's Association (SEWA), initiated in 1972 in Ahmedabad city, and the Working Women's Forum initiated in 1978 in Madras city. Both these today provide credit and other support to poor women surviving on informal sector activities, in these and other cities, and some rural areas as well.

In this context, it is also relevant to take note of several urban-based women's groups which are raising a voice against dowry, family and social violence against women, the negative portrayal of women in the media, etc., and are pressurising for changes in existing laws and legal processes. The efforts of such urban groups are of importance for rural women as well, insofar as they can affect the law and make an impact on existing ideological biases.

The extent to which these grass-roots struggles are likely to prove effective and significant as points of countervailing pressure on existing State policies and structures, however, remains to be seen.

REFERENCES

ACHARYA, MEENA. & LYNN BENNETT: 'The Rural Women of Nepal : An Aggregate Analysis and Summary of Eight Village Studies,' in *The Status of Women in Nepal,* Vol. II, part 9, CEDA, Tribhuvan University, Nepal, 1981.

AGARWAL, ANIL: "In the Forests of Forgetfulness", *The Illustrated Weekly of India,* Bombay, Nov. 13-19, 1983.

AGARWAL, ANIL & PRIYA DESHINGKAR: 'Headloaders: Hunger for Firewood — I', CSE Report No. 118, Centre for Science and Environment, Delhi, 1983.

AGARWAL, BINA: 'Women and Water Resource Development', mimeo, Institute of Economic Growth, Delhi, 1981.

——: 'Rural Women and the High Yielding Variety Rice Technology', in *Economic and Political Weekly* (Review of Agriculture), Vol. 19, No. 13, 31 March, 1984.

——: 'Women and Technological Change in Agriculture : The Asian and African Experience', in Iftikar Ahmed (ed): *Technology and Rural Women : Conceptual & Empirical Issues,* George Allen and Unwin, U.K., 1985a.

——: 'Work Participation of Rural Women in the Third World : Some Data and Conceptual Biases,' *Economic and Political Weekly* (Review of Agriculture), Vol. 20. Nos 51 and 52, 21-28 Dec 1985b.

——: 'Women, Poverty and Agricultural Growth in India', *Journal of Peasant Studies,* Vol. 13, No.4, July, 1986a.

——: *Cold Hearths and Barren Slopes : The Woodfuel Crisis in the Third World,* Delhi, Allied Publishers, and London: Zed Books: 1986b.

AHLUWALIA: MONTEK S. 'Rural Poverty and Agricultural Performance in India, *Journal of Development Studies,* Vol. 14, No. 3, April, 1978.

ASTRA: 'Rural Energy Consumption Patterns : A Field Study', Indian Institute of Science, Bangalore, 1981.

BAHUGUNA, SUNDERLAL: 'Women's Non-Violent Power in the Chipko Movement', in Madhu Kishwar and Ruth Vanita (eds.), *In Search of Answers: Indian Women's Voices from Manushi,* London: Zed Books, 1984.

BANDYOPADHYAY, JAYANTO: 'Beyond the Firewood March', *Financial Express,* September 1-2, 1981.

BARDHAN, PRANAB: 'On Life and Death Questions: Poverty and Child Mortality' in *Land, Labour and Rural Poverty: Essays in Development Economics,* Delhi, Oxford University Press, 1984.

BARDHAN, PRANAB & ASHOK RUDRA: 'Interlinkage of Land, Labour and Credit Relations : An Analysis of Village Survey Data in East India', *Economic and Political Weekly,* Vol.13, Nos. 6 and 7, Feb, 1978.

BATLIWALA, S.: 'Women in Poverty: The Energy, Health and Nutrition Syndrome', paper presented at a workshop on 'Women and Poverty' at the Centre for Studies in Social Sciences, Calcutta, March 17-18, 1983.

BHADURI, T. AND V. SURIN: 'Community Forestry and Women Head-Loaders', in 'Community Forestry and People's Participation,' Seminar Report, Ranchi Consortium for Forestry, Nov. 20-22, 1981.

BHALLA, SHEILA: 'New Relations of Production in Haryana Agriculture',

Economic and Political Weekly (Review of Agriculture), Vol. 11 No. 13, 27 March, 1977.

BYRES, T.J.: 'The New Technology, Class Formation and Class Action in the Indian Countryside', *Journal of Peasant Studies*, July, 1981.

CENSUS OF INDIA: Series 1, Paper 2 of 1983, 'Key Population Statistics based on 5 per cent Sample Data', by Padmanabha, Registrar General and Census Commissioner, India, 1981.

CHAKRABORTY, A.K. *et al.*: 'Health Status of Rural Population of Singur as Revealed in Repeat General Health Survey 1975', *Indian Journal of Medical Research*, Vol. 68, Dec, 1978.

CHEN, LINCOLN C., EMDADUAL HUQ & STAN D'SOUZA: 'Sex Bias in the Family Allocation of Food and Health Care in Rural Bangladesh', *Population and Development Review*, Vol. 7, No. 1, March, 1981.

CSE: *The State of India's Environment 1984-85: The Second Citizen's Report*, Centre for Science and Environment, New Delhi, 1985.

DASGUPTA, BIPLAB: *Agrarian Change and the New Technology in India*, Report No. 77.2, United Nations Research Institute for Social Development, Geneva, 1977.

DANDEKAR, KUMUDINI: 'Has the Proportion of Women in India's Population Been Declining', *Economic and Political Weekly*, Oct, 18 1975.

DESAI, ASHOK V: *India's Energy Economy: Facts and their Interpretation*, Economic Intelligence Services, Centre for Monitoring Indian Economy, February, 1980.

DESHPANDE, ANJALI: 'A New Menace', *Mainstream*, July 24, 1982.

DHAWAN, B.D.: *Development of Tubewell Irrigation in India*, Agricole Publishing Academy, 1983.

DOGRA, BHARAT: *Forests and People*, New Delhi, 1984.

EPSTEIN, T. SCARLETT: *South India: Yesterday, Today and Tomorrow*, London: Macmillan, 1973.

FOLGER, B. & M. DEWAN: 'Kumaon Hills Reclamation : End of Year Site Visit', mimeo, OXFAM America, Delhi, 1983.

GAIHA, RAGHAV: 'Aspects of Poverty in Rural India', *Economics of Planning*, Vol. 17, Nos. 2-3, 1981.

——: 'Poverty, Technology and Infrastructure in Rural India', paper delivered to the European Econometric Society Meeting, Pisa, Aug. 1983.

——: 'Impoverishment, Technology and Growth in Rural India', mimeo, Faculty of Management Studies, Delhi University, 1984.

GHOSH, SHANTI: 'Discrimination Begins at Birth', UNICEF, mimeo, 1985.

GOVERNMENT OF INDIA: Rural Labour Enquiry 1974-75, Final Report on Wages and Earnings of Rural Labour Households', Labour Bureau, Ministry of Labour, Chandigarh, 1979.

——: 'Rural Labour Enquiry 1974-75, Final Report on Employment and Unemployment of Rural Labour Households', Labour Bureau, Ministry of Labour, Chandigarh, 1981.

GORDON, JOHN, E., SOHAN SINGH & JOHN B. WYON: 'Causes of Death at Different Ages by Sex and by Season in a Rural Population of Punjab 1957-59 : A Field Study', *Indian Journal of Medical Research*, Vol. 53, No.9, Sept, 1965.

GUHA, RAMACHANDRA: 'Forestry in British and Post-British India — A Historical Analysis', *Economic and Political Weekly,* October 29, 1983.

GULATI, LEELA: 'Profile of a Female Agricultural Labourer', *Economic and Political Weekly* (Review of Agriculture), Vol. 13, No. 12, March 25, 1978.

——: 'Fisherwomen on the Kerala Coast : Demographic and Socio-Economic Impact of Fisheries Development Project', International Labour Office, Geneva, 1984.

GRIFFIN, KEITH & AJIT KUMAR GHOSE: 'Growth and Impoverishment in the Rural Areas of Asia', *World Development,* Vol.7, Nos. 4/5, 1979.

HOROWITZ, B. & MADHU KISHWAR: 'Family Life — The Unequal Deal: Women's Condition and Family Life Among Agricultural Labourers and Small Farmers in a Punjab Village', *Manushi,* No. 11, 1982.

HOWES, MICK & M.A. JABBER: *Rural Fuel Shortages in Bangladesh : the Evidence from Four Villages,* Discussion paper 213, IDS, Sussex, 1986.

HUGHART, DAVID: 'Prospects of Traditional and Non-conventional Energy Sources in Developing Countries', World Bank Staff Working Paper no. 346, World Bank, Washington D.C., July, 1979.

ILO: *Poverty and Landlessness in Rural Asia,* International Labour Organisation, Geneva, 1977.

India Today: 1984.

Indian Express: 'Tribals Hostile to Social Forestry', July 10, 1983.

ITES: *Rural Energy Consumption in Southern India,* Institute of Techno-Economic Studies, Madras, 1981.

JAIN, DEVAKI & MALINI CHAND: 'Report on a Time-Allocation Study — Its Methodological Implications', paper presented at a 'Technical Seminar on Women's Work and Employment', Institute of Social Studies Trust, April 9-11, 1982.

JAIN, S.P.: 'Mortality Trends and Differentials' in *Population of India — Country Monograph Series No. 10,* Economic and Social Commission for Asia and the Pacific, Bangkok, 1982.

JODHA, N.S.: 'Common Property Resources and Rural Poor', *Economic and Political Weekly,* Vol. 21, No. 27, July 5, 1986.

KHAN, M.E., S.K. GHOSH, DASTIDAR SINGH, & RATANJEET SINGH: 'Nutrition and Health Practices Among the Rural Women — A Case Study of Uttar Pradesh, India' Working paper No. 31, Operations Research Group, Delhi, 1983.

KING, E: 'Time Allocation in Philippine Rural Households', Discussion paper No. 76-26, Institute of Economic Development and Research, University of Philippines, Los Banos, 1976.

KULKARNI, S: 'Towards a Social Forestry Policy', *Economic and Political Weekly,* Vol. 18, No. 6, Feb. 6, 1983.

KUMAR, SHUBH K.: 'Role of the Household Economy in Child Nutrition at Low Incomes', Occasional paper No. 95, Dept. of Agricultural Economics, Cornell University, Dec, 1978.

KYNCH, JOCELYN & AMARTYA SEN: 'Indian Women : Well-Being and Survival', *Cambridge Journal of Economics,* Vol. 7, No. 3/4, Sept-Dec, 1983.

LEVINSON, J.F.: *Morinda : An Economic Analysis of Malnutrition Among Young Children in Rural India,* Cornell/MIT International Nutrition Policy Series, 1974.

MAKHIJANI, A.: 'Economics and Sociology of Alternative Energy Sources', paper presented at the Environment and Development Regional Seminar on Alternative Patterns of Development and Life Style in Asia and the Pacific, ESCAP and UNEP, Bangkok, August 14-18, 1979.

Manushi: 'A New Form of Female Infanticide', No. 12, 1982.

MENCHER, JOAN & K. SARADAMONI: 'Muddy Feet and Dirty Hands : Rice Production and Female Agricultural Labour', *Economic and Political Weekly* (Review of Agriculture), Vol. 17, No. 52, December 25, 1982.

MILLER, BARBARA: *The Endangered Sex — Neglect of Female Children in Rural North India*, Ithaca and London : Cornell University Press, 1981.

MUNDLE, SUDIPTO: 'Effect of Agricultural Production and Prices on Incidence and Rural Poverty : A Tentative Analysis of Inter-State Variations', *Economic and Political Weekly* (Review of Agriculture), Vol. 18, No. 26, June 25, 1983.

MYRES, NORMAN: 'Forests for People', *New Scientist*, December 21-28, 1978.

NAG, M. *et. al.*: 'Economic Value of Children in Two Peasant Societies', in *International Population Conference : Mexico*, Vol. I, IUSSP, Liege, Belgium, 1977.

NAGBRAHMAN D. & SHREEKANT SAMBRANI: 'Women's Drudgery in Firewood Collection', *Economic and Political Weekly*, Jan. 1-8, 1978.

NCAER: *Report on Rural Energy Consumption in Northern India*, Environment Research Committee, National Council of Applied Economic Research, New Delhi, 1972.

PANIGRAHI, L: *British Social Policy and Female Infanticide in India*, Delhi, Munshiram Manoharlal, 1972.

PATNAIK, U.: *The Agrarian Question and the Development of Capitalism in India*, Delhi, Oxford University Press, 1986.

POULSEN, GUNNAR: *Man and Trees in Tropical Africa*, Publication No. 1010, International Development Research Council, Ottawa. 1978.

RAVINDRANATH, N.H. *et al.*: *The Design of a Rural Energy Center for Pura Village, Part I, Its Present Pattern of Energy Consumption*, ASTRA, Indian Institute of Science, Bangalore. 1978.

ROSENZWEIG, MARK R. & T. PAUL SCHULTZ: 'Market Opportunities, Genetic Endowment and Intrafamily Resource Distribution : Child Survival in Rural India', Center Paper No. 323, Economic Growth Center, Yale University, 1982.

QUIZON E.K. & R.E. EVENSON: 'Time Allocation and Home Production in Philippine Rural Households', mimeo, Yale University, 1978.

SAITH, ASHWANI: 'Production, Prices and Poverty in India', *The Journal of Development Studies*, Vol.17, No.2, Jan, 1981.

SCHOFIELD, SUE: *Development and the Problems of Village Nutrition*, London: Croom-Helm, 1979.

SEN, AMARTYA: 'Family and Food: Sex-Bias in Poverty', mimeo, forthcoming in P. Bardhan and T.N. Srinivasan (eds.), *Rural Poverty in South Asia*, 1981.

SEN, AMARTYA & SUNIL SENGUPTA: 'Malnutrition of Rural Children and the Sex Bias', *Economic and Political Weekly*, Annual Number, May, 1983.

SHIVA, V. & J. BANDYOPADHYAY: *Ecological Audit of Eucalyptus Cultivation in Rainfed Regions*, A Report for the United Nations University, Dehradun, Research Foundation for Science, Technology and Natural Resource Policy, 1984.

SINGH, I.J.: *Small Farmers and the Landless in South Asia,* Chapter II, monograph, World Bank, Washington, DC, 1981.

SHARMA, URSULA: *Women, Work and Property in North-West India,* London and New York: Tavistock, 1980.

SKAR, SARAH LUND: 'Fuel Availability, Nutrition and Women's Work in Highland Peru', World Employment Programme Research Working Paper No. WEP 10/WP 23, ILO, Geneva, 1982.

SWAMINATHAN, M.: 'Eight Hours a Day for Fuel Collection', *Manushi,* March-April, 1984.

TAYLOR, CARL E. & RASHID FARUQUE: *Child and Maternal Services in Rural India: The Narangwal Experiment,* Part I, Baltimore and London: Johns Hopkins University Press, 1983.

UNDP: *Rural Women's Participation in Development,* Evaluation Study No. 3, United Nations Development Programme, New York, June, 1980.

VENKATRAMANI, S.H.: 'Female Infanticide : Born to Die', *India Today,* June 15, 1986.

VISARIA, PRAVIN & LEELA VISARIA: 'Indian Households with Female Heads: Their Incidence, Characteristics and Level of Living', paper presented at workshop on 'Women and Poverty', 1983.

WHITE, B: 'Population, Involution and Employment in Rural Java', in G.E. Hansen (ed): *Agricultural Development in Indonesia,* Ithaca, Cornell University Press, 1976.

... TWO STEPS BACK?

New Agricultural Policies in Rural China and the Woman Question

Govind Kelkar

Introduction

In recent years, scholars and activists in the women's movement, particularly in the Third World, have expressed an increasing interest in the household contract system of responsibility in China, and its implications for women. Many outside observers have viewed the system with some misgiving and questioned the process of decollectivisation of agriculture. They have argued that it would undo Maoist achievement in the release of socialist productive energies as well as limit the socialisation of various household/family activities, bringing about an effective change in gender relations and leading to inequalities similar to those found in capitalist settings (Nolan, *et al.*, 1982).

This paper will focus on the gender-specific implications of the household contract system of responsibility in rural China. In specific terms it will : (*a*) examine the general implications of the contract system in promoting inequalities in the countryside; (*b*) trace the erosive effect of the economic reforms and modernisation on rural women in particular; (*c*) analyse the ideological basis of the woman question in China; and (*d*) discuss how the Chinese communist policies for mobilising women and for modernisation have evoked strong reactions from the All China Women's Federation.

The paper is based primarily on my own field work in two communes in Wuxi County of Jiangsu Province, in 1983. During my field work, I observed that women's work does not carry with it control of resources. The greater participation of women in the household contract system of agriculture or in home-based production (which have been the primary characteristics of women's work in Chinese economic policies since 1979) is not sufficient for either ensuring their control over the products of their labour, or for a higher social valuation of their work, since this is dependent upon the existing structural arrangements for the management of the rural economy in the hands of men.

General implications of the household contract system of responsibility

The household contract system of responsibility was introduced in China in December 1978 as a result of a decision in the Third Plenum of the Eleventh Party Central Committee, and has gradually become the principal method of rural management. Towards the end of 1984, the system was reported to have been adopted by 98.3 per cent of the country's production teams. As a result, China's agricultural output is claimed to have risen by an annual average of 7.9 per cent from 1979 to 1983, as against an average of 3.2 per cent in the years between 1953 and 1978 (*Beijing Review,* 1984). There is also noted to have been a general improvement in the peasants' standard of living in the last five years, with a rise in the average per capita income of 67 per cent between 1978 and 1982, from 133.6 yuan to 270.1 yuan (*Xinhua,* 1983). At the same time, there have also been increasing reports of violence against female children and women in rural areas, which has been a cause of concern to both the government and the Women's Federation.[1] As discussed in the paper, this growing violence is linked to the introduction of the

[1] In his report to the Fifth National People's Congress, Premier Zhao Ziyang said:

> Persuasive education must be conducted among the people of the whole country, especially among the peasants to change radically the feudal attitude that views sons as better than daughters and regards more sons as a sign of good fortune. We must, in particular, protect infant girls and their mothers... The whole society should resolutely condemn the criminal activities of female infanticide and maltreatment of mothers, and judicial departments should resolutely punish the offenders according to the law. (See 'Sex Ratio of China's Newborns and Infants', *Women of China,* August 1983, p.11.)

household responsibility system in the Chinese countryside.

The responsibility system in rural production is based on a three party contract signed by the State, the collective (the production team) and the peasant household or a group of households, or an individual. Based on a State plan (for production of certain crops and products in a particular area) the production team contracts out tracts of land to peasant households who in turn agree to grow given quantities of the stated crops. Although there are some regional variations, typically under this system the distribution of produce is organised as follows: the contracting household pays agricultural tax and sells the required quota of produce to the State at a set price; the production team retains a share of earnings from product sales for its own use and for common services (welfare funds); the remaining portion is owned by the peasant household for personal use or sale. In 1984, these contracts were permitted to be extended to 15 years and were made transferrable;[2] reports of hiring labour during the peak periods of agricultural activities have also come in.

The State has a mandatory plan for the production of both agricultural and cash crops. For instance, it is usually suggested that 70 to 75 per cent of the country's farm land be used to sow grain and the rest to sow cash crops. These plans are transmitted to local governments, which are authorised to modify the plans to suit local conditions of production.

There is no direct enforcement of the plans by the State. Local authorities implement these plans by signing purchasing, supply and marketing contracts. Peasants have the freedom to decide on the proportion of grain or cash crop sown. The collective works out the plan for land use and crop rotation and undertakes the responsibility for solving any problems which arise out of the contract system.

The contracting peasants are required to sell about 10 per cent of their contracted output to the State at a fixed price. A certain amount of surplus can be sold to the State at a higher price and the remaining at 'open markets' or fairs where prices can be

[2] See discussion on No. 1 Document of the Party Central Committee in 1984 in an interview of Du Runsheng, Head of the Rural Policy Research Institute, by All-China Journalist Association in March 1984. Also *Beijing Review*, April 30, 1984.

negotiated with the buyers. Besides, peasants must pay an agricultural tax to the State and contribute a set quota to the welfare and management fund of the collective. The taxes and quotas are the same as they were prior to the introduction of the responsibility system. The only difference is that peasants now pay these taxes directly to the State, whereas formerly the collective did so. In the second stage of rural reform in 1985, the State monopoly on purchase of grain and cotton was replaced by a system of purchase through contracts. Now, under the guidance of the State plan, peasants arrange their production according to market demands. The structure of farming has changed accordingly; in 1985, for example, the amount of farm land planted with grain was reduced, thus causing a fall in grain output, while that of cash crops increased. As in the past, the collective still owns land and water conservation facilities; in most cases, it provides heavy machinery, improved seeds, chemical fertilizers and other services such as information and training on new scientific techniques to the peasants, but no longer organises production or distribution.

The two major forms of the household contract system of responsibility prevailing in nearly 74 per cent of the collectives are *bao-gan* (total responsibility) and *bao-ch'an* (output contract). Under the *bao-gan*, the collective fixes the quotas for agricultural tax, State purchase and collective share, and allows the contracting parties (individuals or households) to keep the remainder. The *bao-ch'an* system is a contract for the fulfilment of a fixed output quota: the contract fixes the harvest quotas and requires the contracting households or individuals to turn the yield over for collective distribution.[3] The foodgrain or other produce is redistributed to them by the collective on the basis of work points. However, in the advanced areas of rural and agricultural production, farmwork is said to be in the hands of contracting individuals or households. Therefore, the distribution of collective income and the workpoint system seem to be redundant.

The other forms of household responsibility system are con-

[3] 'Rural Contract System Needs Perfection', *China Daily*, Beijing, March 23, 1983. Also based on my discussions with Chinese officials in the Ministry of Agriculture, in Beijing and Shanghai, May 1983.

tracts by which an individual or household is paid according to the amount produced, and contracts for specialized work that usually require a fairly high level of technique or specialized knowledge. Interestingly enough, the responsibility system has boosted diversification of production in rural areas. Peasants use part of their time for working their contracted land and part in raising sheep, pigs, bees, chickens, snakes, ducks and fish; growing flowers, mushrooms and vegetables; processing grains; planting trees; and taking up carpentry, tailoring and transportation.

Households engaged primarily in these specialized activities are called 'specialized' and 'key households'.[4] Towards the end of 1983, there were 24.82 million specialized households in China, making up 13.6 per cent of all rural households (Lu, 1984). They fall into two categories: (i) contracting households where the means of production remain part of the collective economy; and (ii) self-managing households where the means of production are owned by the households themselves, and in most cases have no relationship with the collective economy. Specialized households may or may not enter into a contract with the collective to work a plot of land or undertake a service activity. Labour productivity and the marketable surplus of specialized households are higher than those of ordinary households. For example, a survey of 2,277 specialized households from different parts of the country showed that they owned 1,772 tractors and 119 motor vehicles (Lu, 1984). Some of them even bought small airplanes.

Another survey of 20,988 prosperous households in Yingxian county, Shanxi Province, indicated that close to 43 per cent of the people who quickly became wealthy in the rural responsibility system were commune members who had once been cadres, educated youths returning to the countryside or demobilised soldiers. Skilled workers and management experts make up five to nine per cent of the prosperous households (Lu, 1984).

The general aims of the household contract system of responsibility in the rural areas were to promote agricultural production and correct the 'leftist' mistakes committed before and during the Cultural Revolution. These were to be achieved by reducing the

[4] Generally speaking, if the main income of a household, that is more than 60 per cent of the total income, comes from a particular activity other than agriculture, then it is called a household specializing in that particular production or service/trade activity.

size of the labour group from a production team to a household or group of households or an individual, and increase peasant incomes by linking the peasants' remuneration with work performance. Moreover, peasants were given autonomy in the management of production and the benefits derived from the produce. It was further considered necessary to eliminate egalitarianism in the distribution of the produce and carry out structural reforms in the rural management methods that had dampened the peasants' enthusiasm for increased production and higher productivity. In the present readjustment of rural policies, structural reforms of the people's communes and the establishment of township government administration, political work and economic management at the commune level are to be separated from each other. This was introduced with the objective of removing the obstacles which 'hindered the initiative of the cadres and peasants and (were) therefore unfavourable to the development of national and cultural wealth in China's rural areas' (*Renmin Ribao*, 1983).

It is important to mention here that researchers and cadres in China, like concerned scholars and activists outside China, have conducted surveys and organised various forums to discuss the implications of the rural responsibility system. While admitting the existence of individual economy and other non-socialist economic forms, Party and government planners have repeatedly emphasised that common prosperity for all the labouring people is the goal of a rural responsibility system. (*Renmin Ribao*, 1983). Notwithstanding the fact of an increasing gap between a prosperous minority and large masses of workers and peasants who have had neither a cadre status nor acquired knowledge or access to new technological resources, the rural responsibility system is not considered a deviation from a path to socialist development. The *means* of production — land and water conservation facilities — are owned by the collective and are not allowed to be leased or sold, so that it checks exploitation caused by the loss of such means. Differences in income resulting mainly from differences in labour strength, technical know-how, diligence, management ability, natural or man-made calamities are permitted to exist and grow in China. Some 'hardworking' and 'skilled' people are allowed first to get rich and are well rewarded for their efforts.

Egalitarianism with its stress on 'politics in command', and continuing massline efforts to enhance 'redness' among cadres, and single-mindedly develop 'large sizes' and, 'high degrees' of public ownership rights are considered to have led to 'chaos' and 'leftism' of the Cultural Revolution type as well as economic stagnation, and thereby hindered growth and modernisation in China. Further, it is said that a socialist society like China is also no exception to the basic contradiction between the forces of production and the relations of production. In fact, this is the main motivating force of progress in all societies. What is evident from these discussions is the lack of concern with the development and institutionalisation of old and new inequalities.

In China at present, there is no attempt to see the dialectic between increased production and transformation of social relations. The main contradiction is not seen as between the socialisation of production and the private ownership of the means of production. It is viewed instead as being between the growing material and cultural needs of the people and the backward social forces of production. The primary emphasis is now on an economic pattern — household based management to update agriculture with modern science and technology and diversify the rural economy by running small scale industries, home-based commercial production, transportation, co-operative enterprises and large-scale animal husbandry, which will help fully develop the forces of production and are acceptable to the local people, enabling them to frequently adjust and forge certain links in the relations of production that are at odds with the development of productive forces in a socialist society.

However, studies of underdevelopment and political economy in the Third World during the last decade have shown that it is usually impossible to dissociate the relations of production from the forces of production. Development of productive forces is usually directed in accordance with the interests of a minority ruling elite which controls (or gradually comes to control) the means of production, and hence wields power. The prevailing productive forces are closely linked to the prevailing social relations, which ultimately reproduce themselves in the interests of the ruling groups or classes. The new economic reforms in China have the potential to give rise to a socio-economic system which subserves the lives and needs of the masses to those of the ruling elite's class and gender.

Household contract system

A more in-depth understanding of the implications of the household contract system emerged from my visit to two communes in Wuxi County, Jiangsu Province, in March 1983. I wanted to see the best that this system of responsibility had to offer to women. Jiangsu is the most economically developed region, situated where the Changjiang (Yangtze) flows into the Yellow Sea. Wuxi County is commonly referred to as the 'land of fish and rice'. Throughout the province, a large number of aid-agriculture industries have been set up. To further promote agricultural production, the government has successfully implemented the policy of 'actively developing a diversified economy' as well as the rural responsibility system. The per capita income from industry for peasants in the rural areas around Wuxi has reached Y323, the highest in China.

The two communes I visited in Wuxi include Meich'un and Ch'ianzhou. Meich'un is located at a distance of 22 kms. from Wuxi city. Women constituted 20 per cent of the commune management committee. Of the 23 production brigades of Meich'un, 22 were engaged in the cultivation of rice and wheat and one specialized in fishing. The commune has adopted the *bao-ch'an* system of responsibility and followed the work point method of produce distribution. Meich'un's management committee was in the process of setting up the township government. Meich'un was called a 'developing' commune, having a medium level of industrial development. The average per capita income for 1982 was 262 yuan, which included income from both collective distribution as well as side-line production. There were nine members in the women's committee at the commune level, Chen Aiwu, its director, is an articulate woman in her early forties who has guided the women's affairs in Meich'un for the last eight years. She was selected to this position in the last commune level election in 1979. A staunch supporter of the new economic changes in the rural areas and in particular of the household contract system, she played a leading role in her family and believed in the existing sexual division of labour in household chores.

Ch'ianzhou, a developed commune, is located at a distance of 40 kms. from Wuxi city. The township government (the former commune) of Ch'ianzhou has 21 production brigades and 300 production teams. Thatched houses were seldom seen in this area and many of the new houses were two-storeyed. Ninety-five per cent of Ch'ianzhou's income came from industry, the remaining five per cent from agriculture, with rice and wheat as the major crops. The average per capita income was reported as 380 yuan. Under the new structural reforms, Ch'ianzhou set up the township government in January 1983. This government handled administrative affairs such as public security, judicial matters, education and culture, family planning and township construction, and the township party committee looked after discipline, implementation of Party policies and organisational and propaganda work. Of the 27 members of the township government, two were women: the head of the government, Ms. Tang and another in charge of family planning.

The economic management of the commune was under the newly constituted economic commission, with its three affiliated commissions for industry, agricultural services and economic diversification. The structural reforms and reorganised economic management in Ch'ianzhou represented a token participation of women: one as a typist in the 13-member economic commission; one as an agro-technician in the 15-member agricultural services comission, two as seri-culture experts in the 14-member commission for economic diversification and two as accountants in the 13-member industry commission. The already inadequate participation of women in decision-making was reported to have further declined from the pre-household contract system period when women's representation was close to 25 per cent in rural Jiangsu.

During my visit to the 12th Production Team of Zhuxiang Production Brigade, which specialized in milk production, I realized that no one wanted to speak of the political meetings and collective efforts of the past. According to the 60 year old team leader, the 'leftist' policies of the past promoted 'equality in distribution or egalitarianism and did not allow anyone to be in a position to prosper. Now, our goal is prosperity for all.' When I raised the point that the new contract system might lead to supporting an inequitable social system, he frankly admitted that during the time that average income has risen, the gap between the rich and poor has widened. About five per cent of the households came within the category of the poor, having a per capita income of less than 100 yuan a year. This is, however, caused mainly by the differences in their ability to work, he added. The team leader, his three sons and their wives were engaged in the specialized activity of milk production. Women took care of cows, and men took charge of the sale of milk, deposits and investments. None of them had any contract with the collective to work a plot of land or to do any specialized work, and have gradually disengaged themselves from working in the fields.

The township government of Ch'ianzhou has developed a three-point plan to narrow the gap between the rich and the poor. First, encouraging some peasants to prosper before others: skilled and hardworking people are provided with funds, technology, and raw materials to specialize in certain lines of business. Their efforts are appreciated, they are given certificates of merit for their prosperity through hard work, and are expected to lead the average peasants. Second, helping poor peasants to prosper through hard labour: the township party committee secretary and the township government make a survey of the poor households and help them through extension of credit, material aid, medical services and the necessary tehnical guidance for their 'prosperity plan'. Third, those who prosper first must help others: prosperous peasants are expected to help other people of their collective who have not been able to do well. Examples of such help are, providing the technical know-how of successful ventures and selling goods at half price to poor, impoverished families.

Erosive effects of the household contract system on women

In the concern for production and economic growth, the woman question has not received any substantial attention. The lack of concern for women in the rural household contract system is illustrated by the numerous examples of reappearance of male dominance and attempts to lock women into their traditional familial roles. I was repeatedly told by economists, rural sociologists, agronomists, journalists and women activists in Beijing, Shanghai, Dalian and Nanging that the different character of China's economic policy in the past five years has accentuated the complex set of issues concerning the debate on women's role in society.

Undoubtedly, the productivity of peasant households has increased as a result of the household contract system of responsibility, and rural women have created more wealth for the State, the collectives and their families. The number of women workers in the State and collectively owned undertakings and enterprises rose from 31.28 million in 1978 to 40.93 in 1982, accounting for 36 per cent of the total number of workers as against 33 per cent in 1978 (*Beijing Review,* 1983). The Fifth National Women's Congress held in Beijing in September 1983, attended by more than 2,000 representatives, commended 10,000 'Five-good Families',[5] and 0.42 million 'March 8th Red Banner Pace-setters'.[6] Despite these achievements, there is, however, no rise in the women's social position in China nor is there an increase in their participation in the decision-making process.

Reports from surveys conducted by the Institute of Agricultural Economics, Beijing, and my discussions with local officials and grassroots women's federations in the countryside of Wuxi County all indicated that after the adoption of the household contract system women's work burden has increased, and their domestication and the sexual division of labour have strengthened. In Ch'ianzhou township, a protocol officer of Wuxi said that only single and career-minded women can compete with men. 'It is evident from past accounts that most of the career-minded women chose to be single or have had childless marriages — also, if all women participate in the work outside the house, the family would be disturbed.' Further he misquoted the present leadership of China, saying that 'Women

[5] 'Five-good Family' is a nation-wide campaign launched since 1979 by Women's Federations at all levels. Five-good family included: *(i)* The family should love the motherland and socialism; *(ii)* every member should work or study hard; *(iii)* family planning should be practiced; and the family should be industrious and thrifty in managing its household; *(iv)* it should practice good sanitation and hygiene; *(v)* it should be a democratic and harmonious family and also cooperate with neighbours.

[6] March 8th Red Banner Pace-setter are those women who *(i)* exemplifed in their great love for the country, the collective and socialism; *(ii)* showed outstanding achievement in labour/production; *(iii)* excelled in knowledge of science and technology; *(iv)* observed the State family planning norms; and *(v)* maintained a harmonious family e.g. showed respect for the aged, love for the young and provided good education to the children. Importantly these criteria for selection did not take into account a dispute or settlement for divorce. (Govind Kelkar, Field Notes, April 1983.)

should devote more time to the household, particularly look after the children and support the husband to do political, social work. These are the women's duties.'

A similar statement about the role of women was the result of a 'frank and informal' discussion with a head of the management committee of Yuanyi Brigade, of Youyi Commune in Jui Xian County. He told me:

> Women in China have equality in all respects .... They do not mind the existing wage disparity as well as discrimination for them in the household side-line production. .... It is the men who have the decisive voice in the family, particularly in the matters of importance, such as building a house or any other major work.... If you give more power to women, they cannot exercise that power or manage the affairs. If a woman could become a brigade leader, I would readily leave this post for her (Kelkar, 1983).

From my recollection of China of 1978, these statements would have been impermissible, both politically and socially, then. The social valuation of man as a better worker and producer has certainly given way to a traditionally strong undercurrent of discrimination against women in a situation rather relaxed from ideological underpinnings.

The production team of Xllich'ou of Sinnan Production Brigade was a known 'specialized village' of Meich'un Commune. All the 26 households of Xllich'ou were engaged in specialized production such as bean curd, bean sprouts, sweet potato cakes, carpentry and tailoring. I visited five households, including that of the production team leader who was a woman and had received a certificate of merit from the county government for earning 10,000 yuan with the family's hard labour in side-line production. In all these houses, women got up early, started work at 4 a.m. or earlier and worked for 10 to 12 hours in the side-line production. Men also worked, but the women's situation was different in the following respects. First, in addition to the 10 or 12 hours work in side-line production, women were responsible for cooking, washing and childcare, carrying night-soil to the pit in the field and bringing the wooden pots back to the houses after adequate cleaning. Surprisingly, men did none of these tasks; 'These are always a woman's work', I was told and if a man were to do it, others would say 'Your wife is lazy. This happens in the cities, too. That's why, men do not do this.' Second, marketing of the produce and the benefits derived from it were handled by men. The husband or the older son carried the produce to the neighbouring Wuxi city or to the 'open market' in Meich'un, and deposited the savings in the commune-run bank there. In four of the five households, I asked if the woman ever saw the bank or operated a joint account with her husband. At first, they did not understand my question; after I explained, they said that in three cases the husband did the banking and in one case the twenty-year old son did it. So a woman's work was subsumed in the household's work and her savings in the household's savings, giving her no additional control or decision-making power in the family or in the production process.

It was repeatedly said that since the introduction of the household contract system, women could arrange their time in such a way that they were able to attend to both housework and contracted work in agriculture and/or side-line production (*Women of China*, 1983). 'In the past due to the "leftist" influence, we stressed full attendance of manpower, that is everyone in the family went out of the house to work. Even some women who were not strong enough to do farmwork, had to go. Now, they can work at home in side-line production.'[7] Strangely, no attempt has been made in the recent past (since the mid-70s) to encourage husbands or other men to share in child-rearing or other strenuous household duties. On the other hand, China's social scientists have come up with the plan to marginalise women and their work:

> It is necessary to lengthen the time for maternity and child-care leave. Raising good children is also a contribution to society. Second, we must begin with the actual state of social production in China and provide more time for women to engage in housework. For example, we could move up the retirement age for women in certain occupations to let younger labour power participate in production. Work schedules could be changed to offer part-time employment,

[7] My interview with the Women's Federation of Jiangsu Province, Nanging April 4, 1983.

> half days or three day workweeks, and so on. Some trades could let women work in spurts as the job calls for, such as the morning or evening markets which could employ women for two to three hours a day. ... In this way, women not only participate in social labour and add a certain amount to the family income, the tension on the home front in terms of housework and childcare is also relieved. This system would enable women to combine their work capacity with their capacity as mothers, so they can do a better job of raising and educating the children (*Social Sciences in China,* No. 2, 1982).

Besides, the remunerative aspects of the household contract system reinforce the traditional superiority of the male. An able-bodied woman is only 80 per cent worth an able-bodied man. This affects the social valuation of women, and is one of the factors leading to the revival of female infanticide in the countryside (discussed in detail later). In Ch'ianzhou, for example, the household contract system was introduced in 1979. In the initial years, peasants continued with the workpoint system. For the past one year however, they have, 'perfected' the *bao-gan* form of the contract system. They no longer follow the workpoint assessment but adhere to the principle 'the more you produce, the more you keep for yourself'. Nevertheless, with regard to women, the wage disparity of the workpoint method continues to be perpetuated. Prior to the introduction of the contract system in Ch'ianzhou, an able-bodied man earned 10 workpoints a days, while an able-bodied woman earned only eight for similar work. In keeping with this tradition, an able-bodied woman could contract only 1.60 mu of land while an able-bodied man would contract two mu of land. The officially stated rationale for this kind of discrimination was that 'a woman is physically weaker than a man'.

During my stay with a peasant family in Xitang Production Brigade and in my informal discussion with the head of the township government, I learnt about the 56-day maternity leave for the first child in the rural areas of Ch'ianzhou. However, in the case of the second or third birth, there was no maternity leave given and the parents had to pay a penalty of 2,100 yuan for the second surviving child and 5,600 yuan for the third. Although in some brigades, one can pay this penalty over the ensuing seven years, in Xitang, the couple has to pay it as a lumpsum. When I asked about cases of female infanticide in the area, I learnt to my surprise that there were few cases. 'But we could not effectively put them down. There was no way we could prove that they had killed the female baby', said Ms. Tang. In the past one and a half years, there were six second and third births in Xitang; only a male baby survived, the remaining five female babies died within five to six days of their birth. At the time of my visit, there were four women who were reported to be pregnant for the second time. Ms. Tang added: 'In the case of a son, one might pay a heavy penalty, up to 5,600 yuan, but in the case of a daughter one might want to get rid of her' (Kelkar, 1983). Traditionally, sons were supposed to continue the family line and provide for their parents in their old age. In contrast, daughters did not continue the family line and did not have the same earning capacity as boys. Girls were lost to another family on marriage and were not in a position to provide for their parents in their old age.

Evidently, the continued preference for sons and the reappearance of female infanticide on a large scale were not mere remnants of the feudal ideology that views men as superior to women, as Chinese leadership sometimes explains (*Beijing Review*, 1983), for there were good economic reasons for the continuing prejudice against daughters and marked preference for sons. The household contract system of responsibility has not merely tended to undo China's earlier efforts at organising the economy along largely sex/gender neutral lines but has strengthened patriarchal structures, putting a premium on the existence of women.

Before the full-scale implementation of the contract system, political and ideological meetings had been institutionalized at the village level. These meetings were particularly directed to raising rural women's consciousness and helping them overcome their subordination and oppression (Kelkar, 1979). With the new strategies of economic development in rural areas, these meetings have been de-emphasised or discontinued, probably as part of the doing away with 'leftist' policies. In an investigation of the implications of the household contract system for rural women's work carried out by a research team from the Institute of Agricultural Economics in Fengyang County in Anhui Province, researchers noted that the women worked from dawn to dusk schemes for economic diversification but they did not meet or collectively discuss amongst themselves. 'There was no time for political and ideological work.' The team concluded that though there was an increase in the income of the households surveyed, 'the women's lot has become worse than before' (Kelkar, 1983). In the Fifth National Women's Congress in September 1983, the All-China Women's Federation regretted the fact that political and ideological work has been neglected with the introduction of the household contract system (and the implementation of the 'one couple, one child' norm). Hence, the ideology of male superiority has been revived among the people, giving rise to ugly practices and 'crimes such as female infanticide, abuse of women and maltreatment of mothers who give birth to girl babies (Kelkar, 1983).

Prior to 1949, female infanticide had been practiced throughout China, particularly during periods of natural and man-made food crises. According to some reports of early twentieth century China, in Beijing alone 24 female infants were thrown out to die and collected by carts at night. In Fujian 20 per cent of female infants were done away with. Missionaries in Guangdong had reported that in certain districts only one out of three female children was allowed to live.[8] The Chinese Communists claimed to have succeeded in nearly ending this practice during the land reform movement that followed the founding of the People's Republic in 1959. Within the first three years of the country's liberation, over a hundred million acres of agricultural land were taken from four million landlords and rich peasants and given to fifty million former landless tenant cultivators (Wilson, 1966). Significantly, women were given the right to own land in their own names which gave them an unprecedented sense of self-worth, in contrast to the traditional system of family property ownership. These land reforms further stipulated that a woman could separate her share from the family land in cases of divorce. This provided economic leverage that clearly strengthened the

[8] For historical accounts of female infanticide in China, See Bernice J. Lee, 'Female Infanticide in China,' in R.W. Guisso and J. Johannson, *Women in China: Current Directions in Historical Scholarship,* New York, Philo Press, 1981; Samuel Couling, *The Encyclopaedia Sinica,* 1917, p.249; Hugh D.R. Baker, *Chinese Family and Kinship,* London, Macmillan, 1979, pp. 6-8.

position of women. Specially illustrative are the following two songs from *The Zhanghe River,*[9] written and popularised at the time of liberation:

'Your place is by the stove. I forbid you to touch my land.'
'But my name's on the title-deed too.'
'In the past year I've made you five pairs of shoes, two suits,
'One padded with cotton. Will you pay for the work?'
'I also wove cloth; you sold it and bought a donkey.
Three parts at least of the beast are mine.
I've washed your clothes, prepared your food
We are equal now, you must give me my due,
Or — shall we ask the court to decide?'
'Laoguai,' she says gently from beneath the quilt
'Nobody heeds your old rules today.'

At sunrise Hoho and the girls set out for the fields.
Ling-ling tells how her husband was silenced.
Her friends sing for joy. The old life is gone, when a woman
Was only a drudge, to cook, wash and bear children.
We are half of the human race. The men forgot that.
A house needs a beam as well as a pillar —
So the world needs women and men.

Ideological underpinnings of the woman question

The Chinese communists considered it necessary to secure equal economic rights and status and equal allocation of land and property for women and men. They intensified educational work among women workers to raise their political consciousness and create a new attitude towards work and production, so that women would fully understand the importance of labour and production work and 'turn themselves into creators of family and social wealth.' Historically, the communist leadership showed a good understanding of the woman question and of the dialectical

[9] The narrative poem *The Zhanghe River* was written in the form of folk ballads popular among the Chinese people, by Yuan Zhangjing in the spring of 1949. Yuan Zhangjing is chairman of the Writers' Association in Beijing. Song of the Zhanghe River is about three women, Hoho, Lingling and Zi Jinying who, like many other women, wished to marry someone they could love and live with in dignity all their lives. These songs suggest women's newly won confidence through their right to land. For some selected songs from *The Zhanghe River,* see *Women of China,* May 1984.

relationship between the politics of women's liberation and socio-economic development. Throughout the period of Maoist leadership in China, particularly during the Great Leap Forward, the Cultural Revolution and the Criticise Lin Biao and Confucius campaign, the party and the government attached great importance to linking economic growth with the creation of a culture and ideology of anti-hierarchical social relations. This did emphasise the issue of women's liberation and the need for a thorough transformation of the family in the course of revolution. In this regard, two legislative measures introduced in the 1950s, deserve special mention. They confronted the structural and cultural bases of the ideology of male superiority. The Marriage Law reduced the power of the male family members by providing for a free choice of partners, monogamy, equal partnership in raising children and altering the patterns of inheritance and custody of children in favour of women. The Chinese Marriage Law did not recognise a 'head of household'; husband and wife had equal status in the family. The Agrarian Reform Law gave women the right to own land and property in their own name. Furthermore, the promulgation of these laws was followed by mass campaigns to make these measures and facilities known to common people throughout the country.

Raising the participation of women in social production, and political consciousness regarding the means to achieve the goals of a socialist society, were fundamental to the woman question in China. Mao Zedong believed that the key to toppling the feudal hierarchical system and Confucian ideology lay in the overthrow of the landlords who formed the backbone of all rural authority. Once the peasants succeeded in seizing power from the landlords, the other authoritarian feudal systems would crumble. At the same time, he felt that the special hardships suffered by women in the traditional patriarchal family invested them with great revolutionary potential.

In his report, 'Women in the Struggle for Land' in *Investigation of Xunwu* (May 1930) Mao noted that women, like men, worked in the toting of grass, in transplanting, hoeing, collecting fuel and firewood, building field ridges, harvesting, and levelling fields after harvest. Women were assisted by men in growing vegetables and in the entire range of domestic work, such as cooking, fetching water, feeding and looking after the pigs and other domestic animals, making shoes, laundering, ironing and washing clothes, sweeping the floors and washing the dishes. They were, however, 'exclusively responsible for rearing children: their burden is much heavier than men's. Women work constantly. Before one job is finished, another comes up. They are appendages to an economic system centred around men (feudal economy and the early stage of capitalist economy', Zhong, 1983). Because of the extraordinary oppression that women suffered, they were an important ally in the construction of socialist China and the fight against feudal ideology. The leadership emphasised that women 'are not only in urgent need of revolution but are also a decisive factor for its success', (Zhong, 1983). The defined task of the party therefore was to launch a new family policy and help women discover their social function. National liberation was consequently to be a liberation from partriarchal structures as well.

Xiang Jingyu was a pioneer of women's organisations and was the first to head a women's department of the Chinese Communist Party in 1922. At her suggestion, the party organised women's associations in the liberated areas with worker — peasant women as the core force. Emphasising the role of women intellectuals in society, she called on them to 'go among the women workers and peasants, work for them and learn from them'. She said the women's movement could be linked with the movement for power to the proletariat: 'Women's rights are not something to be begged for, nor something to be given to us in charity by ruling classes. They are prizes of the struggle that we must seize back from the ruling classes' (Kelkar, 1979). In 1928, Xiang was arrested and sentenced to death by Guomindang.

The party's Plan of Action on Women's Issues in March 1931 asserted that the legal norms of the old society must be destroyed, and asked for the application of political principles to oppose the exploitative relationships of the feudal family, and to guarantee women's equality with men and permit them to acquire civil rights (Kristeva). The 1931 Constitution of Jiangxi Soviet Government went a step further, suggesting the possibility of a society without family. Freedom of marriage was recognized and it was noted that 'measures for the protection of women will assure them the necessary means to dissolve the family bond stage by stage, and fully participate in cultural, political and economic life' (Kristeva).

The new freedom from a forced feudal or bourgeois marriage was considered 'one of the greatest victories in the history of mankind' in the National Congress of Soviets in March 1934. However, after an initial attempt to enforce the Jiangxi Marriage Law in the liberated area in the northwest, the party played down its concern for marriage and family reform. For the first time, during the Yanan period, the party sought the preservation of the family and showed concern for the relationship between husbands and wives. The deputy commander of the Eight Route Army and the CCP North China Bureau in 1942 emphasised the importance of family harmony and sounded a note of caution in promoting women's rights and gender equality (P'eng *et al,* 1942).

Seemingly, there was fear that the integration of the woman question into the process of socio-economic change might complicate the broad base of the anti-Japanese struggle and alienate the male peasantry. Therefore, cadres were urged in other ways to integrate land reform and production with steps towards involving women. It was only towards the later stage of the civil war, in 1947-1948, that the party leadership decided to overcome male resistance and asked cadres to mobilise women for land reform. Since land was distributed on a per capita basis, including women and children, it was considered necessary for women to take part in land reform meetings to help protect their land rights as well as support the class struggle.

The Marxist rationale, central to the woman question in China, is that women are oppressed primarily because they are cut off from social production. In other words, women can gain liberation only through participation in productive labour. The party as well as the Women's Federation have repeatedly stressed that women 'stop looking at economic work as unimportant'. However, in the First Five Year Plan (1952-1957) the method of planning adopted was that of material balances, as in the Soviet Union. The role of the housewife was glorified and women were urged to'do productive labour and run the home thriftily'. Delia Davin makes an attempt to explain this phenomenon:

> It seems probable that the state of economy was a factor in change. In these final years of the Five Year Plan, the last

individual farmer entered the cooperatives. There followed an influx of peasants into the cities seeking to better themselves. Industry could not absorb so many, and there was a sufficiently serious increase in the urban unemployed. In the cities, therefore, there was a feeling that it was unrealistic to ask women to take jobs which did not exist and that it would be better to encourage them to find satisfaction in their traditional roles (Davin, 1976).

In the following years of the Great Leap Forward, 1958-59, the Chinese revolutionists attached great importance to the integration of economic development with the creation of a culture and ideology of anti-hierarchical social relations. The different character of mobilisation and mass initiative in Chinese economic policies in these years emphasised the issue of women's liberation (Zaretsky,1980). The collectivization of agricultural land and the socialisation of housework were considered critical factors in enabling women to participate in productive labour. Millions of housewives stepped out of their homes to work in farms and industries run by the rural people's communes and the neighbourhood committees. (*Chinese Women in the Great Leap Forward,* 1960). Most of the reports published during the late 1950s suggest that 90 per cent of working age women participated in work outside the home in this period; in the 1960s and 1970s there were, however, piece-meal reports indicating that women were involved in social production only to the extent of 54 to 55 per cent in 1958-1959.[10]

Discussions on the family during this period followed the orthodox explication of Engel's analysis: that the abolition of private property, coupled with the socialisation of housework, and the large scale participation of women in social labour would bring about the final demolition of the patriarchal family structure. Thereafter, the family would be established on the more harmonious basis of equality, bringing about a complete liberation of women in a communist society (Johnson, 1983). The Maoist assumption during this period, as at other times, was that the development of social relations and relations of production were a precondition for the development of forces of pro-

[10] For a full-length discussion see Elizabeth Croll. *Women in Rural Development, The People's Republic of China,* ILO, Geneva, 1979, pp. 20-22.

duction; advanced social relations were not the result of developed productive forces.

Against this backdrop, economic growth and higher productivity became the dominant theme of economy and society during the years of the New Economic Policy (1961-1965). Women's participation rate declined sharply. In the policies, the emphasis was again on the role of woman as a housewife and on her reproductive activities, but during the Cultural Revolution, the housewife-oriented campaigns were criticized. The party leadership stressed that 'women hold up half the sky', and that they should be mobilised to participate fully in the socio-economic and political development of the country. In the late 1960s, the essential philosophy of economic and political policies concerning the role of women in the revolutionary society of the Great Leap Forward period was re-established and great stress was laid on mass movement, reducing inequalities and breaking family shackles. Women cadres mobilised other women to smash all inequalities and overcome all obstacles. 'After the overthrow of imperialism, feudalism and bureaucratic capitalism in China, we women had to break down what remained of the feudal authority of husbands' (Tsui *et al.*, 1974).

In China, ever since the Cultural Revolution, the women's movement was re-established as a separate social movement and a major component of the proletarian revolution. Contrary to the uneasy alliance between feminism and socialism and the resultant ambivalence towards women in the First Five Year Plan and the New Economic Policy periods, since the late 1960s there has been clarity in the perception of the woman question in China, namely that the oppression of women is a class oppression (*Beijing Review,* 1973). The women leaders in China pointed out that 'Socialism is not a sufficient condition automatically bringing about a redefinition in the role and status of women in its wake (Croll *et al.*, 1978).' Women will only improve their position if they fight for it themselves 'with a constantly heightened socialist consciousness' (*China Reconstructs,* 1974). They further stressed that participation in social production is a fundamental condition for women's integration in socialist development but it is not a sufficient condition. Consciousness-raising efforts have to be made in order to resolve the pressures emanating from feudal, cultural values and growth-oriented development.

In the mid-'70s the nation-wide campaign to criticise Confucius and Lin Biao went some way towards combining both women's special and class interests. The Chinese treatment of the woman question during this period is particularly striking when we contrast its materialist orthodoxy with an innovative approach to gender equality and the more woman-specific conceptions. There were direct attacks on discrimination against women fostered by a persistent 'feudal-patriarchal ideology' of 'respecting men and despising women' (Soong *et al.*, 1972). A number of specific issues were tied to the campaign, such as (*a*) agitation for more equitable work-point ratings, including a major effort to redefine 'equal work' as 'work of comparable value' rather than the 'same work'; (*b*) household chores and childcare not solely the woman's responsibility: (*c*) promotion of matrilocal marriages and the questioning of patrilocality as a source of gender inequality embedded in marriage practices and family structures. A major contribution of the campaign was the generation of ideological forces that encouraged or legitimised new claims made by women. In the following years, however, the campaign lacked official legitimacy and sustained organisational effort : it therefore failed to accomplish anything concrete.

The Women's Federation protested too against the patriarchal devaluation of housework:

"Conventionally, women are believed to be born housewives, capable of trivial housework only, but the value of housework has never been taken into account. In this way women's position in total social labour is discredited. In reality, the wealth created by men contains the value of women's housework. Investigations show that a woman normally spends 5-6 hours on housework, cooking and looking after children, so that her husband can concentrate on his work in the fields and/or other occupations. This is the point that we should never fail to see while valuing women's work." (Shandong Women's Federation, 1986).

Some of the model women exemplified by the official media were those who demonstrated their excellence both in production and therefore political work and efficiency, and in housework and taking care of husbands and children. This amounts to saying that women who have a revolutionary consciousness can fully demonstrate their zeal and capacity in organisational work as well as in housework, and work effectively in accordance with the right political principles. There was, thus, an implicit assumption that traditional women's work should be retained.

The question then must be: which part of this political code on the woman question should be preserved and developed because of its revolutionary character and which left underdeveloped because of its non-progressiveness? The main contradiction is thus seen as between the women's ideology and their practice, and not between the demands made on them by a political system and their ability to meet these demands. 'A revolutionary policy towards women would have questioned the reasonableness of women's double-work, discussed the social value of the socialisation women carry out and placed the collectivization of housework on the agenda (Hemmel *et al.*, 1984). This, however, did not happen.

In present-day China, the family has received attention both from the party leadership and the All-China Women's Federation. The major task of the recently established Marriage and Family Research Institute is to study problems related to marriage and the family and help formulate policies to promote socialist ethics (Kelkar *et al.*, 1983). While feminist literature and women writers in China did not directly attack the family and marriage, a suggestion was made for a radical transformation in family relationships and in the attitudes of 'bad' husbands with the help of political education and legal measures. No attempt was made, however, to examine women's work in the house and their familial roles — how these are determined by history, social structure and growth-oriented development policies, and how they combine to determine women's position in Chinese society.

Response of the Women's Federation and its changing character

The Women's Federation has launched a resistance movement against the ideology of male superiority and patriarchal norms that oppress and discriminate against women in the family and community. The Fifth National Congress noted a feeling among its participants that they ought to reorient their organisation along gender-specific problems. The Women's Federation must break the shackles of male dominance and increase their political consciousness, professional knowledge and investigative skills to live up to their role of the 'defender and protector of women's rights and interests'.

In order to deal with the recent rise in unemployment in the cities of China, some social scientists suggested that women should devote more time to household chores and to 'raising good children'. As noted earlier they recommended part-time employment for able-bodied female labour and seven-year child-rearing leave for women workers. Women journalists, writers, students and cadres mobilised other worker-peasant women and launched a campaign against these recommendations (Kelkar *et al.*, 1983). In the Fifth National Congress, these recommendations were finally ensured; the representatives emphasised that they would not allow anyone to condemn the Chinese women to household drudgery and child-tending. The Federation's President, Kang Keqing said: 'The idea that "too many people are employed in China now, and as women shoulder a heavy burden in the families, they should return home and perform their household duties" is wrong because it is incompatible with the principle of equality between men and women and is bound to weaken the socialist modernization' (*Beijing Review,* 1983). It was further said: 'If we advocate the viewpoint "women workers go home", does this not mean that we negate the prerequisite of women's liberation? If women workers do go home, they will no longer have independent economic incomes. They will always ask for money from their husbands. Under such circumstances, how can they talk about equality? Without economic independence how can they talk about true independence?' (*Beijing Review,* 1983). However, the Women's Federation considered it desirable to reduce the six-day working week for women in order to give them more time at home with their children and to attend to household chores.

The Fifth National Congress of Women questioned the increasing discrimination against women in the fields of education and employment. In the previous five years the number of women scientists, technicians and professionals rose from 1.67 million in 1978 to 1.93 million in 1982, constituting 31.6 per cent of the total number of scientists and professionals in China. However, only two per cent of the senior positions were held by women, and of the country's 335.6 million illiterates, 70 per cent were women, (*Beijing Review,* 1983). Evidently, the party is also not free from an attitude of male superiority. In the 1980s, there are only 5,200,000 women party members, making up 13 per cent of the total membership (Luo, 1983). Time and again in the last five years, the Women's Federation has complained about the political under-representation of women as well as about their declining number in decision-making bodies. It was said that 'the present local situation of women cadres resembles the shape of a pagoda: the higher the level the fewer the women cadres, and even their number is declining in China today," (*Renmin Ribao,* 1983). To check this decline, the Women's Federation has conducted its own investigation into discriminatory practices in recruitment, training and promotion of women. In one such case in Hunan, in an examination of 1,500 cadres from rural areas conducted by the Personnel Bureaux, the Women's Federation found that no women were permitted to sit for the examination. It reported the matter to the party committee and obtained the guarantee that 20 per cent of the cadres recruited would be women (*Women of China,* 1983).

The main aim of the Fourth National Women's Congress in 1978 was to involve the masses of women in the new modernisation policies: 'The new line of the party was to be the fundamental line of the women's movement' (*Beijing Review,* 1978). Unlike the 1978 Women's Congress, the Women's Federation in the early '80's became increasingly aware of gender-specific problems arising mainly from the new economic reforms and modernising policies being pursued. The Fifth National Congress decided to take resolute action to redress cases of discrimination against women and to combat all ideas and practices that oppress or belittle women or promote the image of a devoted wife and mother. In a recent reaction to the anxiety caused by the rising number of divorces, Lei Jieqiong, a famous sociologist and leading member of the Women's Federation in Bejing, said: 'Why do people assume that the present increase in divorce is a tendency towards the bourgeois way of life? . . . Why do so many literary works advocate that women be satisfied as housewives, setting aside their own careers to further those of their husbands? . . . The increasing rate of divorce is evidence that women are moving towards emancipation from feudal mental fetters.' (*China Daily* 1983). Lie Jieqiong concluded by expressing the need for more research on women's problems.

The Fifth National Congress further stressed the use of socialist ideology to correctly handle the relationships between love, marriage and childcare on the one hand, and work, labour and study on the other. The years 1983-1984 were marked by Law Publicity Week in Beijing and the emergence of legal aid booths to publicise and defend the constitutional rights of women throughout the country. The Women's Federation organised public forums to acquaint women with their legal rights to assist them in their struggle against all sorts of discrimination and persecution, (*Women of China,* 1984). In February 1984, 74 booths were set up in the busy areas of Beijing; over 2000 lawyers, judicial workers, college teachers and students worked in these booths; they played tapes of speeches made by officials of State, judicial departments and party leadership to popularise women's rights, and answered legal questions on intra-familial disputes, the status of women in the family; the inheritance rights of daughters and protection for female victims of violence. Emphasising the gender-specific demands of the Women's Federation, Kang Keqing suggested the need for 'a systematic and meticulous investigation to identify the problems that are harmful to the legal rights and interests of women and children . . . On the basis of this investigation, the Women's Federation was to take the initiative in cooperating with other departments to study, formulate and implement the measures necessary to solve these problems. Only in this way can the Women's Federation hope to deal effective blows at crimes of cruelly injuring and murdering women and children, stop the drowning and abandoning of infant girls and eliminate all those ugly phenomena that should never exist in a socialist China.' (*Renmin Ribao,* 1984).

The Women's Federation implicitly admonished the socialist administration which allows crimes such as female infanticide to go unpunished. Towards the end, to effectively check the rising number of crimes against female babies and women, the Women's Federation carried out investigations in a number of provinces and counties and reported an alarming disparity in the number of male and female infants, thereby highlighting the spreading crime of female infanticide, (*Renmin Ribao,* 1984). The report of the Women's Federation of Anhui Province pointed out the increasing gap between the ratio of male and female babies in the counties of Suixi and Haiyuan during 1979 to 1981, and stated that 'the main cause of disparity in the male-female baby ratio was female infanticide under the influence of male chauvinism which was a vestige of feudal ideology'. The report added that in a production brigade in Haiyuan county more than 40 female babies had been drowned in 1980-81.

To further improve its organisational capacity to deal adequately with the new dimensions of the woman question in China, the Women's Federation, in addition to its existing schools for cadres, plans to set up a Chinese Women's University where women will be trained in both socialist theory and gender-specific programmes.

The party and government leadership have also repeatedly criticized the lingering ideas of patriarchal clan and hierarchy in social relations (*Beijing Review,* 1983).

Recently, the CCP Central Committee issued a directive to all party units, saying that the protection of the legitimate rights of women and children is 'an important matter concerning the observation of constitution and the State laws. It is not the responsibility of a single organization such as the Women's Federation but also the common task of the entire party and the entire people' (*Renmin Ribao,* 1983). Notwithstanding their efforts, what is seen in China today, not unlike many other Third World countries, is the dichotomy between a political system which consciously legislates for improvement and the welfare of women and a development planning which gives priority to economic growth and technological modernization that is detrimental to women's interests and is therefore ultimately against the liberation of society.

REFERENCES

Beijing Review: May 16 1983. Also, YU Guangyuan (ed.) *China's Socialist Modernization,* Beijing, Foreign Languages Press, 1984.
——: September 19, 1983.
——: 'Protecting Infant Girls', Editorial, January 31, 1983.
——: March 8, 1973; March 8, 1974; September 29, 1978; March 9, 1979.
——: September 19, 1983.
Ibid, 'The Viewpoint Women Workers Go Home is Wrong', *Guangming Ribao,*

September 10, 1983 (for translation, see Survey of World Broadcasts (SWB) September 24, 1985 (FE/7447/BII/2).

Beijing Review: September 19, 1983.

——: September 29, 1978, also SWB, April 25, 1978.

——: October 10, 1983.

China Daily: May 12, 1983; *Beijing Review,* September 5, 1983.

China Reconstructs: March 1974.

Chinese Women in the Great Leap Forward: Peking, Foreign Languages Press, 1960.

CROLL, ELIZABETH, *Feminism and Socialism in China.* London, Routledge and Kegan Paul, 1978, p. 330; also the author's interviews with Women's Federations in 1978 and 1983. Field Notes, March-April, 1978; and April, 1983.

DAVIN, DELIA: *Woman-Work, Women and the Party in Revolutionary China,* Oxford University Press, 1976, pp. 110-111.

HEMMEL, VIBEKE & PIA SINDBJERG: *Women in Rural China: Policy Towards Women Before and After the Cultural Revolution,* Curzon Press, Scandinavian Institute of Asian Studies, p. 73, 1984.

JOHNSON, KAY ANN: *Women, the Family and Peasant Revolution in China,* Chicago, University of Chicago Press, 1983.

KELKAR, GOVIND: Field Notes, April 1983.

——: *China After Mao: A Report on Socialist Development,* New Delhi, Usha Publishers, 1979, Chapter X.

——: Field Notes, April 1983.

——: *China After Mao, op. cit.* 1979, pp. 154-155.

——: Field Notes, April 1983; also *China Daily,* February 27, 1983.

——: Field Notes, April 1983; also *China Daily,* February 27, 1983.

——: Field Notes, April, 1983

KRISTEVA, JULIA: *About Chinese Women* (translated from French by Anita Barrows) London, Marion Boyars, p. 120

Ibid, p. 121

LU YUN: 'Specialized Households Emerge' *Beijing Review,* December 3, 1984.

Ibid, November 12, 1984.

LUO QIONG: 'Party Rectification and Women's Rights' *Renmin Ribao,* December 11, 1983.

NOLAN, PETER: 'De-Collectivisation of Agriculture in China, 1979-82: A Long-term Perspective,' *Economic and Political Weekly,* August 6, 1983; Andrew Watson, 'Agriculture Looks for "Shoes that Fit": The Production Responsibility System and Its Implication', Paper presented at the China in Transition Conference, Queen Elizabeth House, Oxford, September, 1982; Marina Thorborg, 'Problems of Theory and Practice. Doing Research on Women in the Chinese Economy' in Myra Lewinter (ed.) *Theoretical and Methodological Problems in Research on Women in Developing Countries,* Copenhagen, Women's Research Centre in Social Science, December, 1982.

P'ENG TEH-HUAI: 'Report Concerning Work in the North China Base Areas' in *Kung-fei Hui kuo shih-lia lei-pien, Collection of Historical Materials on the Communist Bandits,* Vol. 3, pp. 380-382. Also Dingling's Criticism of the Party's Treatment of the Woman Question, (*Liberation Daily,* March 8,

1942), Yanan, 1942.
Renmin Ribao: Editorial, November 7, 1983.
Ibid: also *Beijing Review*, May16,1983 and YU Guangyuan(ed.) *China's Socialist Modernization, op. cit.*, 1984.
——: 'Continuing Discrimination Against Women', March 4, 1983.
——: April 7, 1984.
Ibid, also see Huang I-shu, 'China's Renewed Battle Against Male Chauvinism' , *China Report,* Vol. XIX No. 4, July-August, 1985.
——: April 29, 1983.
Social Sciences in China, No. 2, p.164.
SOONG, CHING-LING: 'Women's Liberation in China' *Peking Review,* No. 6, February 11, 1972; *Renmin Ribao (People's Daily),* March 14, 1975; Kay Ann Johnson, *Women, the Family and Peasant Revolution in China, op. cit.* Chapter 13.
TSUI YU-LAN,: 'How We Women Won Equality' *China Reconstructs,* March 1974; also see *Women Hold Up Half the Sky,* (Reprints from *Peking Review* and *China Reconstructs*), Berkeley, Yenan Books, 1980.
WILSON, DICK: *A Quarter of Mankind: An Anatomy of China Today,* London, 1966, p. 7.
Women of China: November, 1983, *Beijing Review,* November 28, 1983, also November 19, 1984.
——: August, 1983
——: January 1984, *Beijing Review,* October 15, 1984.
——: 'Women Show Their Strength in the Development of Rural Economy', Paper Presented by Shandong Women's Federation at a Seminar on Women in Agriculture and Rural Development, Aunguxian, China, May 1986.
Xinhua: 'Changes in Chinese Living Standards in Four Years', June 14, 1983.
ZARETSKY, ELI: *Capitalism, the Family and Personal Life,* London, Pluto Press, 1980, p. 102.
ZHONG FU: 'Comrade Mao Zedong's Investigations of Women's Conditions in the Countryside', *Women of China,* December, 1983, pp. 4-6.

TWO ROADS TO THE FACTORY

Industrialisation Strategies and Women's Employment in Southeast Asia

Pasuk Phongpaichit

Introduction

Capital accumulation needs efficient, cheap and docile labour, be it male or female. A capitalist State will facilitate the induction of women into wage employment whenever this is necessary for the benefit of capitalism and for achieving the State's industrialisation goals. The integration of female labour into formal wage employment has been a regular feature in countries which have adopted a labour-intensive export-oriented industrial policy in joint ventures with multinational companies, in recent years. In many of these countries, before the introduction of such a strategy, there may well have been religious or conventional household norms which acted as a constraint to women's entry into formal wage employment away from home. In such cases, the State has often found subtle ways to mobilise women away from their households into the realm of social reproduction.

A change in the economic role of women invariably leads to changes in the division of labour within the household. As young women go out to work, older women, older men and young men who cannot find work may have to share in housework. They may moreover, resent women going out to work because the household stands to lose some of the services and comforts previously provided by the women. Such resistance is likely to be stronger if what the young women workers bring in is not substantial. There may be attempts on the part of older women and men to put pressure on young women to combine their traditional role and their new working role in such a way that the rest of the household does not lose out. They may even make the change difficult for young women by not co-operating or not being sufficiently understanding when young girls encounter problems relating to their new life-styles.

Both the State and the household thus make claims on, or make use of, women. The interplay of these claims in the process of on-going economic and social change results in different consequences in different socio-economic contexts, labour market situations, government strategies and industrial policies.

In cases where governments have created an export processing zone or free trade zone, capitalists and governments often co-operate in making use of women workers in a rather ruthless manner. Some States allow companies to take advantage of women workers by officially banning trade unions and dispensing with some of the labour laws.[1] By so doing the State in effect ignores the interests of women and the household, and tends to perpetuate their inequality and subordinate status.

Examples of countries which have pursued labour-intensive, export-oriented industrialisation vigorously include Singapore, South Korea, Taiwan, Malaysia and Hong Kong, and to a lesser extent, Thailand and the Philippines. Where the strategy has

[1] Edgren (1982: 21-22), reported that with the onset of the drive for export-led growth in Asia since the '60s, trade union organisation and collective bargaining which have grown in importance since the Second World War were severely curbed. In Korea, a Provisional Special Law Concerning Regulation of Labour Unions and Labour Disputes at Foreign Capital Firms was introduced in 1970, prohibiting all labour disputes in the Export Processing Zones. Statutory arbitration committees were set up to resolve labour disputes, and a number of exemptions from existing laws were granted in the zones. Trade unions were effectively banned in the zones. In Singapore the introduction of the Industrial Relations (Amendment) Act of 1968 reduced many of the workers' previous rights, such as the right to negotiate on issues like dismissal and reinstatements. Trade union organisations were turned into a business organisation (see also Heyzer, 1982a). Similar regulations were introduced in Malaysia in 1967, and strikes were banned. In the Philippines, a tightening of labour legislation was introduced in 1974. No strikes were allowed in 'vital' industries, which included those of the zones. In Sri Lanka, there was an attempt to empower the Labour Minister to exempt firms in the Free Trade Zones from the provision of the existing labour laws. But this proposal was later withdrawn after much criticism both nationally and internationally, but trade unions were still not allowed to enter the compounds of the Free Trade Zone.

created mass employment for women, their traditional roles have undergone a dramatic change. But the experiences of different countries vary a great deal; where industrialisation did not take off but was eclipsed by the growth of the service sector, many women were instead inducted into informal and service occupations, such as personal services and sexual services (as in Thailand and the Philippines), as well as construction and other labouring work. Even among successful industrialising countries, the position of women differs greatly. In this paper we shall look at the situation in two rather successful industrialisers, Singapore and South Korea. The purpose is to delineate those circumstances which make for a difference in the status of women in both.

We shall look first at the special features of female employment in export-oriented, labour-intensive industries and the reasons which induce women to work in formal wage employment.

Why women enter formal wage employment

There is a mass of literature available on the recent integration of Asian women in labour-intensive, export-oriented industries. Most of it deals with wages, working conditions, and the characteristics of industry and women workers. Recently, there has been an attempt to emphasise the specificity of the experience of different countries in the context of local patriarchal, religious and cultural traditions, government policies and the relative prosperity of the national economy. Sufficient data and information have been generated from these studies for us to obtain a fairly clear picture of what happens when women are drawn from the fields to the assembly line.

It is now fairly well documented that the steady flow of cash income from work in multinationals is the most important inducement to women to work, and to families to accept their new role as workers away from home. The women's incomes benefit not only women themselves but also their families by increasing their material welfare. Women's contribution to the family is strongly felt in Taiwan and Hong Kong where industry has offered them employment for over a decade. In these two countries it was found that the women's families had become so dependent on their daughters' incomes that they resisted their wish to marry. In Indonesia where industrial employment for women is still rather insignificant when compared to the availability of women workers, wages are still very low, but the steady flow of income into the household while the women are working is of great value. Women's wages are used to pay interest on loans, make improvements in the house and clear other payments which would otherwise have been almost impossible.

As far as the women themselves are concerned, the increased earning power confers on them greater financial independence, and higher status in the households. This higher status is visible in the greater freedom that working women have in the choice of marriage partners, in deciding when to marry, and in participating more in decisions concerning the financial affairs of the household.

The advantages of women's employment then, are a greater total income for the family, and improved status within the family for the women. Against these two advantages, however, must be weighed the negative effects of such employment. First, women working in export-oriented enterprises risk damage to their health due to bad working conditions and a high incidence of industrial diseases. Second, the overall welfare of the family and, especially, childcare may deteriorate if other family members or some other agency do not take over some of the functions which the working women can no longer manage. Third, the women and their households face the possibility of severe financial and psychological strain if the women are laid off when the factory shifts elsewhere or are forced to leave work when they have children. In most cases factories employ only single girls, and do not pay enough for women to afford surrogate childcare. Many women find that they are useful to employers only when they are young and highly productive; when they are discarded they find that they have neither the training nor experience for future lucrative employment in the labour market.

The experiences of different countries indicate a rather varied pattern. In all cases, the women benefit on some counts and lose on others; no change takes place without some disrupting forces, however. We will not attempt to discuss the pros and cons of the strategy; rather, we would like to focus not so much on what happens in early attempts to industrialise but on the consequences on women and the household once the country has achieved a certain measure of industrialisation. In the following two examples, we will look at the question of working women and the household in a broad context. The recruitment of women into factory employment was only one feature of a period of rapid and sweeping change in both societies: they were forced to confront the problem of new roles not just for factory women but for women as a whole. We cannot isolate the specific effects which women's employment had on changing attitudes to women in general, or how far other changes in women's roles impinged on the position of factory girls. We merely have to see the experience of the factory girls as part of a wider canvas.

Singapore

Singapore began its labour-intensive industrialisation strategy only in 1960, for which it relied heavily on foreign capital from multinational companies.[2] At that time it had a large pool of unemployed and underemployed workers, and participation rates among women were still rather low. The industrial strategy required female labour, and the government did several things to facilitate their recruitment, such as locating industrial zones near communities with underemployed women workers. In the 1960s, young women workers were mobilised into industrial employment in large numbers. They were subject to long hours of work and relatively low pay, compared to the men. The two main industries at the time were garments and electronics. These industries experienced rapid technological change and retrenchment was common; workers could be laid off very easily, and women workers were the first to suffer. They were also susceptible to industrial diseases. Liberals and feminists wrote several articles against these conditions and the maltreatment of women workers. The government limited trade union activities and prohibited strikes, thus colluding with the MNCs to exploit labour.

The late 1970s, however, presented a rather different picture. Successful industrialisation had created a tight labour market for both men and women, and women's wages began to increase, making for a narrowing gap between male and female wages.

[2] On industrialisation in Singapore see, for example, Datta-Chaudhuri (1982).

The government began to assist married workers in continuing to work by subsidising the cost of childcare in some cases. Attempts were also made to upgrade the skills of both men and women workers. It is not difficult to see that the government's assistance was motivated by the fact that the Singapore economy needed its female labour to keep industrialisation going, as Singapore has a rather small population. But even then the government's move came rather late: from the beginning it was the household which played a very important role in women's continued employment in industry.

According to one study, the factory women who entered the job market during the first phase of labour-intensive industrialisation and managed to remain in the industrial work-force into the second phase, were often upgraded into positions of higher pay, and greater permanence. These were women who had family support for childcare and other household chores, or those who, at the start of their careers, had been educated upto the primary level or above. These two factors were important to the women's careers. Family support enabled the women to continue working long enough, even after marriage, in order to acquire the tenure and skill necessary for further upgrading, as industries progressed from labour-intensive to more capital-intensive operations; a high educational level enabled them to acquire more skills and move up the wage scale in the industrial hierarchy. Higher wages in turn allowed the women to pay for the cost of childcare and remain in the work-force even after marriage. The women who had neither family support nor educational qualifications tended to suffer most as they had to quit work upon marriage.

The '60s and '70s still had the prevalence of the extended family system among the Chinese, and this assisted the women a great deal. Many women factory workers were able to rely on family support because their families were close at hand. Singapore's women workers were mainly recruited from within the relatively small state of Singapore, and government contrived to locate factories close to *kampongs* (village homes) with surplus women workers to ensure a good supply of labour with minimal disruption. This situation differs from that of many other Asian industrialisers, where new industries rely heavily on migrant labour drawn from a wider rural hinterland. Such migrant labour cannot depend on a family support system near at hand.

Towards the early '70s, the extended family system went into a decline as a result of the mushrooming of public housing through the Housing Development Board, which aimed at resettling families from *kampongs* that often housed large extended families, into modern flats designed for nuclear families. In this situation only women who could afford childcare remained in the work-force. Here too, the household played an important role: kin members were prepared to help look after the children of working mothers in return for some compensation, which was usually cheaper than private childcare services.

In the second phase of industrialisation, tight labour markets and higher wage compelled the government to shift its industrialisation strategy from labour-intensive to capital-and skill-intensive enterprises. In order to achieve this the development of human resources was of utmost importance, and since Singapore has a small population, it could not afford to discriminate against women. Thus, public policies to upgrade the educational levels and skills of those who had not had the opportunity to do so in the previous phase, were open to both men and women. In this second phase more women entered professional occupations, and in industry, more were upgraded into supervisory roles and positions. The need for female labour compelled the government to provide assistance in childcare, and even encourage men to play a more active role in household work.

Thus by the early '80s in Singapore, women became a permanent part of the industrial labour force, in every sphere of work from unskilled to skilled and professional. In the realm of human resource development policies, women are now much less discriminated against, compared to previous periods and to other countries.

Factory women now have much more control over themselves and their careers, and participate more in decisions concerning the household's finances. Their wages have been rising and prospects for a career in industry are better, when compared to the situation prevailing before industrialisation, and to the position of factory women in South Korea, another rather successful industrialiser of the last 20 years. By no means am I suggesting that the situation in Singapore is ideal; urban women as a group still feel discriminated against and among them, factory women more than educated women. But on the whole, their position has improved, and as they become more sure of themselves and of their importance in the permanent industrial labour force of the country, State attempts to manipulate them are correspondingly more difficult.

South Korea

In terms of the long-term consequences of industrialisation on women and the household, the case of South Korea is markedly different from Singapore. South Korea has also undergone two main phases of industrialisation — the labour-intensive phase in the '60s and early '70s, and a more capital-and skill-intensive phase from the mid-'70s onwards.[3] As far as women workers are concerned however, they still constitute what may be termed a 'floating' or 'peripheral' labour force.[4]

Women's industrial working lives are still rather short, extending from their late teens upto the time they get married or have children. The reasons for this can be found both in the economic and the social sphere. In the economic context, South Korea has a much larger population than Singapore (40 million as against 2.5 million), and thus in terms of the labour market it has a much larger supply of both male and female labour; the competition between males and females for industrial jobs is thus much keener overall. Further the source of supply of workers, females included, for factories, in the early phases of industrialisation was the large rural hinterland. Migrant women workers had to travel a long way from home and were thus deprived of their family support systems.

Despite the fast growth of industrialisation in South Korea, the rate of labour absorption was still not rapid enough to create a tight labour market situation as in Singapore. It is also possible that the social bias against women was stronger in South Korea, and militated against change, even for example in education. Women are usually educated in the liberal arts, and men in subjects such as engineering, science, computer engineering,

[3] On industrialisation in South Korea see for example, Park (1980).

[4] Information on South Korean women workers are from Yoon (1977), the Federation of Korean Trade Unions, (1978) and interviews with researchers in KWDI, FKTU and Ehwa University in 1983.

economics and law for which there is a greater demand. As industries progress from labour-intensive to capital-intensive technologies, men move up the ladder through re-training programmes and incentives and encouragement to study, while women remain behind, so that those with poor social backgrounds move from outdated labour-intensive industries into jobs discarded by men.

In South Korea, a woman's place is still seen to be very much in the home. A married woman is supposed to look after the household affairs of not only her immediate family, but of her husband's as well. Despite the emergence of the nuclear family this custom is so prevalent that, even where a woman is living with her parents-in-law, she is not in a position to ask them to help with childcare or other household chores, to enable her to continue working. This is in marked contrast to Singapore where, as we have seen, the extended family is very supportive to the working woman.

Without family support, factory women are at a great disadvantage in the labour markets, as they find it difficult to remain in the labour force long enough to acquire tenure and skills. In most cases, therefore, they cannot return to industrial jobs until after their child-rearing responsibilities are over. In the urban slum of Seoul there is now a large number of poor married women in their late '30s or '40s who were factory workers in the labour-intensive industries of the '60s. Most of them came from rural areas as migrant workers, and married and settled down in the outskirts of Seoul. Discarded from the labour force after marriage, poorly educated and lacking the skills now in demand by industry, they end up working as housemaids for middle class families for very low wages.

The unwillingness of the family and society to accept the woman's role in social production disadvantages Korean women in other ways as well. Their household work is not valued in economic terms. This, coupled with the unwillingness of the family and society to accept women's role in the public sphere, acts to lower the economic value of women's work in industry. Thus we find that women's wages in Korean industries (for unskilled and semi-skilled jobs) are about two-thirds men's wages or less (after adjusting for differences in age and length of service), and there is very little sign of a narrowing in the gap between male and female wages. This means, effectively, that women cannot afford surrogate childcare.

Another striking difference between Singapore and South Korea is society's or government's view of women with regard to policies on human resource development. Whereas in Singapore women are not discriminated against in education and professional jobs because of the shortage of labour, in South Korea they do not seem to enter the government's development goals as part of the human resource factor in economic development at all. They are pushed into the labour market when required, as during the labour-intensive phase of industrialisation, but must leave their jobs and return home when their families demand. While government policy in Singapore attempts to upgrade the educational level of both men and women who could not benefit from compulsory education in the early phase of industrialisation there is no such policy in South Korea: all vocational school education and attempts to upgrade skills in the private sector have been concentrated on men.

Rapid industrialisation and the shift towards capital-intensive industry in South Korea have created a rather tight labour market situation for industrial workers in skilled and technical jobs. We would expect that the women would now be in a position to get better jobs and better pay; recent developments however have shown that they inherit only those work opportunities which are discarded by men. Welding is a case in point: traditionally a male occupation, Korean women have recently been encouraged to take it up in shipyards and factories. The Korean Employers' Federation has even suggested that more women be trained in welding techniques. This suggestion, ostensibly a radical move aiming at diversifying women's role in the industrial sphere, reveals itself, on closer inspection, as the old imperative at work again: a shortage of men for this work has raised the demand for women. Welding is characterised by a high turnover rate and, in advanced countries like Japan, for instance, robots are increasingly replacing manpower. The reasons for this are two: the high efficiency of robots, and the difficulty in getting men to weld when they can choose other occupations instead. South Korea cannot afford robots but it can offer women the unpleasant jobs that men no longer want. Doubtless, once robots are introduced, women welders will be discarded and ushered back to their kitchens again.

Thus, in South Korea, women, despite having contributed to its successful industrialisation, have not been able to escape the hold of the household as defined by social custom. The relatively slack labour market situation as compared to Singapore, and a different industrialisation strategy may be said to be the main reasons responsible for this state of affairs. In the period we are studying there was no real imperative to change women's status, as was the case in Singapore, where there was a clear dependence on women workers in the second phase of industrialisation. It should also be pointed out that the subordinate position of women in South Korea is not confined to factory women; even the educated are oppressed. Although more Korean women now have access to education, very few can get satisfactory jobs. In government service, for instance, there are hardly any women in executive and professional grades.

The Korean government is only just beginning to talk about ways to encourage married women to continue working in those occupations where male labour is tight. Yet, neither government nor employer is prepared to subsidise the cost of childcare. The general feeling is that this is the responsibility of NGOs or social welfare organisations, and family norms, as we have seen, provide little support to women.

Conclusions

These notes on the experience of women in a growing industrial labour force in two Asian countries do not make for any definitive conclusions but they do begin to suggest a framework of analysis.

In the newly industrialising countries of Asia, just as in the older industrial countries, women have played a secondary role in the industrial labour force. They have been hauled into the labour market only under special circumstances — when there is an especially strong demand for labour, or when there is a special demand for work at which women are believed to excel — while under other circumstances there is a strong social preference for dividing up the tasks and allotting women the household.

The intensity of labour demand is thus the major factor

regulating women's induction into the labour force.There is however, an interplay between labour demand, government policy and household organisation which affects the way labour demand eventually affects women. In the event of a high labour demand, government can take steps to encourage female recruitment into the labour force, or seek other options. For instance, it could invest in upgrading the productivity of the existing (largely male) labour force to alleviate labour demand, or it could encourage the use of robots. It is quite possible that South Korea would respond to a high labour demand with the latter alternative.

The household is likely to offer initial resistance to female induction into the labour force in order to conserve the benefits which the household gains from its non-working female members. But in the event that women wish to go out to work, they can (with difficulty) use the household as a supportive resource. Their success in doing so is likely to depend on many factors — the accessibility of the household (difficult for a migrant worker), the contribution that their income makes to family welfare, the availability of outside support structures (State-sponsored welfare), and so on.

Earlier studies of the recruitment of women into the industrial labour force in Asian industrialisers struck a pessimistic note: they saw the employment of women as essentially exploitative and short-term. The subsequent experience of South Korea tends to support this prediction, but in Singapore, where labour market conditions were tighter, where the government positively encouraged female recruitment, and where the households offered working women some support resources, women were able to play a role in the labour market which was more than just peripheral. It remains to be seen whether this role will be retained and developed further.

SELECT BIBLIOGRAPHY

BLAKE, MYRNA: *A Case Study on Women in Industry,* Bangkok, Asian and Pacific Centre for Women and Development, 1980.

DATTA-CHAUDHURI, MRINAL: 'The Role of Free Trade Zones in the Creation of

Employment and Industrial Growth in Malaysia', Bangkok, ILO-ARTEP, Working Paper, 1982.

EDGREN, GUS: *Spearheads of Industrialisation or Sweatshops in the Sun? A Critical Appraisal of Labour Conditions in Asian Export Processing Zones,* Bangkok, ILO-ARTEP, Working Paper, 1982.

ELSON, DIANE & RUTH PEARSON: 'The Latest Phase of the Internationalisation of Capital and Its Implications for Women in the Third World', *Discussion Papers* No. 150, IDS, University of Sussex, 1982.

GROSSMAN, RACHEL: 'Women's Place in the Integrated Circuit', in *Southeast Asia Chronicle.* No. 66, January-February, 1979.

HEYZER, NOELEEN: 'The Relocation of International Production and Low-Pay Women Workers' Employment: The Case of Singapore', in Kate Young and Mckintosh (eds.), *Third World Women and Development,* London, Routledge and Kegan Paul, 1982.

—— : 'From Rural Subsistence to Peripheral Industrial Labour Force', in Lourdes Beneria (ed.), *Women and Development: The Sexual Division of Labour in Rural Economies,* New York, Praeger, 1982.

LIM, LINDA: 'Women Workers in Multinational Corporations in Developing Countries — The Case of the Electronics Industry in Malaysia and Singapore', Women's Studies Programme, *Occasional Papers,* No. 9, University of Michigan, Ann Arbor, 1978.

—— : 'Women Industrial Workers: The Specificities of the Malaysian Case', paper prepared for a book on women workers in Malaysia, ed. by Jamilah Griffin and Wendy Smith. Kuala Lumpur, 1984.

PARK, YUNG CHUL: 'Export-led Development: The Korean Experience (1960-1978)', in Eddy Lee (ed.), *Export-led Industrialisation & Development,* Bangkok, ILO-ARTEP, 1980.

SALAFF, JANET & EILEEN WONG: 'Women Workers: Factory, Family and Social Class in an Industrialising Order', in Gavin W. Jones (ed.), *Women in the Urban and Industrial Workforce: Southeast and East Asia,* The Australian National University, Development Studies Centre, Monograph No. 33, 1984.

WOLF, DIANE L: 'Making the Bread and Bringing it Home: Female Factory Workers and the Family Economy in Rural Java', in Gavin W. Jones (ed.), *Women in the Urban and Industrial Workforce,* 1984.

YOON, SOON YOUNG: 'Study on the Role of Young Women in the Development Process, Especially in Industries', Bangkok. ESCAP. Division of Population and Social Affairs, mimeo, 1977.

BABIES TO ORDER

Official Population Policies in Malaysia and Singapore

Chee Heng Leng

Of late, the Prime Ministers of both Malaysia and Singapore have created a furore in their respective countries with certain policy pronouncements on their population programmes. Dr. Mahathir Mohamed, Malaysia's Prime Minister, announced a policy to achieve a population of 70 million in 115 years as a solution to the country's industrialization and domestic market problems. (Malaysia's current population is 15 million, and was expected to stabilise at 33 million in twenty years.)[1] In order to accomplish this feat, Malaysian women are being encouraged to bear five children each. Mr. Lee Kuan Yew, Singapore's Prime Minister, on the other hand, has more eugenic concerns: he has exhorted Singapore's graduate women (the presumed 'intelligent' stock) to have more children in order to maintain and replenish Singapore's supposedly dwindling talent pool. Both announcements have been greeted by public uproar, but nonetheless, have been translated, in varying degrees, into policies affecting the lives of many people, especially women. Particularly insidious is the ideology underlying both policies, and in this paper, we will discuss their impact on women's roles and status in society.

Population policies in general reflect and express the interests

[1] The growth rate dropped from 2.8 in 1960-70 to 2.5 in 1970-82; the projected growth rate for 1980-2000 is 2.0. Based on this, the population is expected to grow to 17 million in 1990, 21 million in 2000 and to stabilize at 33 million in 2005.

and ideologies of the State and ruling classes, while international aid agencies — reflecting the First World's preoccupation with overpopulation as the primary cause of global poverty and deprivation — support and sometimes directly exercise population control on unsuspecting Third World populations.[2] Indiscriminate sterilizations have been known to have been carried out on women without their understanding, and sometimes without even their knowledge, of what is being done to them (Dreifus, 1978). Contraceptives not approved for use in the West are commonly 'dumped' on the Third World whose societies often lack the laws to protect them (Foundation for National Progress, 1979). Usually, however, population policies are carried out through propaganda and the use of incentives and disincentives which are directed towards the family and, primarily, towards women who ultimately bear the responsibility for biological reproduction. Not only do these policies reflect the State's infringement of what should surely be a woman's prerogative — control over her life and body — they also usually reflect the dominant ideology of the ruling classes, particularly with respect to the role of women in society.

Malaysia's 70 million population policy

From the mid-1950s to 1967, family planning activities in Malaysia were undertaken largely by the private sector, under the auspices of family planning associations. Their exclusion from government development plans was primarily attributable to their 'controversial nature' (National Family Planning Board, 1977). In 1964, however, family planning was adopted as a government policy with the stated objectives of (*i*) improving the health and welfare of the family; (*ii*) raising the standard of living; (*iii*) increasing the per capita income; and (*iv*) reducing the population growth rate from three per cent per annum (in 1966) to two per cent by 1985 (i.e. the birth rate per 1000 should decline from 37 in 1966 to 26 in 1985).

In line with this, the National Family Planning Board was

[2] For an elaboration, see the auther's paper entitled 'The Relevance of Science and Technology to Women: Health and Nutrition', written for the Social Development Division of the Economic and Social Commission for Asia and the Pacific.

started in 1967 and allocations were made for family planning activities under the First Malaysia Plan (1966-70). The neo-Malthusian ideology held sway all over the world and the proliferation of birth control studies in developing countries in the 1950s and 1960s pinpointed excessive population growth rates (and resultant large families) as the primary, if not the sole, cause for poverty and underdevelopment in these countries.[3] In many cases, international aid agencies such as the World Bank imposed population control policies on Third World countries, usually as a condition for receiving loans. Malaysia did not escape from such pressures. Allocations for family planning activities increased in absolute terms from 2.0 million ringgit (constituting 1.06 per cent of the total allocations for health and population) in the First Malaysia Plan (1966-70), to 27.0 million ringgit (7.16 per cent) in the Third Malaysia Plan (1976-80) and to 30 million ringgit (4.97 per cent) in the Fourth Malaysia Plan (1981-85).

Against this background, the Prime Minister's announcement on April 6, 1984, of a 70 million population policy came as a surprise. Henceforth, Malaysia's target was to achieve a population of 70 million in 115 years (Government of Malaysia, 1983/84). Subsequent official statements called upon women to have at least five children each in the national interest, (the fertility rate is expected to drop from 3.7 in 1982 to 2.4 in 2000) and the Prime Minister himself stated that women whose husbands could afford it (*sic*), should stay at home to raise their families (*Star*, July 28, 1984).* In addition, Rafidah Aziz, Public Enterprises Minister and chief of the women's section of the United Malays' National Organization (UMNO, the ruling political party), announced that women should get married at the age of 19 so that they could have five properly-spaced children by the time they were 40 years of age (*Star*, August 19, 1984).

Public reaction was wide and varied, but the government did not directly address any of the issues raised in a substantial or

[3] This serves a useful purpose for imperialist powers, as the unequal economic relations between developed countries on the one hand and developing countries on the other can then be attributed to 'overpopulation', rather than be seen in the context of colonialism and imperialism.

*In fact, he is quoted as saying that 'in a situation where there may be unemployment, it will be good for the girls to have babies and let others be employed.' (Mahathir Mohamed, *New Straits Times*, July 28, 1984.)

serious manner. Indeed, it could not offer any explanation as to how the figure of 70 million was to be achieved in 115 years by women having five children each. At the present growth rate of 2.2 per cent, Malaysia's population would reach 70 million in 71 years (i.e. in 2051) or 117 million in 115 years. Having five children per household would raise the growth rate to 3.2 per cent (i.e. the rate prior to the implementation of the family planning programme), and this will mean a 538 million population in 50 years (i.e. 2030). To achieve a 70 million population in 115 years would in fact require a drop in the growth rate to 1.4 per cent, demanding an even more aggressive family planning policy than the one prevailing.

Numerical juggling notwithstanding, it is quite clear that the Prime Minister's message is that he wants a rapid increase in the country's population and that this is to be achieved by an increase in fertility rates. The basic official rationale for this is that for Malaysia to become a great society (presumably like South Korea and Japan), it will require a policy of heavy industrialization. This, in turn, requires a large population to provide both the labour force as well as the domestic market for industrial products.

This line of thinking has been criticised from various perspectives. Essentially, population size is not the only factor which influences the domestic market. The level and distribution of income also play an important role as they affect spending capacity; hence, increasing the population does not necessarily lead to an expansion of the local market. In fact, a country's level of industrialization does not vary proportionately with its population size. For example, Sweden, with a population of less than 10 million is an advanced industrialized economy, whereas Bangladesh and Indonesia, with far larger populations, have remained economically backward (Jomo, 1985).

Furthermore, it has been pointed out that Mahathir's argument holds only if the type of industrialization that is planned is labour intensive (which might not even be a desirable form of

[4] These figures are quoted in Fernandez (1984), and have been endorsed by the Selangor Consumers' Association, Women's Aid Organization, Federation of Womens Lawyers, Selangor Graduate Society, Malaysian Trades Union Congress, and the University Women's Association.

industrialization for Malaysia at this stage). With regard to the expansion of the market for Malaysia's industrial products, the country can tap the ASEAN (Association of South East Asian Nations) regional market which has yet to be fully explored, even if it does not sell beyond the region.[5]

Concern has also been expressed by scholars regarding the effects of a larger population size on the rate of unemployment, the availability of educational, health and social services, and the prevalence of poverty and malnutrition in the country. In the last few years, the unemployment rate has risen from 5.6 per cent (in 1980) to 5.8 per cent (in 1983) for Peninsular Malaysia. Moreover, in the current government policy the thrust is towards shifting out of labour-intensive industries and increasing labour productivity. It may thus be queried: will the increased population be productively employed? (Jomo, 1985).

The system is already facing a crisis in trying to cope with the present demand for educational, health and social services. Schools have to contend with shortages in educational facilities as well as inadequately trained teachers, especially in rural areas (Chee Khoon, 1984). The situation of the health services is hardly more encouraging as government hospitals reach the breakdown point (Jomo, 1983); at the same time, the price of private medical care is soaring in response to increasing demand, and the government's 'solution' is to encourage the privatization of medical care.

Further, over 40 per cent of the population exists below the official poverty line.[6] The *Mid-Term Review of the Fourth Malaysia Plan* does not reveal the official poverty line, but admits that poverty has increased, while malnutrition is rampant in rural areas.[7] It has been argued that the rural poor are most susceptible to government propaganda, and also most vulnerable to the adverse economic effects of having more children

[5] Under the programme of economic regional cooperation, ASEAN preferential trading arrangements have been implemented for a large number of ASEAN produced commodities and products.

[6] The figure of 42.8 per cent is quoted by Ibrahim (1983). The figure is based on a 1983 study carried out by the Socio-Economic Research Unit of the Prime Minister's Department.

[7] This is evident from numerous reports published on recent surveys conducted by the Institute of Medical Research, Kuala Lumpur.

(Fernandez, 1984). Besides, in the context of racially-charged Malaysian society, the 70 million policy also has racial implications. The rural poor are predominantly Malay and if indeed they are the most susceptible then the success of the policy may mean a higher rate of increase for the Malay population relative to the non-Malay population. Speculation is rife that this indeed is the thinking behind the formulation of this policy.[8]

Needless to say, however, the greatest impact of the new population policy will be on women, especially poor women. It is well established that multiparous births take a heavy toll on the mother's body. The maternal mortality rate increases after the fourth pregnancy, and with each successive birth, there is additional risk. The problem is not confined to multiple births; it increases with the age of the mother and with reduced spacing between births. Women who undergo repeated pregnancies, followed by prolonged lactation periods, and who do not have an adequate supply of high quality protein, will experience maternal depletion syndrome — low birth weight, poor lactation and, ultimately, premature ageing and early death.

However, the policy's effect on women's roles and status will have an even greater impact on society. In advocating it the authorities have explicitly, as well as implicitly, reinforced the idea that the primary role of women is to stay at home and bear children. Women in trade unions in particular, have expressed chargin at the Prime Minister's suggestion that women workers should stay at home and have children, and let the others be employed in an economic situation where unemployment is high. This is no less than an open endorsement of the idea that women should come out to work *only when they are needed.* When the economic situation is such that their labour is no longer needed, they are asked to return to their homes. In other words, women are but a reserve pool of labour.

This is detrimental to women of all classes. Even among the better off, access to an independent source of income is very important for women's self-esteem and position in the family, and overall status in society. In a system where the role of homemaker and child-carer is largely still that of a woman's, and where child-care facilities and other supportive systems are lack-

[8] This is not necessarily the author's opinion.

ing, it is difficult for women to combine 'self-development' pursuits, be they careers or other activities, with caring adequately for five children. The implications of this for the standard of living in general will be far-reaching.

For the poor the 70 million population policy has especially dire consequences. Such families are least able to do without an additional income (in many cases, the incomes that women bring in are the primary or even sole means of family support), and are also least able to pay for childcare facilities that upper class women can avail of to free them for economic participation and other pursuits. In the final analysis, therefore, poor families, and especially poor women, will bear the brunt of the new policy.

Singapore's eugenic policy

After many years of an aggressive population reduction policy which successfully lowered Singapore's natural population growth rate, the government has recently instituted a more selective policy to encourage graduate women to have more children, while discouraging others from having more than two.[9] The basis for this new policy is Lee Kuan Yew's concern with the trend among Singapore's graduate women to marry late, or not to marry at all, and to have few or even no children. The fertility rate of non-graduate women, on the other hand, is higher than that of graduate women. According to the Prime Minister, this will lead to a dwindling talent pool for Singapore as he believes that 'intelligence' is genetically determined, and is thus transmitted from highly educated women (presumed to be highly intelligent) to their offspring.

Needless to say, this kind of argument carries with it many assumptions at various levels, and although Lee cites the 'hereditarians[10] to support his beliefs, their arguments have serious flaws. In fact, this matter has been the subject of a considerable controversy within the scientific community since the 1960s. For our purposes here, suffice it to say that scientific evidence does not warrant the conclusion that intelligence is

[9] The mean number of children for women with no qualification is 3.5; primary schooling 2.7; secondary schooling 1.9; and tertiary education 1.7.

[10] The 'hereditarians' advance the argument that mental ability is predominantly determined by genetic factors.

genetically determined.[11] Moreover, it is scientifically unjustified to assume that less-educated people are less intelligent, as achievement in the educational system depends on many other factors (for details, see Blum, 1978).

These considerations notwithstanding, Singapore's government has institutionalised a system of incentives and disincentives which encourage graduate women to have more, and non-graduate women to have fewer, children. Of the most recent measures, one is a cash incentive of $10,000 offered to women of lower socio-economic groups if they get themselves sterilized. Another is the withdrawal of State facilities for third and subsequent children of non-graduate women. The third child of graduate women, on the other hand, is given priority over and above all other children where schooling is concerned. Obviously, these policies will perpetuate and further exacerbate existing inequalities between different socio-economic groups.

These policies also play a significant ideological role. Singapore is a society in which the ideology of meritocracy is employed to the fullest. In a meritocracy, social mobility is generally premised on intellectual or educational achievement or supposed 'ability', usually taken to mean mental ability. If educational achievement is assumed to be inborn and inherited, then the reason why some people are on top of the social and economic structure is usually presumed to be that they were 'born' with the requisite intelligence to be on top! This is the kind of argument which the 'hereditarians' provide for justifying the existing class hierarchy in society. In reality, however, people have to deal with a system in which social mobility is as, if not more, dependent upon factors such as socio-economic status and family background, as on educational achievement.

Ideological implications for the status of women

Family planning policies by themselves will not necessarily raise or lower women's status directly, but they may well contribute to creating conditions which cause an improvement or a deterioration in it. For instance, the primary objective of the earlier family planning movement advanced by Margaret Sanger and her sup-

[11] For a fuller discussion, see Heng Leng and Chee Khoon (1984).

porters was to allow women to have more control over their own fertility and thus offer them the choice of how they want to live their lives. The whole point of family planning, therefore, should be to provide a woman with the means to decide, in consultation with her husband perhaps, the number of children she wants and the times at which she is most ready — financially and emotionally — to have them. On a practical level, if women were to be given the right to choose in this matter, it would entail the provision of facilities and support services — such as contraceptive help, childcare centres, etc. — which are within the reach of all women, as well as a wide dissemination of information. This is necessary to ensure that the question of choice is not merely lip-service, particularly where lower income women are concerned.

Both the Malaysian 70 million and the Singaporean eugenic population policies, however, reflect a fundamental disregard for a woman's right to decide how many children she wants, and to exercise control over her own body and life. Insofar as these policies seek to influence (through the use of propaganda) and to coerce (through the use of a system of incentives and disincentives) women to have a certain number of children, they have the effect of narrowing the range of choices for her (in practical and economic terms) and therefore, of limiting her control over her own body. Needless to say, the extent to which women have choice and control in the determination of the course of their own lives is fundamental to their status in society.

In general, lower income women will be most affected by government propaganda and policies. In the case of Malaysia, for example, the cutbacks in allocations for family planning activities will have the greatest effect on these women as they are the ones who mainly utilize governmental and quasi-governmental family planning facilities and services.[12] Better-off women seek advice and get supplies from private practitioners. The case of Singapore is different, but here too, lower income families will have to toe the government's line as the withdrawal of State facilities will have a great impact on them. In this case, they are discouraged

[12] For instance, the number of women using the facilities of family planning agencies decreased substantially between 1979 and 1982, from 87,000 to 72,000, as a result of a directive to such agencies to present a low profile.

from having more children. Nonetheless, for lower income families, it clearly narrows the choice as to how many children they can have. Moreover, the economic incentives offered to graduate women to have more children will work regressively and increase existing inequalities between the upper and lower socio-economic groups. Both the Malaysian and Singaporean policies, therefore, have a strong, intrinsic element of class bias.

Of course, whether or not population policies have a direct impact on fertility rates in general is questionable. In fact, it has been shown that people make independent and rational decisions in spite of policies — whether government, foreign or other — seeking to influence them in particular directions (Mamdani, 1972). In cases where fertility rates have decreased, seemingly in response to aggressive population policies, standards of living have risen alongside. It is quite probable, therefore, that fertility rates would have dropped as a result of the increase in the standard of living, and despite population policies. Thus, (as has been speculated at a recent conference[13], Malaysia's 70 million population policy might well not have any effect on long term fertility rates, although it will definitely influence short term fluctuations.

At another level, the Malaysian and Singaporean population policies also bring into focus the question of the State's direct incursion into private (and family) life and, by extension, into influencing women's role and status in family and society. This is in addition to the more indirect influence which it exercises through promulgation of the prevailing State ideology in various other ways.

Finally, it should be pointed out that the rationale behind both the Malaysian and Singaporean population policies is a reflection of the way in which people are used to serve capitalism's needs. Instead of creating an industrial policy to serve the needs of the people, the capitalist State in Malaysia seeks to manipulate the population (people) to serve its industrial policy. Similarly, the capitalist State in Singapore seeks to create a talent pool to conform to its self-defined needs, instead of creating policies to serve the needs of the majority of the population.

[13] 'Population in the Year 2000 and Beyond', organised by the Federation of Family Planning Associations in Penang, December 1984.

REFERENCES

ANWAR IBRAHIM: Keynote address presented at United Malays National Organisation Youth Conference on Poverty, Bangi Selangor, December 1983.

BANK NEGARA MALAYSIA: Annual Report, 1984.

BLUM, JEFFREY: *Pseudoscience and Mental Ability: The Origins and Fallacies of the I.Q. Controversy* New York, Monthly Review Press, 1978.

CHEE, HENG LENG & CHEE KHOON (eds.): *Designer Genes: I.Q., Ideology and Biology,* Petaling Jaya, Institute for Social Analysis, 1984.

CHEE KHOON, TAN: 'Without Fear or Favour', *Malaysia Star 1984.*

CHEE, HENG LENG & JOMO K.S.: 'Health Priorities in Malaysia: Medicine in a Sick Society?' in Jomo, K.S. and R.J.G. Wells (eds.) *The Fourth Malaysia Plan: Economic Perspectives.* Kuala Lumpur, Malaysian Economic Association, 1983.

DREIFUS, CLAUDIA (ed.): *Seizing Our Bodies: The Politics of Women's Health,* New York, Vintage Books, 1978.

FERNANDEZ, IRENE: 'The 70 Million Population Policy: Whither Women?' paper presented at the National Council for Integration of Women in Development (NACIWID) Dialogue Session on the 70 million Population Policy, Kuala Lumpur, October 1984.

FOUNDATION FOR NATIONAL PROGRESS: 'The Corporate Crime of the Century', *Mother Jones,* San Francisco, 1979.

GOVT. OF MALAYSIA: Economic Report, Malaysia, 1983/84.

JOMO, K.S.: 'New Medicine for an Old Illness?" in Jomo, K.S. (ed.) *Malaysia's New Economic Policies: Evaluations of the Mid-Term Review of the Fourth Malaysia Plan,* Kuala Lumpur, Malaysian Economic Association, 1985.

MAMDANI: *The Myth of Population Control: Family, Caste and Class in an Indian Village,* New York, Monthly Review Press, 1972.

NATIONAL FAMILY PLANNING BOARD: *The Malaysian National Family Planning Programme: Some Facts and Figures,* Malaysia, 1977.

WORLD BANK: *World Development Report,* New York, Oxford University Press, 1984.

REFORM OR CONFORMITY?

Temple 'Prostitution' and the Community in the Madras Presidency[1]

Amrit Srinivasan

This paper describes the changes that affected an artist community of Tamil Nadu in the wake of reform agitation begun in the late nineteenth century, concerning the idiosyncratic life-style of a section of its women — the devadasis. The term devadasi, a shortened form of the Tamil *tevaradiyal,*[2] was applied to that class of women who, through various ceremonies of 'marriage' dedicated themselves to the deities of temples and other ritual objects. The use of the term 'caste', *jati,* in relation to the devadasis is misconceived; according to the devadasis themselves

[1] The paper draws upon my research work for a doctoral degree at the Department of Social Anthropology, University of Cambridge, England. Data on the devadasis were collected through both field and library research. The documentary material focussed on (i) the specifically British, official and non-official tradition of scholarship on India in the colonial period, and (ii) on the orthogenetic textual tradition. In the field, research was carried out in two stretches covering a total of one and a half years from 1979 – 1981 and focussed primarily on the Tanjore District of Tamil Nadu. The main aim of field research was to contact and interview the devadasis — the living representatives of a changed cultural position, in order to grasp their evaluation and interpretation of the past. All those who could provide eye-witness accounts of the institution of temple-dancing as a working system, such as dance teachers, temple priests, musicians and local landlords, were interviewed as well. Supplementing these interviews was the collection of biographies, extended case-studies and genealogies, archival accounts, temple and social histories, court and temple records and scripts of dance lyrics and ritual songs.

[2] The term translates (not very well) as 'slave of the gods'; literally it means 'at the feet of the lord' which clearly distinguishes it from the cruder term, *tevadiya* or 'available for men', which is used to refer to a common class of prostitute.

there existed a devadasi way of life or professional ethic (*vrtti, murai),* but not a devadasi *jati*. The profession of devadasi was hereditary but it did not confer the right to work *without adequate qualification*. There were certain local communities associated with the devadasis such as the Melakkarar, the Nayanakkarar and the Dasi in Tanjore district, who either recruited (through birth and/or adoption) and trained them or were functionally connected with them in the tasks of temple service. But it was only *after* the reforms that these individual and distinctive service categories merged under the prestigious 'caste' title, Isai Vellala,[3] in a bid to overcome the disrepute attaching to their past association with the devadasis. In a very real sense this marked the transition from a loosely-integrated occupational, temple social system to a highly politicised, communal caste association which utilised the cultural propaganda of the regional non-Brahmin party organisations, the Dravida Kazhagam and the Dravida Munnetra Kazhagam, to achieve corporate identity and prestige.

The first half of the paper reconstructs the devadasi system as it prevailed prior to the legislation of 1947, which banned all ceremonies and procedures by which young girls were dedicated to Hindu shrines.[4] The second half describes the 'reforms' instituted in the social, religious and domestic status of the devadasis in the wake of the legislation, and questions to what extent these changes constituted an 'improvement' over their past position. The colonial context of the devadasi debate which kept the whole issue of reform very much at the forefront of conservative, native political activity is borne in mind throughout the discussion.

In Tamil Nadu, or the Province of Madras as it was earlier

[3] The term *icai* appears in classical Tamil literature and refers to a special music played in the courts of kings. In association with Vellala, a respected caste name for dominant Tamil non-Brahmins, it represents a modern version of the term *icai-karar* or *icai-panar* which referred to the prestigious bards and court minstrels who performed this music in ancient times. (Tamil Lexicon, Vol. I : 272-3). This title was adopted by the caste association, the Isai Vellala Sangam, at a conference in Kumbakonam in 1948.

[4] The full text of the Act is found in the archives of the Government of Madras, Law (legislative) Department G.O. No. 23, January 26, 1948: Acts — The Madras Devadasis (Prevention of Dedication) Act, 1947, Publ. Madras Act XXXI of 1947.

known, it was the devadasi, or D.G. (short for dancing-girl in Anglo-Indian coinage) who was the *nautch* girl of elsewhere, With appropriate variations, she danced this style before the deity in the temple and also at royal courts, the domestic celebrations of the local elite, public ceremonies of honour, and temple festivals. The performance of the *nautch,* the *cinnamelam*[5] or *sadir kacheri*[6] as it was variously called in Madras, was obligatory and a matter of etiquette at society occasions. Besides, of course, it proclaimed the wealth and prestige of patrons who maintained the dancing-girls (as concubines) and their bands of musicians, all at great cost.

The campaign against the dedication of women to temple service began in earnest in 1892. Articulated primarily by educated Hindus, Brahmin and non-Brahmin alike, the campaign formed part of the whole complex of reforms relating to women, such as the ban on *sati,* female infanticide, the encouragement of widow-remarriage and the raising of the age of consent, which had earlier been pressed forward by the English missionaries and officials themselves. The overall moral, political and scientific 'experiment' tried out in India by the Utilitarians and enlightened Protestants, had however proved to be a dangerous failure. The 'mutiny' of 1857 and growing local protests had brought home to the British Parliament the impracticality of interfering with their subjects' private lives. In 1858, the governing of India was transferred from the East India Company to the Crown, and Her Majesty, Queen Victoria, promised the Indian people tolerance and non-interference in all matters relating to religious faith and observance. The equal and impartial protection of a rational system of civil law was, in the same breath, offered as a privilege available to all.

The move for greater neutrality in the religious affairs of the Indians had been initiated by the missionaries, who saw in the government's 'protective' attitudes towards the Hindu temples, for instance, a patronage of precepts and practices at variance

5 The band which accompanied the dancing-girl, as against the *periamelam* which accompanied the male, temple-pipers.

6 The term *sadir* is not a Tamil one; some derive it from the Urdu or Hindustani word, *sadar* meaning public court. In usage it referred to the public, solo concert (*kacheri)* dancing at rich mens' homes on ceremonial occasions.

with Christianity. As early as 1833, the Directors of the East India Company sought to withdraw all control and sever connections with the management of religious institutions. Despite the enormous complications of such a move (given the government's deep involvement in temple affairs) they set about it, while yet continuing to draw what benefits they could from the temples, as for instance, the utilisation of surplus endowments on matters requiring public spending. Her Majesty's assurance consequently was increasingly viewed by the Indian public as a desire on the part of the government to withdraw from the responsibilities of rule. If earlier the people had made their anger felt at the comprehensive programmes of religious (Christian) attack on idolatory, caste practices and other social customs, they now went about letting the government know that its duty lay not in indifference but in the ratification of the people's wishes and expectations even in private and/or religious matters.

The government's proclaimed policy of neutrality combined with its potential power to legislate was destined to greatly politicise the Indian people who competed with one another to somehow gain official attention. Beginning in the second half of the nineteenth century, the tremendous spurt in both constitutional and unconstitutional agitations for secular and religious reform has been well documented by political historians. Lobbies, associations and other pressure groups were formed to let the 'consensus' be known, on which government action could be based and were, in a sense, encouraged by the British. It is in the context of this greatly accelerated political activity that many of the older questions relating to women's issues were regenerated, this time largely through indigenous initiative. There was nothing particularly new in this for Indians; the tradition of liberation and reform was as much a part of shared history as conservatism and conformity and went back to a period much earlier than the advent of the British. What *was* new was that given the alien impersonal bias of British law, these movements were more likely than ever before to be couched in terms of a universalistic jargon essentially insensitive to socio-historical complexity.

If sacrificial infanticide and *sati* had been banned earlier as 'murder', then by the late nineteenth century temple-dancers were being presented as 'prostitutes', and early marriage for women as 'rape' and 'child-molestation'. Given the dual role of the British, both as administrators and legislators, there was a premium on social issues being presented in a 'language' understood by them, on which their actions could be based. This imposition on all manner of public activity, of an alien framework of understanding, played up the apparent contradictions within Indian social reality permitting the politicisation of many civil issues. In the case of the devadasi controversy, if some viewed it as a pernicious social evil, there were others who viewed it as a perfectly valid religious profession with the devadasi having her own distinctive code of conduct. This sympathy extended even to a defence of her legal rights:

> 'Raising the consent age above 14 in extramarital cases would be unfair to devadasis as that would prevent them earning their livelihood.' (Testimony of Mr. Pandit, Asst. Commissioner of Belgaum, Age of Consent Committee, Poona hearing. Appearing in Associated Press despatch, Bombay *Daily Mail,* 1928, November 5.)

As history informs us, however, the vigour of the reform movement was such that the devadasi had stopped dancing much *before* formal legislation was enacted against temple dedication in 1947. A reconstruction of the devadasi system as it actually worked in the Tamil region may reveal the nature of the incomprehension that underlay the huge success of the reform campaign.

Traditionally the young devadasi underwent a ceremony of dedication to the deity of the local temple which resembled, in its ritual structure, the upper-caste Tamil marriage ceremony. Following this ceremony she was set apart from her non-dedicated sisters in that she was not *permitted* to marry and her celibate or unmarried status was legal in customary terms. Significantly, however, she was not prevented from leading a 'normal' life involving economic activity, sexual activity and child-bearing.[7] The very rituals which marked and confirmed her incorporation

[7] In Christian traditions of celibacy for the priesthood and consecrated life, sexual chastity is a normative aspect of the vows taken. Before the Reformation, however, the prevalence of priestly concubinage provides sufficient evidence to indicate that in an earlier period the institutionalised stipulation against marriage was more crucial than rigorous sexual chastity. There is no

into temple service also committed her to the rigorous emotional and physical training in the classical dance, her hereditary profession. In addition, they served to advertise, in a perfectly open and public manner, her availability for sexual liaisons with a 'proper' patron and protector. Very often, in fact, the costs of temple dedication were met by a man who wished thus to anticipate a particular devadasi's favours after she had attained puberty.

It was, crucially, a woman's dedicated status which made it a symbol of social prestige and privilege to maintain her. The devadasi's sexual partner was always chosen by 'arrangement' with her mother and grandmother. Alliance with a Muslim, a Christian or a lower caste man was forbidden, while a Brahmin or member of the landed and commercial elite was preferred for the good breeding and/or wealth he would bring into the family. The non-domestic nature of the contract was an understood part of the agreement, with the devadasi owing the man neither any householding services nor her offspring. The children in turn could not hope to make any legal claims on the ancestral property of their father whom they met largely in their mother's home when he came to visit.

The temple institution's sanction to the pursuit of feminine skills and the exercise of sex and child-bearing functions outside the conventional domestic *(grihasta)*[8] context was evident in many ways. Till 1910 the rituals of dedication were public and elaborately advertised ceremonies which required the permission

---

denying, however, that the ordinary understanding of celibacy today implies sexual abstinence. Particularly in the case of nuns the passionless ideal is more strictly enforced and adhered to. For the reform, strongly influenced by Christian monastic ideals in the colonical period, it made more sense consequently to publicise the devadasi system as a degenerate one. Ancient ideals of sexual purity it propogandized had been corrupted by the strength of commercialism and modern-day immorality. But if one is to understand the devadasi system, it is crucial to accept that though the ceremony of dedication prevented her from contracting a legal marriage, it never demanded sexual abstinence. If anything Tamil bhakti traditions, of which the devadasi was an integral part, rejected puritanism as a valid religious ethic for its female votaries.

[8] In the indigenous tradition, *grihasta* refers specifically to householding life based on the marriage of a man and woman, and the duties and rights that flow from it. The devadasis always lived as members of a household but it was not a 'domestic' *(grihasta)* structure.

and full cooperation of the religious authorities for their proper performance. The *pottukattu* or *tali*-tying ceremony which initiated the young *dasi* into her profession was performed in the temple through the mediation of the priest. The insistence on the pre-pubertal state of the girl was in imitation of Brahminical custom which saw marriage as the only religious initiation *(diksha)* permissible to women. Similarly, the *sadanku* or puberty ceremonies of the devadasi which confirmed her 'married' status as wife-of-the-god, were performed with an emblem of god borrowed from the temple as stand-in 'bridegroom'. On this occasion the procreative and nuptial rites performed at the time of actual consummation of a Brahmin marriage (shortly after the girl attains maturity) were also carried out and auspicious wedding songs celebrating sexual union sung before the 'couple'. From now onwards the devadasi was considered *nitya sumangali,* a woman eternally free from the adversity of widowhood, and in that auspicious capacity, she performed for the first time her ritual and artistic duties in the temple. The puberty ceremonies were an occasion not only for temple honour but for community feasting and celebration in which the local elite also participated. The music and dance and public display of the girl was meant to attract patrons just as amongst upper-caste non-Brahmin groups they served to invite marriage proposals from the family network.

A variety of competitive social pressures and traditional community obligations worked towards the setting up of particular arrangements between dancing girls and rich landed or business households. The men of the patron class were expected to accept a young devadasi as a concubine despite the enormous expense it eventually entailed. The fact that it was the eldest son alone (and that too one who was already married) who had the right to take on such a partnership showed the normative co-existence of a private 'decent' way of life with one that was more wayward and idiosyncratic. For the devadasis their temple attachment granted sectarian purity and the promotional avenues to pursue a prosperous career. The economic and professional benefits were considerable and most importantly, not lacking in social honour.

'Touching the dancing women, speaking to them or looking at them,' was mentioned as a ritual offence in the sectarian texts laying out the etiquette to be followed by worshippers when visiting temples. This misconduct was considered equivalent in blame to other varieties of desecration such as spitting in the temple, turning one's back to the shrine, looking covetously at consecrated property, etc. Life honours were granted to the devadasi at the time of her death. Flowers, sandal paste and a garland from the god of the temple were sent on the occasion of her last rites. In some temples the fire of the kitchen in the temple was used to light her pyre and the deity observed 'pollution' for a token period of one day when no puja was performed at the shrine. Usually, a funeral procession is not meant to stop anywhere, but in the case of the devadasi the bier was placed for a moment on the floor near the entrance to the temple when the gifts mentioned above were made.

As *nitya sumangali,* a woman with the protection of a living husband — the deity and lord of the temple corporation — the devadasi was provided with the excuse to enter secular society and improve her artistic skills amongst the connoisseurs and their families who were obliged to respect her and treat her with chivalry. What in ordinary homes was performed by the *sumangalis* of the family — ceremonies welcoming the bridegroom and guests, singing songs of festivity at marriage and puberty ceremonies, tying the red beads on a woman's marriage necklace, etc.—were in the big houses of the locality performed by the devadasi. As a symbol of good luck, beauty and fame the devadasi was welcome in all rich men's homes on happy occasions of celebration and honour. Her strict professionalism made her an adjunct to conservative domestic society, not its ravager. It is this which lay behind the customary acceptance of married and financially secure family men as patrons. As the wives of men who had maintained dancing women often said, they far preferred a devadasi to a second wife as a rival, as the latter would make domestic life intolerable. Even amongst some non-Brahmin groups where the devadasi could assume the status of a common-law wife of her patron, she never resided with him.

By cooperating in the ceremonies which conferred prestigious *sumangali* status on a section of its female personnel, the temple permitted the most intimate connections to develop between sectarian specialists and the laity. Crucially, however, its mediation helped to simultaneously institutionalise and depersonalise these dyadic, erotic relationships. The triple-cornered communication between the temple, the devadasi and her patron permitted the legitimate pursuit of interests even in the absence of 'market' conditions. For the civil elite a sexual relationship with temple women did not reflect secret needs of a ritual or orgiastic nature. As far as my field information goes, the man did not go to her to get special powers *(sakti)* or other such magical returns. The very publicity and singularity of the connections between a devadasi and her patron ruled out the cultic context more typical of Tantrik rites which involve high-caste men with female partners who are 'low' with a vengeance — usually untouchable. The competitiveness of the enterprise was evident from the fact that it was the devadasi's original sacramental husband, the Lord of the temple, who provided the momentum for her subsequent attraction for men who wished to approximate and imitate it in human terms. The fascination of a 'wife-of the-god' may be mythic just as the fascination for a bed in which Napoleon slept or for a saint's relic. But what is crucial for us is that it converts itself into exchange value when the socialite-client, collector or believer wishes to own the commodity in question or touch it for himself. Intimacy with a devadasi consequently demonstrated public success which visibly marked a man apart from his peers.

Seen in this light, the devadasi represented a badge of fortune, a form of honour managed for civil society by the temple. Land grants were given to individuals by rulers and patrons expressly for meeting their 'entertainment' expenses — the upkeep of a devadasi and her band of musicians. The whole idiom of temple 'honours' *(mariyadai)* in which the devadasi participated permitted a privileged contact with the deity and/or his possessions to have a more clearly secular significance and value. The temple for its own part was no disinterested participant, for the patronage extended to the devadasi was by no means passive. It recognized that her art and physical charms attracted connoisseurs (in the garb of devotees) to the temple eager to promote her as their protegee in the world at large. The devadasi acted as a conduit for honour, divine acceptance and competitive reward at the same time that she invited 'investment', economic, political and emotional, in the deity. In this way the competitive vanities of local patrons, their weakness for one-upmanship with their equals and rivals become inextricably linked with the temple institution. The efficacy of the devadasi as a woman and dancer began to converge with the efficacy of the temple as a living centre of religious and social life, in all its political, commercial and cultural aspects.

The temple's sanction to the system of extra-marital alliance described above was particularly evident from the fact that it was the offspring of these 'mixed-unions' who were given prime monopoly over temple service. The temple also ensured in this way a permanent task-force committed to temple duties over all others. In an inter-caste context, the religious sanction given to female celibacy institutionalised sexual intimacy between devadasis and patrons. In an intra-caste context, it enforced sexual separation in excess of incest prohibitions normally operating within the kin group. The devadasi was permanently denied to any and every man of her community as a marriage or sexual partner. The artificial dichotomy within the community between the householding and the celibate female population gave rise to the 'pure' or 'closed' and the 'mixed' or 'open' sections of the community. The former perpetuated itself through marriage, the latter through both marriage and 'mixed' sex. (The sons and brothers of the devadasi were permitted to marry as also the non-dedicated girls of the group.) These internal divisions were closely linked to aesthetic specialisation within the community.

The allied arts of Tamil bhakti worship — *sadir* (dance), *nagaswaram* (instrumental music) and *nattuvangam* (dance-conducting) — were traditionally organised into two orchestras: the *periamelam* (in Tamil, literally,' 'big drum') and the *cinnamelam* ('small drum')[9]. The *periamelam* was focussed around the male *nagaswaram* virtuoso and was the hereditary specialisation of the 'pure' section of the community. The *cinnamelam,* on the other hand, was focussed around the devadasi or female dancer and her male guru or *nattuvanar,* and was the hereditary specialisation of the 'mixed' section of the community. The requirement for both heredity and skill in temple positions was evident in that it was not enough to be born into the community, one had to be competent in order to gain rights to temple service, just as it was difficult to be competent in the particular

[9] The *periamelam* was constituted of the *nagaswaram* (a kind of oboe), the *tavil* or 'big', outdoor drum, the *ottu* (drone) and cymbals. The *cinnamelam* was constituted by the *mukha-vina* (a diminutive *nagaswaram),* the *mridangam* or 'small' concert drum, the *tutti* (a bagpipe shaped drone) and cymbals.

service unless born or adopted and resident in the community with its internal training facilities. Professional divisions such as *peria* and *cinnamelam* reflected an involution and greater sophistication of the artistic services rendered by the community under the influence of the Bhakti temple institution. Both the technical instrumental organisation as also the aesthetic and functional speciality of the music provided by the two orchestras reflected this fact. The statutory requirement to live proximate to the deity intensified local community relations which (as they saw it) had helped 'concentrate' and develop their skills. Art as a corporate function and mode of livelihood ensured competence and continuity of practice. An extremely telling metaphor used to justify their artistic capacities was that of the plantain (*vazai)* which kept perpetuating itself over the year from the original parent stock *(vazai-adi-vazai).*

What is significant for our purpose, however, is that in the context of an otherwise shared community culture where the *sadir* 'people' (also referred to as the *cinnamelam)* and the *nagaswaram* 'people' (also referred to as the *periamelam*) lived, married and worked together, it was the female profession which instituted competitiveness. Most of the *nagaswaram* players remarked on the greater wealth, fame and glamour that had been possible for the dancing girls as compared to themselves. Significantly, they claimed this to be the effect of an unfair advantage arising out of the natural attraction of women. According to them the temple authorities gave the dance pre-eminence at festivals knowing that the people would flock to see the devadasis. The devadasis were certainly permitted privileges and honours and a physical closeness to the deity denied to the men of their community. The artistic and monetary dominance of the female art form was also linked to its earnings as a concert item — before the 1940s *nagaswaram* played only at outdoor occasions. Even their sense of comparative social superiority ('we take our father's initials . . .') offered the *nagaswaram* artists little recompense since they were forced to acknowledge that it was the devadasi's distinctive life-style which permitted her greater artistic and worldly success. In addition, one cannot help feeling, the privileged access of women artistes to rich patrons and their wealth underscored more sharply their absolute non-availability to their own men. The antagonism felt for the *cinnamelam* was in recognition consequently of the power and influence the devadasis had *as women* and as artists. The leading role played by the men of the community in the subsequent reform campaign to abolish the female profession of temple-dancing cannot be understood without reference to this potent fact.

It was the radical factor of female celibacy which permitted the group to go beyond a purely domestic organisation of internal social relations. The professional division within the community between the male and female art forms was not restricted to household specialisation. In the *nagaswaram* tradition the women of the group were scrupulously kept out of public, professional life. In the dance tradition, too, despite the involvement of both men and women in the occupational tasks of the group, various mechanisms operated which kept the relationship free of any domestic obligations. As we have seen, married girls were not permitted to specialise in the classical temple dance and its allied music. Conversely, those girls who were dedicated to the deity were not permitted to cook or perform mundane domestic tasks either for the men of their own household or for their gurus. The latter in fact were necessarily men from a separate household tradition to that of their students even though they might reside together for the period of training.

The *peria* and *cinna* social divisions clearly did not reflect the mechanical repetitiveness of a uniform domestic structure. The 'rationalisation' of diffuse kinship ties and the 'pre-industrial' economy seen as characteristic of caste society was most evident in the structure and organisation of the devadasi household. The methods and means employed here to encourage artistic excellence, monetary profit and a greater systematisation in the achievement of life's goals reflected an unusual household and cultural tradition which saw itself as perpetuated in a natural *and* moral/social sense, by its women. The direct link that obtained between women as the bread-winners, the kind of income they fetched and their household supremacy, not only in spending and managerial matters but in a political sense as well, will now be briefly described.

It was conscious economic motivation which lay behind the temple dedications, whatever the voiced religious reasons for their performance. Although the temple cooperated in the rituals, pressures to perform the ceremony remained internal to the household and reflected not only the self-interest of the family against 'outsiders' but also internal mechanisms of competition and rivalry which often raised disputes over claims.[10] The insistence on the minor status of the girl to be dedicated reflected this fact since it ensured the retention of hereditary rights by her to service and land benefits in a given temple. The temple tenurial system of pre-colonial India granted a service allotment or *maniam* which was meant for the enjoyment, 'over the generations' *(vamshaparambirayam)*, of a set of dasis attached to a given shrine. They had no right to alienate it since it was not in their name but the temple's, more specifically in the name of the deity or the head of the controlling *matha.* The organisation of shares *(panku)* in this land, just as the organisation of training and arrangement of daily duties, was a matter of internal management by the community. The property transmission within the household recognized the joint and inalienable nature of privileged land-use which could only remain with the family so long as there was a member actively employed in the temple.

The clear desire to keep the economic backbone of the household a female one was consequently linked to the fact that it was the women who were the primary source of both earned and ancestral property. But it was also in recognition of the fact, with no recriminations involved, that the moment a boy made good in an independent career, be it in music or dance or trade, he would move out and maintain a separate household with his own wife and children. Men stayed on as appendages of their sister's or mother's household only on sufferance. A man who had made his own name in his particular field of musical specialisation could not allow professional pride to be compromised by continuing to depend on his women. In any case in purely economic terms, he would be able to move out only once he had established his own reputation and consolidated his earnings. Under ordinary circumstances, it was the women who provided the men with a

[10] In the section on devadasis in his prodigious work on the ethnography of South India, E. Thurston, Superintendent of the Madras Government Museum, gives evidence of the increasing involvement of secular law with the devadasis and their disputes in the late nineteenth century. (*Castes and Tribes of Southern India* in seven volumes, 1909, Madras.)

livelihood, arranged their marriages and gave them a home. The men, it was further felt, always had the choice and the opportunity to make their livelihood elsewhere, not necessarily in the art field, but the women were restricted and had no freedom in the matter. For these various reasons women were favoured over men in property matters. Devadasis were the only women allowed to adopt a child under customary Hindu law and often an adopted daughter was favoured over an only son in the matter of inheritance.

The dominance of women even at the level of formal authority within the home was in a large measure due to the very nature of its economic base. Household property was largely earned income acquired in the form of cash, jewellery and goods, and it was through its women that the household made profits in this sphere. The land endowments, by the very terms of their enjoyment, could not be alienated or capitalised on. Neither did the community have the agricultural skills necessary to profit from the land they owned — they saw themselves primarily as artists and professionals.

The person 'in charge' in the dasi establishment, the *taikkizhavi* or 'old mother', was the seniormost female member who was normally one of the more renowned dancers of her time who, after retirement, exercised control over the younger members. The strict discipline of this old lady over both the private and professional lives of her relatives, her control over joint income, its pooling and expenditure, provided the fundamental source of unity for the dasi household. The critical role she thereby played in the status and prestige of an establishment was appreciable. Considering that much of the income brought into the house was made on an individual basis it was the intervention and managerial control of the old woman which prevented household fission. All community members agreed in this and referred to their mother's or grandmother's special gifts with honour and reverence. Most homes had photographs on the walls of previous such leading lights of the family before whom daily worship was offered.

Quite clearly, it was the women who were considered precious in any given household for its social and professional reputation and continuity. The men acquiesced in the priorities of the household for they too saw their future prosperity as inextricably linked with the emergence of a beautiful and talented sister or niece who would consolidate resources. The alliances made by one's female relatives were significant both for the material and symbolic wealth of the household, and the caste status of the 'father' provided a kind of axis along which different members of the group were graded. Given the peculiarities of the domestic economy in the charge of women, it would not be far wrong to say that it suited men to stay in the background. For not only was household wealth linked to the rather shaming (for men) category of 'women's earnings' but it reflected an area of insecurity and periodic want.

The money flow into a devadasi household remained rather uneven and individual prosperity varied greatly. The excessive life style and lavish spending on hospitality, food and clothing rarely left anything over to be invested in more profitable ways. The *taikkizhavi,* though head of the household, did not gain public recognition or any specific material advantage for her troubles. Given all this, the brothers and uncles of the devadasis acquiesced in their subordinate position because it relieved them of economic cares and responsibilities.

Significantly, these various matri-centred features of the devadasi household encouraged a greater functional specificity and technical excellence of the dance tradition. As mentioned earlier the sexual division of labour underlying the dance was of a non-domestic nature. Despite female household authority, in the professional sphere it was the male guru who exercised control over the dancer. Even when a *nattuvanar* resided with his mother or sister, his superior authority vis-a-vis the female student was ensured by the fact that she came from a separate household. With the achievement of a special renown, however, his subordinate position in his own household clearly led to an ambiguous situation. Given the strong force of the *taikkizhavi* and her complete authority in the household, any man with self-esteem would, it was considered, move out whenever possible and rule supreme in his own domain. Financially as well, the *nattuvanar* who set up on his own had much to gain since he was under no further obligation to pool his earnings with his mother and sisters. Residential separation consequently for the dance guru who continued to be associated with women professionally, conclusively asserted his position of dominance over them.

The self-conscious and competitive functional division within the dance tradition between 'male' (teaching) and 'female' (performing) skills was reflected most dramatically in the emergence of two distinct structures of household organisation. The socio-spatial forces underlying this process related specifically to men and their need to develop an independent tradition for themselves, matching that of their illustrious womenfolk in wealth and prestige.[11] The dasi or matrifocal household was characterised by the following features : (*i*) large size (an average of thirty residents) and excess of female residents (women married into the house but few married out; besides girls were adopted for professional purposes); (*ii*) dichotomous power structure (female members exercised household control, male members exercised professional control); and (*iii*) dichotomous ethical structure (conjugal and celibate codes both coexisted within it). The guru or patrifocal household on the other hand, displayed a consistency of political and moral structure and had a smaller size, made up on an average of an equal number of males and females.

The flexibility and heterogeneity of the dance social organisation described above paid considerable artistic and economic dividends. Members of the community often related the sophistication of their art as a concert item to the teaching of the dance. It was the access of the women of the community to closely related gurus, specialists in the female classical dance, which made the *sadir* tradition aesthetically perfect. Dance teaching was more closely modelled on the Tamil sectarian traditions of spiritual teaching and secular education which required a close and intimate life-long relationship between the adept and the student. The devadasi, we must not forget, was permitted to learn to read and write and pursue vocational skills traditionally denied to all other women in India. The dasis feared and respected their gurus *as teachers* and artists and informal religious leaders of the community whose curse could ruin a girl's career and prospects. At the same time the community context prevented the inherent asymmetry of the guru-shishya relation-

[11] The discussion, rather than view the process of household formation as wholly influenced and controlled by customary, kinship factors, seeks to emphasise the play of rational choices and competitive pressures in areas of internal caste organisation.

ship from becoming exploitative. Households very often stood in a 'student' relationship to some and a 'teaching' relationship to others. The chances of permanent structural asymmetry within the dance organisation were in this way obviated. The continuity of marriage exchange, furthermore, between gurus and undedicated women of student households balanced the tensions inherent to the *gurukulam*.

It was the more wealthy and prestigious patrifocal *nattuvanar* households which showed a marked tendency not only to prohibit their women a professional career but also to restrict the circle of marriage exchange. Quite understandably this aggravated specialisation and claim to 'purity' was seen by community members as being detrimental to art. According to them such extreme professionalism on the part of gurus made it unprofitable for the girls to dance. The accumulation of wealth and power through the exploitation of students and their earnings destroyed community and its 'give and take'. It was only through the continuity of the *gurukulam* — the transgenerational exchange between the teaching and practicing adepts and their respective households — that the excellence of a particular 'school' of dance could be maintained. Real motivations of economic self-interest lay behind this professional and community code of conduct. The skill of a particular *nattuvanar* belonging to a famous tradition could directly affect a student's 'market' both in the dance and entertainment world for the better and enhance her household's prosperity. Equally, for the *nattuvanar,* she was the proverbial goose that laid the golden egg whose talents, if handled properly, yielded steady financial dividends over the year in the shape of fees and gifts.

The unusual social gradation described above sanctioned: (*i*) a particular model of women which constituted a unique religious office — the conscious theological rejection of the harsh, puritanical ascetic ideal for women in the bhakti sects, softened for the devadasi the rigours of domestic asceticism in the shape of the widow, and the religious asceticism in the shape of the Jain and Buddhist nun; (*ii*) a particular community or 'caste' which was a necessary corollary to the institutionalisation *both* of celibacy with sexuality in the devadasi's person. The devadasi stood at the root of a rather unique and specialised temple artisan community, which displayed in its internal organisation the operation of pragmatic, competitive and economic considerations encouraging sophisticated, professional and artistic activity. The innovations introduced into the community through the fact of independent *female* professional skills contrasted well with the more conservative male profession which was also poorer, economically. The abstract sectarian truths of Hinduism which see the male element as 'passive' and the female as 'active' in their cosmologies appear here to receive confirmation on the sociological plane.

For the reform lobbyists — missionaries, doctors, journalists, administrators and social workers—strongly influenced by Christian morality and religion, it was precisely these features of the devadasi institution which were reprehensible in the utmost. The publicisation of the devadasi system as prostitution sought to advertise the moral grotesqueness of the subject population for political ends. For those who supported imperialism on the grounds of its 'civilising' function, programmes of reform, it must be remembered, were not without their ideological rewards. The movement urging the abolition of all ceremonies and procedures by which young girls dedicated themselves as devadasis to Hindu temples, was articulated in the first instance as an anti-*nautch* campaign. The very use of the term *nautch* (a corruption of the Hindi term *nach*, a dance performed by a more common class of northern dancing girl) suggested the smear campaign that was to follow.

The Anti-Nautch supporters, largely educated professionals and Hindus, began their attack on the devadasis' dance, using the declamatory and journalistic skills at their disposal to full effect. Collective public action took the form of signature protests and marches to the homes of the elite who refused to heed the call for boycotting the dance at private celebrations. At the official level memoranda urging legislative action and a ban on the dance were presented to the Viceroy of India and the Governor of Madras who were assured that these performances were '. . . of women who, as everybody knows, are prostitutes, and Their Excellencies hereafter at least must know to be such . . .' After much pressure and recrimination both from the missionaries and the lobbyists, the government agreed to take sides, and by 1911 a despatch was issued desiring nationwide action to be taken against these performances.

The emergence of a vigorous reform movement focusing on the devadasis' dance was a consequence of its politicisation. The so-called 'reformist' approach which characterised Indian political activity in the latter half of colonial rule was reflected in its organisation. By the 1920s the Anti-Nautch agitation had become inextricably linked up with the communal politics of the Dravidian movement. The abolition of the practice of female dedication became a powerful political and legislative cause espoused by the backward non-Brahmins as part of the over-all self-respect campaign initiated by Ramaswami Naicker in 1925. The extraordinary success of the reforms was not unconnected with the fact that the community menfolk stood to gain by the legislation. Given the shastric sanction to the devadasis' celibate, professional ethic and duty, their marriages could not become valid till the passing of the Act in 1947. In the interim period, the tremendous social disabilities they faced worked to the advantage of the men of the community. For most devadasis there was opposition to their getting married particularly if they had been through the dedication ceremony already. To flout the prohibition placed on profane marriage by the sacrament of dedication was viewed as equivalent in moral blame to remarriage for an upper-caste widow. Community members took advantage of this 'blot' on the girls' character and would either demand sums of money as dowry before agreeing to marry the girl or offer opposition in other forms: the astrologer would tell the boy's family that, if married, such a girl would surely die, and so on. At the time of the reform campaign some eminent men did take devadasis as wives, but these exceptions (as in the case of the few reported widow re-marriages of the time) only served to prove the rule. It was the very beautiful or gifted dasis alone who managed to make good matches — M.S. Subbulakshmi, today's renowned singer, married a Brahmin despite her dasi parentage; Jayalakshmi, the famous dancing girl of Pandanallur became the Rani of Ramnad, to mention only two. For the majority however, marriage remained an expensive and difficult proposition.

The reform campaign forced the devadasis to acknowledge the moral supremacy of domestic values; even more importantly, it obliged them to relinquish all rights to temple service and its privileges. The men on the other hand continued to perform both in the temples and in people's homes. The immense patronage they received from the DK/DMK regional party organisations favoured them financially. The *nagaswaram* even today is performed as a concert art. With respect to land rights as well, as explained below, the abolition of the devadasi system benefitted the men of the community over the women in direct contrast to the historical situation.

In the 1920s the non-Brahmin Justice Party (the more elitist precursor of the DK) had taken great care to protect service benefits in terms of lands and buildings attached to the devadasi's office before finally pushing through theLegislature Bill in 1930. The Madras Act of 1929 enfranchising *inams* and *maniams,* as the tax-free land privileges were called, was justified on the grounds of social justice: the devadasi 'bond-slave' to the temple authorities could now own the house and land without the extortion of service. The process of converting traditional usufructury rights to public land (attached to office) into private taxable 'property', however, favoured the men over the women in that they, too, could now inherit the shares earlier kept aside for their dedicated sisters. With land coming into the market through the introduction of the *patta* (land deed) system under the British, the economic and moral infrastructure of matri-centred householding suffered. Internal strife over property division increased and the wealthier sections of the community benefitted over the less fortunate. Most interestingly, however, the processes of rational, western, social change initiated by the reform campaign, far from reducing casteism actually increased communal tendencies within the community. The imperial census data of the 1901-1921 period reveal this process of transition of the devadasi community from a professional class with a *higher* percentage of women (quite unusual for India) to a 'caste with a more typical sex distribution.[12]

The resentment freely expressed by the devadasis at the loss of power and privilege through the legislation provided ample, verbal testimony that the 'reforms' had been pushed through

[12]The census returns showed the following statistical variations for the Dasi group:

largely by a politically aware minority of the community, predominantly men. By contrast, the far greater resistance at the time to reforms seeking to change Brahmin female institutions such as dowry, virgin-widowhood and child-marriage was a consequence of the threat they posed to the interests of elite men. The aggressive anti-Brahminism and anti-ritualism of the Backward Classes Movement of the south provided the men of the devadasi group with a powerful ideology to overcome the humiliation of the Anti-Nautch campaign and fight for dominance both within the household and in the wider political society.

British officialdom's stake in encouraging regionalism and cultural divisiveness directly linked them with those who pressed for its ban. The colonial framework of formal confrontation not only greatly politicised the Indian people but also provided the very rhetoric and 'facts' on which reform action was based. It was essentially alien currents of thought that were utilised by the reform lobby to advertise its public campaign. Even in sensitive areas such as women's reforms it was the power of 'facts' and arguments based on western rationality and reason, and not the authority of the Sanskrit *shastras,* that was increasingly invoked by Indians to bring about socio-cultural change. The reform movement associated with the Hindu temple-dancer continued on the scientific plane, 'civilizing' arguments pushed forward earlier (with far less success) on the religious plane by the missionaries and the British government. The atheist programme of the Backward Classes Movement clearly stressed the benefits of western education and 'rationalism' to bring about desired social change.

Science, religion and the politics of reform became absolutely intertwined in the person of the female missionary/doctor

Census Year	*Dasi*	
	Males	*Females*
1901	1568	5294
1911	1691	3290
1921	5050	5970

Sources: Francis, W. *Census of India 1901,* Vol. XV-A Pt. 2, Madras 1902: 158
Molony, J.C. *Census of India 1911,* Vol. XII Pt. 2, Madras 1912: 112-13
Boag, G.T. *Census of India 1921,* Vol. XIII, Pt. 2, Madras 1922: 114

towards the close of the nineteenth century. Through the sensational and selective publicisation of the medical 'facts' of immature sex, missionaries sought to discredit upper-caste customs and habits on humanistic grounds. The patronage of temple dancers and the practice of pre-pubertal marriage were declared equally abominable, and despite official policies of neutrality in civil affairs, the prestige of science gave missonary interference a renewed legitimacy. It is significant that even with direct community involvement, it was a professional doctor, Dr. (Mrs) S. Muthulakshmi Reddy, who headed the legislative battle for the abolition of temple dedication.

Paradoxically, however, almost simultaneous with the reform movement there emerged a movement urging the 'revival' of the devadasi's dance. Those seeking to abolish the devadasi system had utilized the British machinery of regional party politics and the rhetoric of empiricism to achieve their local ends. Those urging the resurrection of the devadasi's art, separated from her way of life, on the other hand, consciously stepped outside the requirements of state electoral politics and western scientific traditions to achieve their particular ends. The Theosophical Society's[13] notoriously anti-official stance and interest in an Indian cultural and political renaissance bound them with the revival of the dance. At the same time, the nationalisation of Indian art and life and its almost 'religious' idealisation by the Theosophists and thinkers such as Coomaraswamy, Havell and Tagore was in no small measure itself an effect of westernisation. The re-classification of regional, artistic traditions within a unique territorially-defined framework of unity was now proposed in terms of the spiritual and civilisational advantages of Indian and eastern philosophies and techniques.

[13] At the time of its inception, the leading lights of the Theosophical Movement, Madame H.P.Blavatsky and Colonel H.S. Olcott, had toured the southern parts of India and gained support from all sections of the native elite by their public denouncement and denigration of western Christian morality and materialism. In 1882, the Society had set up its headquarters in Adyar, Madras, with the set goal of working towards the restoration of India's ancient glory, her art, science and philosophy. The support later given to the revival of *sadir* as Bharatanatyam by the Theosophical Society was largely due to the efforts of Rukmini Arundale, an eminent Theosophist herself. The direction the dance took under her protective wing cannot be severed from the all-embracing influence of theosophy on her life and career.

The British government officials and missionaries were not slow to play up non-Brahmin suspicion of Indian nationalism, coming as it did from the largely Brahmin-dominated Theosophical circles and Congress alike. With political lines drawn in twentieth century Madras between the British (official)-Christian missionary-'Backward' non-Brahmin complex, on the one hand, and the British (unofficial)-Theosophist-Brahmin[14] complex on the other, it should not be difficult to understand why, by the time the former had done their best to kill the dance and its 'caste' of performers, it should be the latter who would promote it as a 'national' art. When Dr. Reddy's Bill of 1930 asking for the abolition of temple dedications finally came to be passed into law (1947), it seemed to have been pushed through not so much to deal the death of the Tamil caste of professional temple dancers as to approve and permit the birth of a new elite class of amateur performers.[15]

The legislation came at a time when the practice of dedication was already quite dead and it was the official sponsorship and patronage of traditional arts which was at a premium. With newly-won independence to spur on the Congress Party ministry of that time, the Bill was passed into law with the qualification that... 'This legislation should not cut at the root of art and culture... This culture has come to us from generations past.... These things should not be killed in our jealousy for social reform.' (The Hon.Dr.P. Subbarayan in the Legislative Assembly Debates on the Bill, October 9, 1947.) By 1947, the programme for the revival of *sadir* as Bharatanatyam, India's ancient classical dance, was already well underway with the patronage and support of Brahmin dominated Congress lobbies of elite Indians drawn from all parts of the country.

All revivals, however, present a utopian view of the past which

[14] In the existing literature on the Theosophical Society's activities in India, it is their anti-Christian image which is constantly portrayed to justify its appeal to the Hindus. Theosophy was rebelling, however, not against Christianity *per se* but against a particular version of it — non-conformist Protestantism, espoused by the missionaries in India.

[15] For background information on the implications of the Brahmin-non-Brahmin conflict of south India for the Nationalist Movement as a whole, readers are referred to: M.R. Barnell, *The Politics of Cultural Nationalism in South India*, Princeton, 1976; R. Suntheralingam, *Politics and Nationalist Awakening in South India 1852-1891*, Arizona, 1974.

is usually an interpretation fitting in with a changed *contemporary* situation. Given the upper-class Christian religious biases of the Theosophists and the deep influence of evolutionary theories on their 'science', it was the model of the ancient temple-dancer as a pure and holy, sexually chaste woman which was stressed in their performance. By thus marking her off from the 'living' devadasi, they hoped to attract the right sort of clientele for the dance. The argument that without the attendant immorality the dance was a form of yoga — an individual spiritual exercise—abstracted it from its specific community context, permitting its rebirth amongst the urban, educated and westernised elite. The pre-eminence of the women of this class in the field of Bharatanatyam today conclusively indicates that the art has come to be preserved in that very section of Indian society that had been drawn to theosophy in the first place. The modifications introduced into the content of the dance-style were a consequence not so much of its 'purification' (as the revivalists liked to see it) as its rebirth in a more 'proper' class.

In Tamil Nadu today, the art of *sadir*/Bharatanatyam is monopolised by Brahmins who clearly see themselves as having 'rescued' it from the fallen 'prostitute', the devadasi. Yet in a very real and practical sense it is only the devadasi dance they are perpetuating. In essence the dance technique remains unchanged and was learnt from the very community *nattuvanars* and performers who had become redundant after the reform agitation. In the absence of any textual choreography, the widespread renaissance of the dance was really only possible with their help. Many of the best known artists in the field proudly acknowledge training in the secrets of the art from old, defunct devadasis. In the midst of new forms of vulgarity surrounding the dance profession today, such as the commercial cinema, it is the devadasi tradition alone which is propagated by the elite schools as representative of the ancient and pure Bharatanatyam. But we may ask, if the devadasi's dance was a sacred tradition worth preserving and the legislation (justified though it was on the grounds of anti-prostitution) came down with a punitive hand not on prostitutes in general but on the devadasi alone — why did the devadasi need to go?

HIDDEN WOUNDS, VISIBLE SCARS
Violence Against Women in Bangladesh

Roushan Jahan

Introduction

Of late, violence against women has become a highly visible social issue in Bangladesh. This is partly due to the sharpening focus on women's issues after the UN declaration of the Women's Decade, and partly to the publicity given by the media (especially newspapers) and women's organisations, to the abuse of young married women for non-payment of dowry. The latter is a recent phenomenon among Bangladeshi Muslims, and has been instrumental in bringing to public attention problems seldom discussed earlier for fear of social stigma or loss of face. Though violence against women, especially by men (such as wife-abuse, rape, molestation, abduction) both in the home and outside remains largely unreported or under-reported, even the limited coverage suggests that the number of such cases is considerable. The rising pressure from women's organisations for exemplary punishment expressed through organised protests has resulted in a recognition of the need for action both by the government and the public, but policy formulation and programmes intended to reduce violence remain ineffective due to an imperfect understanding of the problem and the factors contributing to it.

So far, very few attempts have been made to study this multidimensional problem in Bangladesh. Jahan first drew attention to the need for research on this issue (Jahan, 1983). Akanda and Shamim's single-year study limited itself to violence leading to murder (Akanda and Shamim, 1984). UBINIG's study on rape covers news reporting between 1981-1984 in two daily papers and raises issues pertinent to media reports (UBINIG, 1985). Islam and Begum (1985), while covering a wide variety of male violence reported between 1975-84, limit themselves to one newspaper. All of these point to the need for further research so that the serious information gap may be closed.

The present paper aims to review the current situation briefly, especially emphasising the role played by the household and the State in the perpetuation and/or reduction of gender violence. While holding violence in repugnance, Bangladeshi society, like all other civilized societies, not only accepts and tolerates it, but also legitimises it in certain prescribed forms and given contexts. The underlying premise defining those permissible forms and contexts is the perpetuation of the existing social order and fundamental social institutions. Gender inequality, leading to gender violence, is deeply embedded in the Bangladeshi social structure; all Bangladeshi social institutions permit, even encourage, the demonstration of unequal power relations between the sexes and try to perpetuate the interests of patriarchy. We propose to look at the manifestation of this phenomenon at the two extreme ends of the social spectrum — in the family, the smallest social unit, providing examples of gender violence in intimate circumstances and relations, and by the State, the ultimate social authority, providing examples from policy formulations, legislation and implementation of laws at the national level. Related to this is a brief examination of socio-cultural devices designed to control women's mobility and sexuality, e.g. sex-role stereotyping, gender division of work, norms of family life, family hierarchy, and so on. As changing socio-economic processes often disrupt existing power relations, both in the public and the private sphere, it is proposed to look at the effects of such factors on women's vulnerability in Bangladesh. As violence against women is regarded here mainly as a social problem, it is assumed that the problem would be amenable to intervention through organised social action. Some alternate strategies for such action are also suggested. The discussion therefore focusses on the following points: (*i*) a brief morphology of violence against women, describing trends in frequency and type, locality, profile of victims and aggressors, based on statistics compiled from newspaper reports; (*ii*) a discussion of factors contributing directly or indirectly to violence in general and violence against women in particular, emphasising Bangladeshi society's perception, tolerance and acceptance of violence in private and public life, and the extent and nature of protection accorded by law to women; (*iii*) an assessment of recent efforts by government and non-government agencies to reduce violence; and (*iv*) suggestions for alternate strategies for action. Two rather obvious points may be mentioned here. Firstly, though the wider socio-cultural context of violence is emphasised here, it is recognized that the immediate context and personal factors, such as psychological make-up and the family history of the aggressor, are equally important in triggering each individual act of violence. Secondly, it is also recognized that gender inequality is only one among other basic inequalities in Bangladeshi society. While men, as the dominant group in relation to women, seldom suffer from gender violence, a considerable number of them fall victim to other types of violence, as the discussion will show.

Ideally, a discussion on gender violence should encompass all oppression and abuse, especially as field experience shows that various types of abuse — physical, sexual, psychological — often closely precede, follow or occur simultaneously, especially in cases of spouse abuse. However, in Bangladesh newspapers and police files usually contain reports on physical/sexual violence. Therefore, in the first section of this paper, violence is taken to mean assaultive behaviour against persons with or without a weapon, with intent to inflict injury. Thus where female victims are concerned, all incidents of violence, physical and sexual, including murder, injury, beating, stabbing, rape, molestation, abduction or hijacking, committed by family members or outsiders, in the home or outside, reported in the newspapers over a five-year period (1980-84) are considered here. For a comparative perspective, statistics on all incidents of violence committed against males will also be presented.

The data[1] used here is taken primarily from material collected for an on-going study on violence against women in Bangladeshi

1 All tables presented in this paper, unless otherwise acknowledged are taken from this research project, sponsored by Women for Women and funded by the Ford Foundation, Bangladesh. At present I am working on an analysis of the data.

families. The material contains statistics from newspaper files and police files, augmented by interviews with a selected sample of persons likely to be concerned about, and involved with, violence in their professional capacities, including police officials, lawyers, judges, social workers, journalists, doctors, nurses, representatives of women's organisations, social scientists and also several victims of violence and their families. Though police files and the files of several weekly magazines were occasionally consulted for cross-reference, the principal sources are two popular Bangla dailies, *Ittefaq* and *Sangbad.* This brings us to the problem of getting reliable data about violence against women. The absence of a sex-wise break-up of figures on crime in the government-sponsored annual reports of the police department is a severe constraint on the researcher. This is only partially alleviated by selective and incomplete newspaper reports. As the volume of news coverage on any given topic seems to depend heavily on the availability of space on the one hand and the relative importance of each news item as perceived by the news editor on the other, a certain unevenness inevitably occurs. Morever, in comparison with official statistics, the limited nature of newspaper coverage fails to reflect the gravity of the situation.

A related problem is the inevitable confusion of categories which arises when different sources are used. The conventional categories used in the police files are found by researchers to be quite inadequate to cover the varied forms of violence against women (Islam and Begum, 1985). Suicide, for instance, is not included in the police files. Female suicide, invariably resulting from oppression should be included in any meaningful discussion of gender violence. We have therefore included this category in the discussion, though for the rest, the paper follows the police definition of violence. Finally, the sensitivity of the issue and personal bias in the respondents may have affected the information received through interviews.

Morphology of violence against women

(a) Trend in frequency and type of violence against women. Information gathered from newspapers shows that the volume of all forms of violence against women has increased over 1980-84.

Though the absolute number of male victims has also increased between 1980-84, the proportionate rise in female victims has been significant:

Table 1

DISTRIBUTION OF VIOLENCE 1980-84

Year	*Incidents*	*Location*		*Action*		*Victims*		*Total*
		Rural	*Urban*	*Reported*	*Unreported*	*M*	*F*	
1980	677	462 (68.2)	215 (31.8)	90 (13.3)		1192	168	1362
1981	747	503 (67.3)	244 (32.7)	117 (15.7)		1445	112	1670
1982	811	575 (71.0)	236 (29.0)	247				
1983	942	582 (61.8)	360 (38.2)	164 (17.4)	778	608	360	968
1984	599	408 (68.0)	191 (31.9)	107 (17.8)	492 (82.2)	436	212	648

Note: Figures in brackets denote percentages
Source: Newspapers

In 1980, the total number of victims in 677 incidents of violence was 1362; of these only 168 (12.4 per cent) were female. In 1984, 599 violent incidents were reported, and the total number of victims was 648; of these 212 (32.7 per cent), i.e. roughly one-third of all victims were female.

Table 2 shows that murder reports have increased over the years. Other forms of violence against women may be roughly ranked in the following order: murder, followed by suicide, rape, kidnapping/hijacking, acid-throwing, beating/stabbing, and others. Crimes against males show a different pattern: murder, beating/stabbing, miscellaneous, kidnapping, suicide, acid-throwing. Thus, sexual violence is directed solely against women; women also figure prominently as victims of suicide, acid-throwing and kidnapping.

Table 2

DISTRIBUTION OF VICTIMS BY TYPE OF VIOLENCE 1980-84

Year	*Murder*		*Suicide*		*Rape*		*Kid-napping*		*Acid-burn*		*Beating/stabbing*		*Others*	
	M	*F*	*M*	*F*	*M*	*F*	*M*	*F*	*M*	*F*	*M*	*F*	*M*	*F*
1980	314	73	36	32	—	29	31	9	3	5	437	4	455	11
1981	275	42	13	16	—	18	27	11	—	5	829	7	301	13
1982	296	103	44	54	—	21	26	37	2	8	165	13	—	—
1983	366	105	10	122	—	51	75	15	2	6	76	16	79	45
1984	179	80	25	55	—	31	62	9	—	8	94	9	76	20

Source: Newspapers

It is unclear, however, whether the noted increase in crimes reflects an actual increase in the number and frequency of incidents of violence during this period or whether it reflects better coverage resulting from pressure from women's groups. In informal interviews, conducted as part of a broad opinion survey, the majority of the respondents (80 per cent), including police officials and media men, felt that for certain crimes such as rape, the increase reflected better coverage due to the increasing willingness among people to discuss previously 'hidden' facts like a rape in the family. However, they were on surer ground with figures for acid-throwing and gun-shot injuries/death, which they think reflect an actual increase.

(b) Profile of victims. Newspaper reports are not uniform in their presentation of information about victims. The age of the female victims is not given in 44 per cent of the reports on violence in 1980-84, due partly perhaps to the general ignorance about age in rural Bangladesh. However, reports which give the age show that the majority of victims are young women below 30. Islam and Begum mention that roughly 50 per cent of the victims of all violence fall in the age group of 15-24, about 22 per cent in 25-30, and nine per cent in 5-15 (Islam and Begum, 1985).

An examination of violence involving sexual assault (attemp-

Table 3

NUMBER OF RAPE VICTIMS IN RURAL AND URBAN BANGLADESH 1983-85

Consequence	*Rural* *below 9*	*Age* *10-19*	*20-39*	*Urban* *below 9*	*10-19*	*20-39*	*40+*	Total
Rape followed by murder	4	35	8	—	8	—	—	55
Rape causing severe injury	23	76	33	9	36	17	1	195
Rape causing mental illness	1	1	—	1	3	—	—	6
	28	112	41	10	47	17	1	256

Source: Adapted from Akanda & Shamim (1984) Table 6, p. 20, Dhaka, Women for Women.

ted/accomplished) which is committed against women only, shows that the majority of victims (of rape, molestation, abduction) are under 20 years of age, as shown in Table 3:

In the three year period, 1983-85, out of 256 rape victims, 197 were 20 years of age. A matter of graver concern however is the high proportion of minor girls (below nine years of age) raped. A related issue is the discrepancy between the figures from police files and those of Islam and Begum (Islam and Begum, 1985). According to the former, in 1984 where the age of the victim is indicated 75 per cent were adult, whereas according to Islam and Begum, 35 per cent were below 15. This illustrates the need to adopt uniform definitions and categories by the police and the media.

Though not uniformly reported marital status emerges as the most frequently mentioned identification in over 60 per cent of the cases in reports which show that the majority of victims are married. Given the prevailing pattern of early marriage for girls (13 years in the rural areas) this is inevitable.

Socio-economic status, as indicated by profession, is frequently mentioned in politically motivated assaults. However, the victims in such cases are mainly male (see Table 8). Additionally, in many instances of robbery, hijacking and kidnapping, victims are identified by name, age, marital status and, in the

Table 4

DISTRIBUTION OF VICTIMS OF SPECIFIC CRIMES BY MARITAL STATUS 1983-85

	Rural		*Urban*		
	S	*M*	*S*	*M*	*T*
Murder	45	184	11	30	270
Rape	130	51	55	20	256
Acid-throwing	21	20	11	8	62

Note: S = Single; M = Married; T = Total

Source: Akanda & Shamim (1984).

case of male victims, profession.

(c) *Profile of the aggressor.* The age and marital status of aggressors are mentioned in a few cases of violence outside the family. Reports vaguely refer to 'certain miscreants' or, more frequently, in the case of abduction/hijacking and sometimes rape, to a certain young man/men (the shadow features of outsiders are sometimes more clearly revealed in cases of politically motivated assaults). This is a serious gap in information. However, a pattern is discernible in the distribution of aggressors by relationship and nature of aggression. Generally, outsiders figure as aggressors in reported cases of sexual violence, and family members in cases of physical violence. In the latter, where reports indicate the identity and relationship of the aggressor with the victim, the husbands emerge as the major aggressors, especially in cases of murder and beating.

(d) *Modus operandi.* Information on this is not always clear from the reports. However, available data on murder show that the most common forms are physical torture, beating and the use of sharp weapons; less common are hanging, use of fire-arms, acid, rape or poison, in that order.

In cases of suicide, apart from those where the mode is not reported (10 per cent of cases reported during 1980-84), the known modes may be ranked in the following order — use of poison, hanging, dying under wheels, drowning, use of sharp instruments, and burning (Islam and Begum, 1985). The wide-

Table 5

DISTRIBUTION OF MURDER VICTIMS BY CAUSE OF DEATH
1983-85

Cause of death	*Victims*	
	Number	*%*
Physical torture	105	39
Beating	79	9
Use of sharp weapons	50	18
Hanging	13	5
Use of firearms	3	1
Use of acid	4	2
Rape	9	3
Poisoning	7	3
	270	100

Source: Adapted from Akanda & Shamim (1984).

spread use of insecticide as a mode of poisoning points to the relatively easy access to it in rural areas. In some cases of abnormal death, autopsies performed at the insistence of natal relatives have revealed that some other mode was used for killing the woman first, and that the body was either hanged or insecticide poured into the mouth later, in an attempt to simulate suicide. Prompt investigation by the police and routine autopsy in cases of abnormal death should help resolve doubts and queries related to such deaths.

(e) Location of violence. An overwhelming share of the reported violence takes place in the rural areas. Table 1 indicated that during 1980-84, 60 per cent of all crimes were committed in rural areas. This is to be expected, as much of the Bangladeshi population is rural-based. Also, since landlessness, unemployment and illiteracy characterise rural Bangladesh, one is tempted to deduce that many of these female victims belong to rural poor households. However, as field experience shows that gender violence, especially wife-abuse, cuts across classes, further research needs to be undertaken to ascertain the relationship of

class violence to gender violence. While violence by husbands and other relatives (both in-laws and blood-kin) appears to take place mainly inside the house, assault by outsiders happens both within and outside it. Instances of outsiders breaking into a house and raping, molesting or abducting women are not infrequent. This raises grave questions about the safety and security currently provided to women by Bangladeshi households and the nature and extent of protection offered by law (the State) against male violence.

One point related to location is, of course, the extent of coverage which a particular area receives in the newspapers. As Table 6 shows, there is a pattern here:

Table 6

DISTRIBUTION OF LOCATION OF VIOLENCE BY NEWS COVERAGE

Location			*Year*		
	1980	*1981*	*1982*	*1983*	*1984*
Dhaka Metropolitan	151	135	174	103	71
	22.03	180.07	22	10.74	11.85
Dhaka Division	90	111	126	249	167
	13.29	14.85		26.43	26.88
Khulna	99	101	157	180	110
	14.62	13.52		19.11	18.36
Chittagong	79	91	92	93	93
	11.66	12.81		9.87	15.53
Rajshahi	85	108	80	57	50
	12.53	14.45		6.05	8.35
Unspecified	174	201	182	260	114
	25.70	26.90		27.60	19.03

If we ignore the unspecified category (which shows the incomplete and vague nature of reporting) Dhaka (metropolitan area and division combined) stands out as the most reported area, followed by Khulna, Chittagong and Rajshahi.

(f) Seasonality in violence. The following table shows that the incidence and frequency of violence ascends from March-April to a peak in the summer months (May-August) and declines appre-

Table 7

DISTRIBUTION OF VIOLENCE 1980-84

Month			*Year*		
	1980	*1981*	*1982*	*1983*	*1984*
January	61	74	66	55	44
February	31	70	52	54	39
March	33	58	74	67	32
April	54	61	37	97	67
May	87	76	58	98	84
June	61	31	109	107	93
July	85	85	94	91	32
August	57	84	120	78	49
September	59	39	43	83	59
October	60	57	54	81	33
November	60	51	46	66	35
December	29	61	58	65	32
Total	677	747	811	942	599

ciably in the winter (December-February). The psychologists interviewed for the opinion survey, felt that this pattern of seasonality may be related to the negative influence of heat on human tolerance levels. Another related phenomenon, also noted by Islam and Begum, may be the breakdown in communication due to monsoon rains in the height of summer (Islam and Begum, 1985). This perhaps interferes with routine law-enforcement activities in relatively isolated and inaccessible rural areas, thus indirectly encouraging illegal activities, including acts of violence.

The two months which show an exceptional drop in the summer, i.e. June 1981 and April 1982, could perhaps be explained in terms of sudden political changes at the top. The first is related to the proclamation of a state of emergency on June 1, 1981 following the assassination of President Zia-ur Rahman on May 30, 1981, which however, was soon lifted. The second seems to be related to the promulgation of strict martial law on March 23, 1982 when General Ershad took over. This situation also eased relatively soon.

(g) Immediate reasons. These are not always reported. However,

where they are, there is a notable difference by sex in the type of reason triggering the violence. While men are preponderantly victims of political violence (national politics or local level power clashes), conflicting property rights and robbery, women are the main victims in violence arising out of family quarrels, due to the non-payment of dowry, rape, conflicting property interests, spouse abuse, enmity with neighbours, lack of consent in marriage, and so on. It should be noted that 'family quarrel' is an ambiguous term; these often result from intra-family stress or tension caused by such varied factors as long-standing conflict over property rights, non-payment of dowry, jealousy, the feeling of inadequacy in a family member who is normally expected to play a dominant role in the family, conflict in decision-making, and challenge to 'established' authority in the family hierarchy. This would doubtless also explain the large number of male victims in the category (see Table 8).

Factors contributing to increased gender violence

The respondents in the opinion survey pointed to several social, cultural and political factors which, according to them, are likely to result in the increased vulnerability of women to male violence. These are (*a*) an increase in the general level of acceptance of violence in society, due mainly to certain historical-political factors; (*b*) increasing stress in male-female relations in the family, brought about by changing socio-economic processes; (*c*) the State's basic reluctance to change laws and policies which perpetuate male dominance over women.

(a) General increase of violence. Respondents pointed to the fact that Bangladesh is not a conspicuously peace-loving or peace-maintaining society. The teachings of Islam which allow for the possibility of violent confrontation with those of other beliefs, and the remnants of feudalism provide the historical backdrop. Also, as many argue, politically motivated violence is on the increase. The breakdown of law and order during the long period of public and political unrest beginning with the Bangladesh movement (1966) which culminated in the war of liberation in 1971, and the 'might is right' position taken by the military government of Yahya Khan has left a legacy of atrocities. Political instability resulted in widespread corruption, the patronage

of musclemen, the application of rigorous repressive measures and violent public reactions to such measures, and the elimination of political opponents through intimidation, abduction and even murder. All these were resorted to by successive regimes in their efforts to grab and retain power. That during a two-month period (September 1-October 31, 1984) the number of politically motivated incidents of violence amounted to 11, and claimed seven dead and 263 injured, is itself revealing (*Sangbad,* 1984). While in the '50s, politically motivated murders were rare, in the '70s and '80s they were more frequent. Examples include the shocking massacre of Sheikh Mujibur Rahman and his family by a group of army officers on August 15, 1975; the killing of four national leaders held in the presumably secure and well-guarded Central Jail on November 3, 1975; the assassination of Zia-ur Rahman by a group of army officers in Chittagong on May 30, 1980; and the stabbing and killing by opposition musclemen of Moyezaddin Ahmad, an Awami League Leader, in broad daylight, while he was leading a protest march in his own constituency (Mascarenhas, 1986). The irony lies in the fact that all such violence happened when the country was intermittently under strict Martial Law, supposedly promulgated to bring about an improvement in law and order.

The murder, abduction or torture of political leaders, trade union workers and other dissidents has not spared women. The scandalous case of 'Imdu', conducting a reign of terror during which he committed multiple murders and abducted the wife of a poor man and kept her away from her family for a long time, illustrates the extent of political patronage used in protecting party musclemen, especially in rural areas.[2] The increase in violence is noticeable in campus politics as well. While the respondents could not recall a single case of politically motivated murder on university campuses during the late '50s and early '60s, instances of stabbing, gun-shot wounds/death, even pitched battles with hand-grenades and automatic rifles, have featured frequently in campus politics during 1975-85. Intervention by law-enforcement agencies has not noticeably reduced such vio-

[2] The daily *Dainik Bangla,* 9.2.1982. Imdu was arrested from the residence of a State minister. He was found guilty of premeditated murder of six persons and sentenced to death. The sentence was carried out on 3.8.1982.

Table 8

VICTIMS OF VIOLENCE BY SPECIFIC CAUSES AND SEX: 1983

	Property		Dowry		Family quarrel		Political		Public unrest		Immoral purpose		Personal grudge		Theft		Other		Total	
	M	*F*	*M*	*F*	*M*	*F*	*M*	*F*	*M*	*F*	*M*	*F*	*M*	*F*	*M*	*F*	*M*	*F*	*M*	*F*
Murder	38	3	1	7		25	4					5	8	7	7	2		4	58	53
Suicide				2		43											4	2	4	47
Throwing acid																				
Rape												48							48	
Molestation												9								9
Beating/stabbing /	103	4					221		5				3				54		386	4
kidnapping/ abduction									1										1	
Robbery	2	1	1													69			3	70
Clash																				
Others	1																		1	
	144	8	2	9		68	225		6		62	11		7	7	71	58	6	501	183

lence; in fact the methods used have themselves been violent and include forcible entry into student hostels and campus residences during the student protests of 1983, 1984 and 1985, the manhandling of students, including female students, by dragging them by their hair, and using intimidating and offensive language to women students and even women teachers in Dhaka University.[3]

According to the respondents, the factors contributing to such general violence include easier access to firearms, acid and other lethal weapons and the increasing exposure to violence through popular literature, theatre, films and television, modelled on foreign material. The large quantity of firearms acquired by the freedom fighters, which successive regimes failed to recover, has been augmented since then by weapons smuggled in or even locally produced, e.g. pipe-guns (Mascarenhas, 1986). Moreover, while the influence of media exposure on young Bangladeshis has yet to be studied in-depth, the increased incidence of the hijacking of cars, kidnapping (accompanied by ransom letters), purse-snatching by youths on motor-bikes, bank looting by gangs of youngsters, gun-shot injuries, and murder of students indicates a rise in violence among the urban middle class which was absent in the early '60s. Many (75 per cent) of the respondents expressed the concern that the repeated occurrence of violence may result in a deadening of sensitivities, leading to an increase in the level of acceptance and tolerance to violence. According to them, such a climate of growing violence augurs ill for Bangladeshi women.

(b) Socio-economic and cultural factors contributing to women's increased vulnerability in the household. Against this increased level of violence we should place certain socio-cultural and economic factors which contribute to the increasing vulnerability of women. Respondents pointed out that violence against women is neither new nor unique to Bangladesh. Women are vulnerable to exploitation, oppression and physical violence from men in all societies where, irrespective of national affluence or levels of development, traditions and legal systems sanction

[3] Personal interviews with several female students and teachers at Dhaka University.

women's subjugation to men in all spheres of life. As has been mentioned earlier, sexism has always been part of the Bangladesh social order. 'In the patriarchal, patrilocal, patrilineal society of Bangladesh, socio-cultural values sanction segregation of the sexes, impose strict gender division of labour and foster a systematic bias of male supremacy' (Jahan, 1983). The emphasis is on women's biological role, defined in terms of reproduction and associated social functions. As the bearer of the heir and carrier of the line, women are held to be vulnerable, needing to be jealously guarded from the lust of strangers. Chastity and modesty in women are placed at a premium and early marriage is still perceived to be the best strategy to provide 'symbolic shelter' to young girls, especially in rural areas. Strict adherence to purdah customs maintain the sharp distinction of 'male' and 'female' spaces (Jahan, 1983). The double standard of sexuality resulting from this dichotomy rears its ugly head when the pattern is broken, e.g. when a woman 'transgresses' into 'public' space. This is clearly seen in the explanation offered by many Bangladeshi men that a woman's presence in public spaces provokes sexual violence against her. While it is obvious that female presence in public spaces certainly makes 'access' to them easier than if they were enclosed within their homes, women find such male attempts to shift the blame on the victims' shoulders particularly offensive, as it assumes that a man is totally unable to control his sexual impulse and a woman has no right over her body, nor any choice in sexual matters. A woman is thus reduced to becoming a sexual object to be used (abused) for male sexual gratification. The socially legitimised way of acquiring the object and keeping it in possession is through marriage. Bangladeshi families, through elaborate socialisation, ensure that children, both male and female, carry on this patriarchal order.

The very structure of the Bangladeshi household, especially in the rural areas, permits socially acceptable violence against women in the form of physical chastisement of the ward (wife) by the guardian (husband). Religious sanction reinforces this social sanction and, unfortunately for women, the 'prescribed' limit is often exceeded in actual practice.[4] Of course the natal family,

[4] *The Holy Quran,* Allama Yusuf Ali (tr.): Sura 4 (women), Verse XXXIV, 'As to those women on whose part ye fear disloyalty and ill conduct,

especially the mother of a girl, tries to raise her daughter in such a way as to minimise the necessity of such chastisement after marriage. From very early childhood a girl is conditioned to accept a sex-bias in the allocation of intra-family food allocation and access to resources and opportunities (Chen, 1981). Formal education is perceived to be irrelevant for her role in life which is to provide unpaid labour for the family and, by bearing and rearing children, to ensure the supply of future unpaid labour. Her lack of education increases her dependence on male guardians who traditionally control all cash flow. Non-formal education, received at home, emphasises the acquisition of these domestic skills and virtues relevant to her position, such as obedience, docility, modesty.

This is very necessary because the position of a young bride, an outsider among in-laws (a close-knit blood-kin) is an especially isolated and vulnerable one in a multi-generational extended family. Patriarchal interest and solidarity of blood-kin are maintained by minimising the opportunities given to the potentially disruptive influence of the bride over the husband. This is done through purdah customs which include elaborate rules of avoidance and the deliberate playing down of overt manifestations of the special and intimate bond between the couple (Papanek and Minault, 1982). The fact that both mother-in-law and daughter-in-law need and compete for the support of the same man heightens the tension between them. For a daughter-in-law open conflict with the mother-in-law, who has a strong hold on her son's loyalties, often ends in strained conjugal relations or abusive behaviour from the husband and other members of the household. In many instances, the in-laws and co-wives, instead of intervening, actively aid and abet the husband in his violence against the wife. In some cases, especially in the rural areas, in the absence of the husband, the in-laws may take on the responsibility of chastisement, which may end in severe injury or even death. The most publicised of such cases is that of Sufia, whose throat was cut by her brother-in-law with the help of four other relatives in an unsuccessful attempt to kill her for non-

admonish them first, (Next) refuse to share their beds, (And last) beat them lightly, But if they return to obedience seek not against them means (of annoyance).'

payment of dowry.[5] The grave consequence of such violence lies in the cyclical pattern of abuse which runs as follows: the husband or other male relatives (and in some cases, female relatives) abuse the wife and the wife abuses the children, with each socially dominant group abusing the next weaker group in the hierarchy. This tacit acceptance of violence in intimate relations, especially in rural households, is likely to perpetuate violence among future generations. Children of these families who grow up witnessing and experiencing such violent behaviour and are taught to accept it not only as normal but 'proper' and 'right', are likely to behave similarly in later life, as research done elsewhere on wife-beaters has shown (Straus, *et al.* 1980).

Moreover, the traditional subservient and vulnerable position of rural women is worsened by the recent disruption of the traditional economic process through increasing landlessness and pauperization, and the concentration of wealth and power in the hands of a few. In rural poor families many men who are socially expected to support their families as heads of household and primary earners, find themselves unable to do so because of increasing landlessness, unemployment and illiteracy. The resultant tension, frustration and feeling of inadequacy are often vented in assaults on wives, the most easily accessible victims. The substantial contribution made by wives to the family income through manual rice-processing, is shrinking in the face of increasing introduction of mechanisation via rice-mills in this area (Salahuddin, 1983). This phenomenon adds to the 'devaluation' of a woman in male eyes and makes her appear a greater liability in times of economic stress. Male migration to the cities for jobs has been an accepted phenomenon of rural life for quite some time. The recent trend in rising divorce and desertion, however, seems to be related to the 'economic devaluation' of women mentioned above.

A related phenomenon in rural family life is an increase in demands for dowry, a very recent trend among Bangladeshi Muslims.[6] It seems to operate on two contrary perceptions of the

[5] DM case no. 793/83 u/s 354/326/307/34 of Bangladesh Penal Code, Case of State vs. Abdul Jabbar and others. The suspects were found guilty and sentenced in 1985.

[6] According to a survey conducted by Salma Sobhan, many villagers declared

meaning of marriage: that of a girl's natal relatives and that of her husband and his relatives. On the one hand, many poor families still want to provide 'shelter' to young girls by marrying them off to eligible grooms of families who seem capable of providing comparable, if not better, levels of living. On the other hand, the eligible groom and his family, in view of the changing economic pattern, may attach little value to the bride's potential contribution to the family as unpaid labour, and may regard her simply as an additional mouth to feed. Many rural families find it necessary to entice prospective bridegrooms by promising a considerable dowry, usually payable in both cash and kind. When parents fail to give the promised dowry after marriage, the bride is tortured and abused, and the marriage often ends in divorce or the abnormal death of the girl by murder or suicide. The daily *Ittefaq* reported that in Pabna (a northern district), in 1981-82, of a total 204 female suicides, 182 were caused by domestic quarrels or the non-payment of dowry (*Ittefaq,* 1982).

(c) The State and women's vulnerability. Theoretically, the State in Bangladesh regards men and women as equals. The Constitution of 1972 (now suspended under martial law) grants all citizens, irrespective of sex, race or religion, equal rights in all spheres of life. However, a closer look reveals that State policies reflect the basic social attitude that all citizens are equal but some (men) are more equal than others (women). Certain clauses in the Constitution regarding the suitability of certain types of jobs for women, the barring of women from the civil service, foreign service and armed services, the emphasis on women's role as reproducers in national development policies and the First Five Year Plan are all indicators of the State's underlying concern in preserving the existing patriarchal social order. This concern of the State becomes especially clear when we examine how the laws relating to violence against women operate.

The law and women

So far, the Bangladeshi legal system, based on the British Penal Code and Common Law, has done little to diminish women's vulnerability to male violence. The legal requirement of proving

that thirty years ago (in the '50s) dowry was very rare among Muslims. Salma Sobhan, 'Women's Issues in Bangladesh', *Law Asia,* Vol. 2, no. 2, 1983.

rape through the physical examination of women places the victim under an intolerable burden. Moreover, as many reports have revealed, delay in such matters often provides suspects with loop-holes to evade deserved punishment. We are in favour of giving the accused the benefit of doubt on reasonable grounds, and also agree with the basic Bangladesh legal stance that a person is to be assumed innocent until proven guilty. However, the fact that in many instances of rape, molestation and abduction, technicalities deprive women of justice, while women who are accused of having hurt or killed their assaulters are promptly arrested, indicates a sex-bias in law enforcement. This is manifest in the case of Kalpana Rani (a young Hindu widow) who killed Subash Chandra Ghosh (a Hindu neighbour) when he tried to rape her.[7] Her prompt arrest by the police the next day stands in glaring contrast to their failure to arrest the male suspect, identified formally by the female victim. This is common in cases of rape/abduction. We may also consider the report in the daily *Ittefaq,* (June 6, 1984) of the rape of a maidservant by a bank manager in mid-May, 1984. The report mentioned that no action had been taken against the aggressor till the day of reporting, almost a month after the event. It is to be noted that, in rural areas, such instances of inaction occur mostly where suspects are members of the village elite, and in the urban areas where they are the employers, supervisors or householders, or their sons or relatives. In many instances, specially in the case of married women, the raped or abducted women, through no fault of theirs, are abandoned or divorced by their husbands because public knowledge entails a loss of face.

The precedence accorded to the Sharia't (the personal law of the Muslims) curtails women's rights in marriage, divorce, inheritance, custody and guardianship. Men are given the right to polygamy, unilateral divorce, twice the share of inheritance, and guardianship over wife and children, including the right of physical chastisement. The Family Law Ordinance of 1961 (amended in 1982) has modified these sweeping male rights to some extent. But women's socio-economic powerlessness and widespread legal ignorance limit the scope of effective legal

[7] The daily *Sangbad,* Oct. 10, 1984. Kalpana Rani's case was taken up by the Mahila Parishad and she was acquitted.

protection from male oppression and violence. For instance, Muslim marriage is contractual in nature and no marriage of Muslims of marriageable age (the legal age is 18 years for men and 16 years for women) would thus be valid without the consent of both parties in the hearing of responsible witnesses. Yet guardians, especially in rural areas, still exercise the right not only of arranging marriages but also of declaring consent on behalf of the bride without consulting her. The only effective protest for the majority of such girls is suicide. In one year, in one district, 11 girls were reported to have killed themselves to avoid forcible marriage to persons they found objectionable (*Ittefaq*, 1982).

Women are also obstructed from exercising their right to divorce, granted by religious laws. The absence of effective agencies offering intervention or support and the inordinate time and expense involved in litigation prevent many women, especially poor and uneducated ones, from seeking redress from domestic violence through divorce or criminal proceedings. Even a woman from a liberal urban background faces many difficulties as friends and family try to persuade her to go back to her husband for fear of the social stigma that a divorce entails (Bhuiyan, 1983). Though Muslim marriage is not sacramental, strong repugnance to divorce and widow remarriage is obvious among middle class Bangladeshi families. As this accentuates female dependence, even the *mullahs* seem not to notice the obvious un-Islamic undertones of this phenomenon. The many difficulties attached to divorce initiated by a woman were evident in the prolonged divorce proceedings of Runa Laila, the well-known young singer who accused her husband of drunkenness and physical abuse. The case went on from 1983 to 1985.[8] Women, even when hospitalised for severe injuries, often prefer to go back to live with the husband or in-laws who inflicted the injuries, than exchange this dubious (but known) 'security' for the uncertain and unfamiliar advantages of 'freedom'. Consider the case of Shahida (fictitious name) interviewed personally by the author. She was hospitalised in April 1984, with severe burns on her body, especially on her back and buttocks. Her brother

[8] Case of Runa Laila vs. Javed Kaiser, T.S. No. 246/83, under the Dissolution of Muslim Marriages Act, 1939.

who brought her to hospital after being informed by the neighbours of Shahida's condition, said that her mother-in-law, with whom she was not on good terms, had emptied a pot of hot water on her back because she was 'disrespectful'. The young woman when asked to comment, kept silent. When asked what she would do after her release from hospital, she said that she would go back to her husband's house. Her brother wanted to file a case but she did not co-operate, and has since returned to her husband.

At the best of times, litigation does not guarantee justice. This is true not only for rape and molestation, but for other forms of violence as well. For instance, Johura Begum filed a suit of dowry demand against her husband under the Dowry Prohibition Act of 1980. The judgement in the lower court was in the wife's favour but upon appeal by the husband the learned judge in the sessions court aquitted the husband on grounds of benefit of doubt, as the time stipulated by the law for dowry cases (within one year of marriage) appeared to have been over when the case was filed.[9]

Thus religious sanctions and traditional values safeguarding the interests of patriarchy operate through family norms, State policies and law, to keep women in a vulnerable position, further accentuated by socio-economic processes over which they have no control.

The Bangladeshi response to violence against women: some observations

The agencies actively concerned with violence against women are (*a*) the Government of Bangladesh; (*b*) non-government organisations especially women's organisations; and (*c*) the media. Let us briefly assess their effectiveness.

(*a*) *Government efforts:* The Government of Bangladesh has recently taken certain steps especially designed to reduce violence against women. The major ones are:

(*i*) The enactment of the Dowry Prohibition Act of 1980 (Act No. XXXV of 1980), later amended by the Dowry

[9] Complaint case no. 639 a of 1982 under the Dowry Prohibition Act, 1980; Most. Johura Begum vs. Dr. M. Haque.

Prohibition (Amendment) Ordinance, 1982 (Ordinance No. XLIV of 1982).

(ii) The promulgation of the Cruelty to Women (Deterrent Punishment) Ordinance, 1983.

(iii) The Ordinance of October 1983 specially designed to prevent acid-throwing.

(iv) The Family Court Ordinance, 1985.

The Dowry Prohibition Act provides that the punishment for giving, taking or abetting the giving or taking of dowry, is 'imprisonment which may extend to one year or with fine which may entend to five thousand taka, or both'. The penalty for demanding dowry is also the same. However, we have already seen that instances of dowry death still occur frequently.

Under the Cruelty to Women Ordinance the penalties are as follows: (*i*) for kidnapping or abducting women for unlawful or immoral purposes, transportation for life or rigorous imprisonment extending up to 14 years; (*ii*) for trafficking in women, also as above; (*iii*) for causing a dowry death, death or transportation for life or rigorous imprisonment extending up to 14 years; (*iv*) for causing death while committing rape, death or transportation for life; (*v*) for attempts to cause death or causing grievous hurt while committing rape, transportation for life or rigorous imprisonment extending up to 14 years; (*vi*) for abettment to above offences, same as for the offence itself. However, this ordinance is too recent for its impact to be apparent. The tables show that the number of reported cases of violence for which rigorous punishment has been provided has not decreased appreciably.

As a manifestation of the government's concern, legally, these prompt enactments are appropriate steps. However, they contain loopholes which permit men to take advantage of their dominant position and escape punishment. Moreover, none of the laws is designed to change or challenge the basic gender-inequality which underlies gender-violence. In the absence of such steps the government's commitment and political will for effective implementation can be questioned. Of course many top officials, including those in the Women's Affairs Ministry, have repeatedly tried to draw public attention to the recent women-specific steps designed to promote the integration of women in national development. Admittedly, the rhetoric of the Second Five Year Plan shows more awareness of the need to increase women's participation in the development process, and various steps to facilitate this have been undertaken during the Second Plan period (1980-85). Yet one suspects that the policies and programmes did not emanate solely from a genuine concern for the gender gap. Rather they were the result, at least partly, of pressures from such disparate groups as western donor agencies and local women's groups, and partly of efforts to fulfill the goals of the UN Decade for Women which the government is obliged to undertake as a signatory to the World Plan of Action. The limited success of the UN Decade efforts, as found even by the government-sponsored evaluation made before the End of Decade Nairobi Conference (Ministry of Social Welfare and Women's Affairs, 1985) is attributable not least to this deep-rooted reluctance on the part of the government to radically change the existing socio-economic-political order, especially as it affects gender relations.

This reluctance is apparent in the government's contradictory policies — on the one hand women are encouraged to participate increasingly in national development, and on other, the top officials and media simultaneously exhort women to uphold traditional values and conform to traditional stereotypes. The blame for the growing incidence of sexual violence against women is placed on the shoulders of the women themselves. More subtle ways of using modesty and decorum as excuses for putting restraints on women in public life are apparent in the recent instance of women TV news readers covering their heads during the holy month of Ramazan (the month of fasting). Moreover, despite repeated demands by women's organisations in many seminars, conferences and over the media, the government has steadfastly refused to entertain recommendations for changing the Sharia't which discriminate against women and contradict the State's fundamental law — the Constitution. While ratifying the UN convention of 1979, reservations were made in all the articles which called for women's equal rights in family matters, on the grounds that these contradict the Sharia't. It has been argued that this reluctance towards stirring up fundamentalist resentment is sound politics, especially taking into account the considerable aid offered by Saudi Arabia and other Islamic fundamentalist States to Bangladesh. However, the Cabinet's rejection of the proposal made by the Minister for Women's

Affairs for establishing family courts in 1983, on the grounds that this involves expenses and logistics which are overwhelming, indicates a basic lack of concern for women's issues.[10] This becomes clear when we note that the same Cabinet had earlier decided to decentralise the legal system (including the high courts), a scheme for which financial and other logistic necessities are likely to be at least as great as those for establishing family courts.

The failure of the government to take any punitive action against certain officials who have abused their official position and sexually violated women in custody and in subordinate positions also, raises questions about the sincerity of the government's concern for reducing violence against women. Instances have also been noted where women who accused men in positions of power, especially in the rural areas, were not even given a hearing. The rank misuse of power by the bureaucracy, political parties, law enforcing agencies and the rich through mutual collusion and patronage, is likely to encourage the abuse of women, especially rural poor women. In such a context, the inevitable conclusion one reaches is that, barring some legislation, the State's role has been one of perpetuating rather than reducing violence against women.

(b) Women's organisations. Women's organisations feel the need for taking a strong joint stand against violence. Some of their notable attempts to publicise their stand on gender violence are as follows: in 1980, the Mahila Parishad (women's organisation) organised a campaign to pressurize the government to pass anti-dowry legislation; 17,000 women signed up for the campaign which led to the Prohibition of Dowry Act, 1980. In 1982, a national seminar on Prevention of Oppression Against Women was jointly organised by 18 major women's groups in the country and inaugurated by the Minister for Women's Affairs. A regional seminar on femicide was organised by the Bangladesh Jatiyo Mahila Ainjibi Samity (Bangladesh National Women Lawyers Association); this generated several short papers on violence against women. On September 23, 1983 a press conference was called by the Mahila Parishad where a 20-point list of demands

[10] The Family Courts Ordinance was finally promulgated in 1985.

was read out. This was later presented to the government. On March 7, 1983 a rally organised by the Mahila Parishad was attended by hundreds of women. In 1985, a demonstration was organised by the Nari Nirjaton Pratirodh Committee (Committee Against Gender Violence) which, ironically enough, failed to break through the barrier created by blue-clad policewomen. Legal education courses related to the rights of women, granted under the Sharia't, have also been organised by various groups active in rural development and human rights. Conscientizing and mobilising women for preventive action has been undertaken by several groups at the field level.

So far, however, the organisations have failed to *politicise* their demands effectively. The professed non-political stance of the organisations is a structural weakness which affects their mobilising strategy adversely. Mahila Parishad, the only politically conscious women's organisation, has taken a bold public stand on several occasions. One such instance was the case of a young medical student from a rich family in Dhaka who killed his wife because she protested against his sexual relations with the maid-servant.[11] During the trial he tried to influence the doctors and other witnesses in his favour. The Mahila Parishad conducted a signature drive to mobilise public pressure for a re-trial and collected 30,000 signatures.[12] At the re-trial, the judges found the suspect guilty and sentenced him to death. In one year the Parishad has taken up 32 cases of violence, two of dowry, two where women were used for immoral purposes, one of murder, five of rape, some acid-throwing cases, one of abortion, two of divorce and three of property-related litigation (Mahila Parishad, 1985). However, the fact remains that women's organisations have failed to make violence against women a political issue, nor is it a major issue on the platform of any political party.

The limited scope of the programmes and the isolated nature of their efforts weakens the stand of women's organisations. Insufficient attention to certain basic needs such as the need for documentation, research, public education, the setting up of

[11] Case of State vs. Iqbal Hossain, 1980 BSCR (2) 39

[12] Personal interview with Maleka Begum, General Secretary of the Mahila Parishad.

clear objectives, and the failure to provide supportive services also adversely affect their activities.

(c) Media. The role of the media has been noticeable in publicising and awareness-building. Despite shortcomings such as sensationalism, selectivity and incompleteness, the reports fill an important information gap. A recent television feature presented various aspects of law-enforcement and legal proceedings in a programme entitled *Ain-Adalat*; the regular focus on women's rights in family matters is also excellent. However, in a country where literacy is low and electricity is often made available to cities only, the media campaign inevitably reaches only a fraction of the population. Its effectiveness is further reduced by the simultaneous use of the media by conservative elements who articulate the traditional attitudes and ideas, thus strengthening the ideological base of gender-inequality.

Some suggestions on action and alternative strategies

The above review leads us to conclude that attempts designed to reduce violence in Bangladesh have had very limited success. Much more needs to be done. Some possible measures are discussed below. Basically it is essential to formulate an integrated programme. In a hierarchical society, points of friction are likely to spark off violence. The elimination of sex-discrimination is the only effective way to reduce violence against women. For a start, progressive legislation is necessary, and for this a climate of opinion favourable to such legislation needs to be created. The mass media could play a significant role in this. Further, public education courses on women's legal rights, and laws protecting them against the infringement of these rights, are necessary. Also the mention of some types of violence is still considered taboo. Open discussions on this would help to change such attitudes and facilitate the course of justice and the rehabilitation of victims. Here again the mass media can play an active role. Women's organisations and the government could perhaps provide the necessary financial and human resources.

Adequate resources need to be allocated too to enable law-enforcing agencies to handle emergencies arising out of violence, especially domestic violence. Police training needs to be geared to handle such situations more effectively. Also, women's organisations strongly advocate the setting up of supportive services and agencies such as 'homes' or 'shelters' for battered women, family courts, and marriage counselling. While the need for this is obvious, the financial cost, additional personpower and other logistical problems may discourage and delay the undertaking of these step by the State. One alternate strategy would be to mobilise community resources and utilise family networks. In the absence of formalised supportive/intervening agencies, family members, friends and neighbours could service as intervening agents and supportive systems. Women's organisations could hold special courses in marriage counselling, legal aid, referral services. Given the social context of Bangladesh, a battered woman is likely to prefer a relative or a friend's house as a socially acceptable 'shelter' rather than a 'battered women's home' run institutionally by strangers.

Development agencies involved in rural women's programmes could have a legal aid cell and a team for monitoring violation of existing laws related to violence against women and take appropriate action to intervene and support when necessary. The Grameen Bank and Nijera Kori have already started action against dowry. Better research and documentation of crimes against women is also a crying need.

Of course, there will be many obstructions in the implementation of these and other similar measures. For example, mobilising family members in Bangladesh would be difficult because the in-laws would tend to aid and abet a husband (their blood-kin) in aggressive behaviour against a wife (an outsider). To break the social pattern and motivate them to be sympathetic to the wife would need a tremendous campaign in changing social attitudes.

Moreover, no amount of public education campaigning can alter the basic *social fact* that everybody in a society inherits different degrees of power depending upon his/her sex, age and material wealth. As long as such inequalities remain, the chances of violence against women remain high. Ultimately, therefore, steps towards radical social and economic change become crucially necessary for stemming gender violence.

REFERENCES

AKANDA, LATIFA & ISHRAT SHAMIM: *Women and Violence: A Comparative Study of Rural and Urban Violence Against Women in Bangladesh,* Dhaka, Women for Women, 1984.

BHUIYAN, RABIA: 'Divorce is Difficult', in Akanda & Jahan (eds.) *Collected Articles,* pp. 54-58, 1983.

CHEN, L.C. *et al.*: 'Sex-bias in the Family Allocation of Food and Health Care in Rural Bangladesh', *Population and Development Review,* March 1981.

ISLAM, SHAMIMA & JAKIA BEGUM: *Women: Victims of Violence, 1975-1984* CWD, Dhaka, 1985.

Ittefaq: 1.8.1982

JAHAN, ROUSHAN: 'Family Violence and Bangladeshi Women: Some Observations', *Collected Articles,* Dhaka, Women for Women, 1983.

——: 'Women in Higher Education', *Paper on Higher Education,* Dhaka University Alumnae Association, Dhaka, 1983.

MAHILA PARISHAD: *Mahila Samachar,* Dhaka, June 1985.

MASCARENHAS, ANTHONY: *Bangladesh: A Legacy of Blood,* London, Hodder and Stoughton, 1986 . Also Maidul Hasan: *Muldhara, 71* (Mainstream, 71), Dhaka, University Press Ltd., 1986.

MINISTRY OF SOCIAL WELFARE AND WOMEN'S AFFAIRS: *Situation of Women,* Government of Bangladesh, 1985.

PAPANEK, HANNA & GAIL MINAULT (eds.): *Separate Worlds: Studies of Purdah in South Asia,* Delhi, Chanakya, 1982.

RURAL POVERTY IN BANGLADESH: A Report to the Like-Minded Group, Universities Research Centre, Dhaka, 1986 (Unpublished).

SALAHUDDIN, KO: 'Dhan prakriyajat karane . . . Adhunik prajuktir Babohar,' in Latifa Akanda & Roushan Jahan (eds.) *Collected Articles, op. cit.*

Sangbad: 1.9.1984 — 31.10.1984.

STRAUS, MURRAY, RICHARD GELLES & SUZANNE STEINMETZ: *Behind Closed Doors: Violence in the American Family,* New York, Anchor Books, 1980.

UBINIG: *Report on News-covering of Rape,* unpublished, 1985.

BEHIND THE VEIL

The Public and Private Faces of Khomeini's Policies on Iranian Women

Haleh Afshar

Many women in Iran equated the Pahlavi regime with political corruption and cultural degradation and, consequently, actively supported the 1979 revolution. They expected the new revolutionary government to guarantee their legal independence and give them the dignity and honour that Islam bestows on all women, and to eliminate the westernised tendency to degrade them into sex objects (Mosalman, *et al.* 1980). What they failed to see was that the dignity so obtained made them the custodians of family honour — a fragile concept quite incompatible with social independence and liberation for women. As the single most important symbol of family honour, women have in fact become the most vulnerable members of the household, assumed to be in need of constant paternalistic control and protection. The emergence of the clergy as the new political authority in Iran has resulted in the considerable extension of this control. Thus, ironically, the revolution has deprived Iranian women of most of their hard-earned civil rights and has reduced them to the status of privatised sex objects required by the new religious order to be at the disposal of their husbands at all times.

In the hundred years that preceded the Islamic revolution Iranian women had slowly and tenaciously fought for equality. They gained access to education in 1910, the abolition of the veil in 1936, the vote in 1962, a curb on the unequivocal male right to divorce and custody of children in 1973, free abortion on demand in 1974, and a ban on polygamy and a right to alimony after divorce in 1976. Thus by the late 1970s many Iranian women expected to find their path to liberation made somewhat easier.

There were, however, divisions among women. The educated middle classes were able to exert considerable private and public influence in support of their demands. They organised street demonstrations and strikes which brought school-teachers and office workers out in their thousands. Since many of their demands reflected the Shah's modernist position, women found it less difficult to achieve some of their aims, and by the mid-'60s had gained access to public spheres. By the early 1970s they began seeking control over their own sexuality and the freedom to express it. The ban on polygamy and free abortion on demand were significant steps in this direction. However, the devout and less wealthy women equated sexual freedom with immorality, imperialism and corruption, and found the pecuniary rewards for their menial jobs insufficient compensation for the loss of moral dignity. Access to paid work became more of a loss than a gain for many women who often supported an idle husband as well as their children on meagre incomes. The process of modernisation had, in many instances, displaced male labour by cheaper female labour without leading to alternative jobs for men. Unemployment, however, did not significantly erode the absolute control of fathers and husbands over the household; in many cases it merely intensified the subordination of women. Those women who worked in factories did have direct access to their wages, but the substantially larger group working in the informal sector as servants, washerwomen and cleaning ladies often had their pay negotiated by, and paid to, their male relatives. In all cases the women continued to do all the domestic work. Hence, many impoverished working class women felt that they had lost the honour and dignity bestowed on them by their religion without gaining any material benefits in return. As a result the advocates of domesticity for women found a large support base among the poor and working classes, both male and female. Women expected a respite from drudgery and the men assumed that by domesticating women they would themselves be able to return to full employment and regain the dignity of paid work. Khomeini, on his return in 1979, exploited this situation and embarked on an intensive campaign to drive women back to the sphere of domesticity. Within months of his return women had been redefined as 'unequal' and 'impetuous' and naturally 'inferior'. Their mere presence in public was described as 'seditious' and they were required to don the *hejab* (usually consisting of head scarf, baggy clothes and trousers), covering them from top to toe, and to return to the home fires. This was readily accepted by urban working class women who had always worn the *chador* (Iranian veil which covers the head and body completely) in public and by fundamentalist and intellectual Muslim women who had, since the early 1970s, acquired a less enveloping *hejab* as a symbol of resistance to the Shah.

Legal inequality

The new theocracy in Iran has based its legislations on the laws of retribution, *qassas,* which require an eye for an eye and a tooth for a tooth. In this context, however, the conviction that women are biologically and socially inferior has resulted in legislation which does not recognise women as independent adults and allow them equal access to law and justice. On his return to Iran, in March 1979, Khomeini issued a decree dismissing all women lawyers, judges and advocates and barring women from teaching at or attending the faculty of law.[1] Subsequently, the entire secular legal structure and administration were dismantled. The Law Association, Kanouneh Vokalah, closed down, and lawyers were required to follow the instructions of newly-appointed religious judges who were usually second year theological students promoted to preside over the courts (Afshar, 1985). Henceforth, murderers could only be punished if the relatives of the victims were able and willing to pay *diyat* (blood money). Otherwise *qassas* laws only entitled them to receive *diyat* in lieu of retributional justice. Thus, only the wealthy could afford justice while the poor had to be content with receiving blood money (Qassas Laws, 1982). Unfortunately women are entitled to only half the blood money of men, and children murdered by their fathers do not receive blood money at all (Qassas Laws, 1982).

Furthermore, a woman's evidence is not accepted by Iranian courts, unless corroborated by that of a man. Women who, nevertheless, insist on giving independent evidence are assumed

[1] A further decree on this subject was ratified by the Cabinet on October 5, 1979.

to be lying and liable to punishment for slander (Qassas Laws, 1982). The Iranian clergy argue that women by their very nature are unable to act as independent adults and are so overtaken by their emotions as to render their evidence invalid. Such a view is not only unjust to women but also un-Islamic in essence and in words. The Koran clearly accepts women as witnesses but equates the evidence of two women to that of one man: 'Call in two male witnesses from among you, but if two men cannot be found, then one man and one woman whom you judge fit to act as witnesses' (2/82). Also, where a woman denies accusations made against her by a man, particularly in the case of adultery, then the Koran asks only that she should swear to God that she is not lying; her fate is then decided by god and men's justice is no longer allowed to intervene (24/7). Sadly, the Iranian clergy have chosen to forget the Koranic statement that 'women should have rights similar to those exercised against them' (2/229). Like many other religious pundits, the Iranian clergy view women as the source of all evil and the specific cause of the downfall of men from grace. This fear of women's power to corrupt is shrouded in rhetoric which equates females with innocence and gullibility, but they are portrayed as unwitting agents of their own seditious natures which can only be checked by strong male authority. Thus, men who are described as being, by their very nature, calm and authoritative are interposed between women and the 'hiatus caused by (their) unruly passion' (*Zaneh Rouz,* 1984).

Employment

The dismantling of much of the modern sector of the economy and the resulting unemployment problem could be resolved to some extent by the exclusion of women from the public sphere. At the same time, Khomeini has been careful to retain the massive support of those slum-dwelling women who both took to the streets in the announcement against the Shah and voted for him in subsequent elections (Tabari, 1979; Afshar, *et al.,* 1983). As a result, women have not been disenfranchised nor formally banned from the labour market. They are, however, discouraged from working in any area other than the traditionally female preserves of nursing and education. In particular, there has been a massive propaganda campaign to drive women out of office jobs.

Khomeini has compared women office workers to a destructive whirlwind and denounced them as painted dolls who 'displace and distract' men and bring 'sedition and degradation' to the workplace (*Kayhan,* 1983). In this he is backed by some of the women he has brought to eminence. Thus, Mansureh Tayeb Zadeh Nouri, a member of the Central Council of Teachers, has declared that 'women should leave government offices where they spend their days drinking tea and leading men astray' (*Zaneh Rouz,* 1984).

In the early post-revolutionary days, there were a few women who dared to criticise the regime publicly for its draconian measures against women. Tehran Majlis deputy, Maryam Behrouzi, protested about women's rights being trampled upon by 'half-baked prejudices disguised as Islamic belief' (*Kayhan,* 1983). As she correctly pointed out, not only were women 'squeezed out of the public sphere', but two years after the formation of the revolutionary Majlis 'not a single law, nor even a single clause has been passed to ameliorate the position of women in this country'. All that had happened was 'un-Islamic and distasteful treatment (was) meted out to women civil servants' along with administrative instructions which 'undermine these women and the future of their jobs' (*Kayhan,* 1983). These instructions include the order compelling all women to wear the *hejab,* the closure of all workplace nurseries and the forbidding of full-time work for all mothers of young children. Motherhood, however, though a prescribed duty, remains unpaid, a situation which makes it imperative for many mothers to seek paid work to secure their livelihood. The problem is so serious that the generally tame *Zaneh Rouz* felt it necessary to publish an article stressing the plight of working mothers (*Zaneh Rouz,* 1984). All the women interviewed stated that they worked to make ends meet; many pointed out that their entire salary merely paid the rent. Women civil servants, who, like the men, had taken a pay cut when the Islamic regime came to power, talked about the steady erosion of the benefits they receive. Despite paying 30 per cent of their income in tax and seven per cent for medical insurance, they received no tangible benefits. Government health schemes seemed incapable of providing any satisfactory medical care or childbirth facilities. Furthermore, married women civil servants had been deprived of food tokens, one of the few fringe benefits they had before the revolution. Because of food shortages and difficulties of shopping during working hours, civil servants had been granted food tokens which could be exchanged at government-run cooperatives situated at or near government offices. These women pay exactly the same taxes as their husbands, and as the designated 'home managers' are expected to buy the food. But the regime's view of women as 'dependents' of their husbands overrides any such considerations and allocates the scarce fringe benefits to the 'deserving' men.

Education

The withdrawal of food tokens compelled many women civil servants to resign from their jobs and join the food queues to exchange their ration cards for provisions. Some of these women were teachers and their decision to leave the profession has had a direct impact on the government policy of sexual segregation of schools, thus further affecting education for girls. Hasty measures introduced to woo women back to the classroom however, met with unforseen resistance from husbands; impressed by the barrage of propaganda about the shame and dishonour incurred by being a woman civil servant, many husbands exercised their legal right to bar their wives from returning to work. The situation was further aggravated by the government's policy on domesticity which confined mothers of young children to the home.

In a country where only 15 per cent of women are literate and only five per cent ever reached tertiary levels of education, it would always have been difficult to introduce segregated schooling without seriously damaging the future of education for women. Currently, of the total 320,000 women civil servants, 180,000 are employed by the Ministry of Education. Of these 120,000 work as primary school teachers, 20,000 are in secondary schools and the rest have administrative posts.[2]

The banning of male teachers from girls' schools has unavoidably resulted in an inferior *bantu* education for women. The problem was grave enough for *Zaneh Rouz* to take the unusual

[2] In the absence of official statistics, these figures were arrived at from reports in the Iranian press in the period June to September 1984.

step of criticising government policies in an editorial: 'Is it right to expect childless women or those with only one child to give all their time and effort to their domestic chores?' 'Why should society be denied the invaluable labour of women because of the unwillingness of their husbands ... who place their personal comfort above that of society and the requirements of our revolution?' (*Zaneh Rouz,* 1984).

The government is intending to resolve this problem by barring women from studying subjects deemed fit for men only, a measure reminiscent of Nazi policies (Afshar, 1983). Accordingly, women are not allowed admission to scientific and most technological university faculties. In a country where women play an essential role in agricultural production and are central to the cultivation of staples such as rice, tea, cotton and other products, the only subject deemed relevant and suitable by the regime for women to study at university is rural dialects — no doubt to enable them to work as interpreters for male agricultural extension workers.

Girl students have proved surprisingly resilient in the circumstances and the impact of their pre-revolutionary education is still reflected in their success in examinations. The Ministry of Education currently refuses to release any data giving the male/female breakdown of examination candidates. However, a survey conducted by *Zaneh Rouz* in 1984 showed that 38 per cent of the successful candidates in the entrance examination for the preparatory courses for university were women. These included 49 per cent of entrants for experimental sciences, 48 per cent for social sciences and economics, 42 per cent of those in education and literature, 41 per cent of arts and only 8 per cent of those who passed in mathematics and physics (*Zaneh Rouz,* 1984). The latter reflects both totally inadequate teaching standards and the reluctance of women to join courses which have been declared unsuitable for them. The future of women who pass the entrance exams remains uncertain despite their current success. To sustain their momentum they need to fight against practical and ideological obstacles which make their life prospects both uncertain and uninviting.

Childcare

One of the successful campaigns by women in Iran led, in 1965, to legislation requiring the establishment of nurseries at all work places, rural as well as urban, employing 10 or more nursing mothers.[3] Although this statutory obligation was frequently ignored by private firms, the public sector was under enormous pressure to comply with it. An increasing number of government funded nurseries and day-care centres catering not only to civil servants, but also to working class women living in slum areas were set up. As early as 1967 some 15,000 children were using such State-run facilities. Each unit generally accommodated about 200 children and kept a number of emergency places vacant for mothers unexpectedly requiring short term childcare (*Kayhan,* 1973). In the poorer quarters of town there were either minimal or no charges, while civil servants were entitled to subsidised nursery facilities.

Unfortunately for Iranian working mothers, Khomeini regards nurseries as 'dens of corruption', and within five months of his return from exile all government funded nurseries were closed. By 1984 most employed women could no longer afford to pay for childcare. With nursery fees accounting for upto 50 per cent of the average government salary, the only alternative for many women was 'God's vigilance'.

Given the policies of the subordination of women, no State agency is prepared to reopen government assisted childcare facilities. *Zaneh Rouz,* in a despondent editorial in the summer of 1984, admitted that the men in charge of the State apparatus 'who should be wise and broad-minded and able to appreciate the gravity of the problem' are of the view that 'our sisters should abandon public ambition and aspirations and concentrate on motherhood and domesticity' (*Zaneh Rouz,* 1984). As far as the government is concerned it is the sole responsibility of women to provide childcare — although those who have the material means and the natural talents to set up nurseries are permitted to do so. (*Kayhan,* 1984). But even private nurseries have not been allowed to operate freely; in 1983 many were closed by the Improved Living Organisation, *Sazemaneh Behsisti* and will remain so pending the legislation of further regulations (*Kayhan,* 1984).

[3] Labour Law of Iran, article 19 as amended on February 9, 1965.

Hejab

As the public representatives of the government's religious convictions, all women, whether Muslim or not, are required to cover themselves with the *hejab*. This may or may not be the all-enveloping *chador* but must cover all but the face and the two hands and thus protect women from dishonour. Iranian women have made several concerted attempts at opposing the imposition of the veil, but despite public demonstrations and protests, they have become the reluctant upholders of the public face of the Islamic regime. Khomeini issued a decree banning unveiled women from all workplaces in 1979, within two months of his return to Iran. Since then the ban has been extended to shops, restaurants, cinemas and all other public places as well as all thoroughfares. Roaming vigilantes, members of the so-called God Party, *Hezbolah,* have taken it upon themselves to attack any woman thought to be insufficiently covered. This is enforced by the provisions of *qassas* law: an instant punishment of 74 lashes to be meted out to unveiled women. Every summer there is an attempt by women to lighten the burden of the veil, to wear less enveloping garments, and each time their resistance is met by riots organised by the *Hezbolahi* who indulge in 'spontaneous' demonstrations against the shameless nudity of women.

The *hejab* has been identified by the regime as the very cornerstone of its revolution. It is described as basic to Islamic ideology and prescribed by God himself as a 'duty' for women (*Kayhan,* 1984). Strictly speaking, it is open to discussion whether the Koran requires women to cover their entire body all the time.[4] But the theocracy in Iran has chosen the most fanatical interpretation possible and is equating treachery, heathenism and prostitution with divergence from its ruling on the veil. The shrouding of the body is seen by them as denoting deliverance from the yoke of imperialism 'and as representing' a symbol of liberation and resistance to capitalism and of revolutionary aspirations

[4] The relevant verses in the Koran require women to cover their 'adornments' and instruct women who are related to the Prophet to 'draw their veils close around them' (The Koran, 24/31 and 33/59). Few Iranian women can claim to be descendents of Mohammad, while the rest are unlikely to think of their arms and legs as 'adornments'.

(*Kayhan,* 1984). Thus women who so much as bare an ankle are accused by the clergy of 'flaunting their naked bodies' and denounced as 'corrupt, seditious, dangerous and destructive of public honour and chastity' (*Kayhan,* 1983). These 'wayward women' are said to be instrumental in the foreign-inspired plot to undermine revolutionary puritanism, and the clergy calls upon the nation to punish such shameless women with the same vigour as we oppose other terrorists who have sought to sabotage our revolution (*Zaneh Rouz,* 1984). This has resulted in public executions of women accused of 'prostitution', though their male accomplices appear, by and large, to have escaped condemnation. Similarly, there have been reports of numerous 'honour'-related murders where men have killed their female relatives accused of extra-marital sexual relationships. The concepts of shame and dishonour are so pervasive that such killings are condoned and these men pitied rather than punished for their acts of wilful murder.

Behind this rhetoric of female honour there lies a deep-seated subconscious fear of women and their sexuality. It underlines not the vulnerability of women, as publicly stated, but the fragility of men. The stated assumption of the regime is that the only fundamental threat to male sanity and rationality are anger and sexual arousal, the latter caused exclusively by women. Their mere presence is said to undermine men's better judgement. It is not only a woman's body, but also her face, her movement, the tone of her voice and even the colour of her garments which can arouse men (*Zaneh Rouz,* 1984). The imposition of the *hejab* is hailed as a timely brake applied to the 'dishonorable ways' of 'loose women' and as a 'shield to their honour' (*Zaneh Rouz,* 1984). In reality, the Iranian clergy fear the power of female sexuality — the satanic power that femaleness exerts which, they assume, can annihilate the male species by its very presence.

Marriage

According to Khomeini the only practical way of curbing the destructive powers of women is to marry them young and make sure that they have their first menstruation in the hunbands' house (Toziholmassael, 2459). To ensure that the prospective husband is actually able to curb the irrational tendency of the woman to appear naked in public and flaunt herself by using make-up (*Zaneh Rouz,* 1984, Afshar, 1983), the groom must obviously be much older than the bride. Khomeini is aware that some girls may be traumatised by the experience of sexual intercourse at the age of nine which is the Islamic legal age of marriage, so he wisely counsels the groom that in such cases he should refrain from repeating the act with the same girl. There is no impediment on his doing the same to other unsuspecting child brides (Toziholmassael, 2459).

This is a far cry from the Islamic concept of marriage which, according to the Koran, should be a contractual agreement between consenting adults stipulating terms on which they would both be prepared to embark on a marital relationship. Women must negotiate a price for the consummation of marriage. This price, the *meher,* is payable to the bride on marriage. Furthermore, women should expect to be kept by their husbands in the style to which they have been accustomed, and to be paid for suckling their babies. Nor is marriage seen as necessarily lasting a lifetime; men have the right to divorce their wives at will, but women too can stipulate in their marriage contract the right to divorce their husbands. There is no stigma attached to divorce, though women who have not reached menopause must wait up to three months before marrying someone else. In the 20 years that preceded the religious takeover, Iranian women had succeeded in gaining the rights granted by Islam and denied them by tradition. In addition, the laws were revised to increase the minimum legal age of marriage for girls to 18 years, to ban polygamy, and make divorce a subject of decision by Family Courts. Furthermore, men lost their automatic right to custody of children and were required to pay alimony as determined by Family Courts.[5]

Within months of his return, and before the election of representative bodies, Khomeini revoked all these laws. Polygamy has been legalised and encouraged through religious sermons as well as by the mass media. Men have regained the right of divorce and Family Courts have been reduced to mere rubber-stamping of male decisions in these matters. The legal age of marriage has been reduced to 13 for girls embarking on formal marriages, and there is no control whatsoever on arrangements made for temporary marriages, which are once more becoming

[5] Family Protection Law 1976.

commonplace.

There is enormous pressure on all women to marry as a matter of national duty. They are hailed as prospective mothers of martyrs, and the clergy and media have joined forces to convince them of their obligation to marry and return to the sphere of domesticity. They are repeatedly exhorted to do their bit for the war, and since they are not at the front holding the invading enemy at bay, they must do their duty at the base and produce more warriors to protect their threatened nation. The regime carefully fosters war hysteria, as well as the feeling that the entire world and particularly the great powers of Satan, namely the United States and the Soviet Union, are poised to attack. Women are advised to avoid too much education, not to become too high-brow and to concentrate on their roles as wives and mothers (*Zaneh Rouz,* 1984).

Within marriage, women are expected to combine the functions of saints and harlots, becoming malleable sex objects and at the same time retaining their attributes of shame and modesty. They must however be aware that ardour is the preserve of men and that women are no more than a means of satisfying the uncontrollable male sexual urge; wives are told to learn to give themselves unquestioningly to their husbands (*Zaneh Rouz,* 1984). Women's magazines and bookshops abound with publications telling women how to become good wives; they are instructed to be 'generous in giving themselves to their husbands and satisfying his every desire'. They are also told to augment his lust and then set about satisfying it. Good wives, we are told, 'seek out his secret fantasies and by enacting them gain hold of his heart'. It is only through absolute satisfaction of his most secret lusts that women can maintain their hold over their husbands and thus obtain a livelihood for themselves and their children (Zibayi, 1984).

But these expert sex objects are required to remain the private and sole possession of one husband, who is entitled to have as many wives as he chooses. All the expertise learned and practiced by each wife remains the property of her husband. It is hard to see how women are expected to survive the experience, particularly since by becoming sex objects they are supposed to gain housekeeping money.

Domesticity

The Prophet is quoted as contrasting the good wife, the virgin who bears children with the bad one, the barren woman who lacks all external beauty, a loud-mouth wife who never stays at home and is forever walking out of the house. Accordingly, the perfect wife is the obedient one who 'protects her soul and his wealth and looks after his house in his absence'.[6] The relationship in this marriage, as described by an Iranian religious leader, is close to that of a master and slave. This is not merely implied by the clergy, but openly stated. In a series of articles on the ethics of marriage, Hojatoleslam A.A. Akhtari categorically says that the greatest mistake of ungodly materialistic societies is the assumption that marriage is a partnership and a collaboration between spouses. Such an assumption denies all the feminine attributes and ignores the female characteristics of shame, chastity and modesty (*Zaneh Rouz,* 1984). Iranian women are reminded that it is their duty to avoid all activities which endanger the husband and seek to please him and be absolutely faithful to him in his presence and his absence, to be respectful and never to laugh at him or belittle him or criticise or make him unhappy; never to leave the house without his permission and to make themselves beautiful and desirable for him (*Zaneh Rouz,* 1984).

This total subordination is prescribed because men are declared to be shouldering the heavy burden of paid employment and are required to respond to the call for participation in the holy war, *jihad.* The Prophet is once more quoted as saying domesticity is the women's holy war — fought, no doubt, against the restless and lustful bodies of men. Husbands are described as turbulent spirits seeking peace, peace created by women who must make the home an enclave of tranquility and happiness. It is in such calm and secure surroundings that men can express their sexual desires and enjoy the bodies of their wives. Where there is no peace there would be no sexual satisfaction for men, and where there is no sexual satisfaction there is no housekeeping

[6] Akhtari Akhlaq ... *Zaneh Rouz* August 4, 1984. No specific reference is made to the Hadith. The Shiia Mojtahed have the right to interpret the laws of Islam for the faithful and do so generally without providing their lay followers with exact reference to source materials.

money. The image of the perpetually aroused male drawn by Muslim pundits to justify early marriages and the veiling of women, is conveniently transformed into that of an exhausted husband unable to perform unless soothed and caressed by his wife. It is argued that once a man shoulders the heavy responsibility of marriage he faces the terrible task of earning a family wage all on his own and that the burden is almost more than he can cope with. He is the embattled public figure against society struggling to survive and gain a livelihood for his family; the combat is so intense that he 'deserves rewards similar to those of martyrs'. It is curious how the imagery of martyrdom has become all pervasive, yet women who are thought to be capable of initiating treason by their very presence are not, nevertheless, thought of as suitable material for martyrdom — this remains a male preserve.

A woman who rewards her husband well and is said to make him selfless, hardworking and generous gains safety because of his ardent wish to maintain this haven of happiness. The wish is so powerful that it sends him out even in extremes of climate 'to work and provide his family with food, clothing and a roof over their heads'.

But the domestic haven is not a protected corner for all good wives. Even the State propaganda machine cannot hide the insecurity of many current marriages in Iran. Threatened by polygamy and easy divorces women concentrate on the only occupation deemed suitable for them, child-bearing, and production of future warriors, paid for by the father. Widows and unmarried women have no recognised contribution to make to the welfare of the State and must be bundled off into marriage to render them productive.

As a result professional single women, even those who are gainfully employed and economically independent, have begun to doubt their self-worth and absorb the State's views on femininity and marriage. As an indication of the success of its propaganda campaign, *Zaneh Rouz* published a long and anguished letter from an 'old' spinster — a 28 year old professional woman who said that she was educated, gainfully employed and ideologically 'pure and committed', yet unmarried. 'Where is my wasted youth?' she is quoted as asking, 'What is left for me in this life? I have saved my purest and most beautiful moments for a man ...

yet the men prefer to marry pretty young girls and leave me to suffer the unbearable longing for motherhood and to shed my tears in solitude. I am the casualty of the men's obsession with beauty and fear of intelligence and intellectual women' (*Zaneh Rouz,* 1984). Iranian women who had earlier struggled against the oppressive institution of marriage find it hard to accept that such a fundamental change could occur in the mentality of their sisters in such a short time, particularly since the prescribed marriage is far from a partnership between equals. *Zaneh Rouz*'s response to this letter included the stern admonishment that 'too much education has made you too highbrow, that is why 13 years after the proper age of marriage you are still single'.

In terms of the ideology of the clergy, the only possible solution for such highbrow women is to be married either polygamously to older men, or to the war heroes who return mutilated and are in need of constant care. In the absence of a national health service, the government is providing small 'dowries' for women to marry these disabled soldiers and relieve the nation of the burden of their costly health care.

Just as marriage has been equated with a national duty for women, so polygamy has been identified as an important duty to be performed by all devout men who can marry women for as short or long a time as they please. The important consideration here is the sexual satisfaction of men who, once the marriage prayer has been said, are legally entitled to use the women as they please. The provision of an inheritance for any children that may ensue is their only obligation; women's interests, particularly in the case of temporary marriages, are non-existent. But whereas men can and do marry as many women as they wish and do so concurrently, women must wait for a period ranging from three months for formal marriages to two for informal ones before embarking on the next one. This waiting period, *eddeh,* ensures that each man knows his child, but temporary wives who, during this time, are not entitled to maintenance, remain unpaid and unprotected.

Yet, strictly speaking, the Koran does not permit polygamous marriage and does not refer to concubinage except in the case of slaves. With the abolition of slavery one can be forgiven for assuming that devout Muslims would no longer find any justification for temporary marriages. Similarly, the relevant verse in the

Koran permits polygamy only for those who can be totally fair and love their four wives and treat them all equally; even so, the verse concludes with the injunction to 'marry only one,' because 'try as you may you cannot treat all your wives impartially'. (Koran 4/129). But the family courts in Iran are only too willing to allow polygamous marriages. The objections of the first wife are never sustained and she is usually denigrated for not being sufficiently patriotic to realise that her husband is only performing his national duty and preventing other women from falling into the pernicious clutches of seditious ways. The only consideration for the courts is whether the man's income is large enough to support an additional wife. Once again in post-revolutionary Iran, we find that it is rich men who can avail of the full benefits of Islamic justice!

Since parents are no more immune to the widespread propaganda on marriage and domesticity than their daughters, there is now enormous parental pressure on women to marry. Young girls are callously married to polygamous old men who proceed to abuse them and discard them when their sexual urges have been satisfied. Iranian women's magazines are full of letters from abandoned or divorced second wives, many still in their teens. No longer wanted by their husbands, and signed away by their parents they are left to perish in the comforting knowledge that they have fulfilled their prescribed duty to the nation. Many of these women are pregnant, but even the sacredness of motherhood does not protect them; husbands frequently refuse to support their children and literally throw their unwanted wives out on the streets. A letter to *Zaneh Rouz* provides a heart-rending example: 'My father married seven wives, he just threw us out when he married the next one.' The wife, her son and daughter found themselves homeless and, according to this letter, 'have never had a roof over our heads since that day' (*Zaneh Rouz,* 1984).

Divorce

Divorce has become the unequivocal prerogative of men. Few women in Iran have marriage contracts that enable them to initiate divorce proceedings: for most the only security is their *meher*. In practice however, women have to forgo their *meher* to gain the consent of the husband to an irrevocable divorce. Those women who have children find themselves in an even more difficult predicament as the husbands have automatic custody of sons at the age of four, and daughters at the age of seven, and there are no legal provisions for access to them for mothers. Here the right of custody in practice implies absolute right over the lives of the children. The *diyat* of children is a symbolic sum payable to their fathers or male ancestors; thus fathers who murder their children cannot be prosecuted: they merely pay the *diyat* to themselves. Mothers who leave their children in their husbands' custody, do so in the knowledge that they may, lawfully, murder them. In a recent infamous case the father gained custody of his three children, despite strong protests from his divorced wife. He proceeded to kill all three, but when a journalist raised this case with Ayatolah Moussavi Boroujerdi, a well known member of the judiciary, the latter stated that according to religious and legal requirements the father is entitled to have custody of his children after the stipulated age. The courts can only implement the law as it stands (*Zaneh Rouz,* 1984).

Understandably, mothers are on the whole very reluctant to divorce their husbands, and in any case are generally unable to start the proceedings. There are only three acceptable grounds for divorce initiated by women: male impotence, male sterility and desertion. The latter has become so commonplace that the government was finally obliged to relax its previous requirement of a four year waiting period for women. Now five days absence without good cause is sufficient ground for assuming that the husband is not returning and initiating divorce proceedings. Male sterility remains subject to a five year trial period to make sure that the husband is not suffering from a temporary incapacitation. Impotence, if certified by a doctor, is generally accepted as ground for rapid divorce.

Conclusion

The Islamic republic was heavily biased in favour of men, in its very conception. Women, though not specifically classified as slaves are required to behave in complete accordance with the wishes of men, who are in a superior position. Degraded into sex objects and demoted to mere wives they have no recognised function other than motherhood and no protection other than the doubtful solace of polygamous marriages.

For middle class women the situation is becoming increasingly difficult, not only because they resent and oppose the regime and its draconian measures against women, but also because they have been singled out as a major target for retribution and oppression. The theocracy has chosen to measure its success in Islamisation by the degree of submission shown by middle class women. In particular *hejab* has become an important issue for struggle; revolutionary guards as well as self-appointed righteous men roam the streets and attack middle class women who are accused of un-Islamic behaviour; this usually means not being sufficiently covered or even wearing bright colours. All colours other than black, dark brown and navy blue are considered immodest and women wearing them are often labelled 'seditious'. Interestingly, lower class women who cannot work under the total cover of *hejab* escape criticism. Quite correctly the State has identified middle class women as the potentially most dangerous group. To lower class women and slum dwellers, the Islamic government, both in its rhetoric and in material terms, gives some recognition and a place which, small though it is, is more than they ever gained from the Shah. They now benefit from more generous rations and food provisions which have also served, to some extent, to buy the allegiance of this class of women. But the continuation of the war, lack of employment, rising prices and the inability of many of them to support their families, or find a man to support them, is gradually eroding their faith in the revolutionary regime to improve their quality of life.

It is however the middle class women who form the firm kernel of opposition. They had spearheaded the reforms under the Pahlavis and fought hard for their rights. These women are all too aware of the losses they have sustained, but are sufficiently organised still to begin another long struggle against the theocracy. It took women in Iran over 80 years to fight the veil and inequality before the law and in society. Although they have lost all but their vote in less than seven years under the new regime, they have not lost hope: a long tradition of underground struggle, of secret societies, and of firm convictions sustains the women's groups in Iran. Urban middle class women succeeded once and can succeed again, but the struggle will prove long and hard.

REFERENCES

AFSHAR, H.: 'Khomeini's Teachings and Their Implications for Iranian Women' in A. Tabari and N. Yeganeh (eds.) *In the Shadow of Islam*, London, Zed Press, 1983.

——: 'The Iranian Theocracy' in H. Afshar (ed.), *Iran, a Revolution in Turmoil*, London, Macmillan, 1985, pp. 220-244.

AKHTARI, HOJATOLESLAM A A: 'Akhlaqeh Hamsardari Eslami (Ethics of Islamic Marriage), serialised in *Zaneh Rouz*, July 28, 1984.

BEHESTI, A: 'Andar Maquleyeh Zibayi' (On the Subject of Beauty) serialised in *Zaneh Rouz*, July 21, 1984.

BOJNOURDI, AYATOLLAH MOUSSAVI: *Kayhan*, July 26, 1984.

KASHANI, AYATOLLAH M. EMANI: *Kayhan*, July 8, 1984.

Kayhan International: June 13, 1973.

Kayhan: February 3, 1983.

——: February 22, 1984.

——: March 14, 1983.

——: March 14, 1983.

——: July 23, 1984.

——: July 26, 1984.

——: July 26, 1984.

The Koran: Chapter 2, Verse 229.

——: Chapter 2, Verse 282.

——: Chapter 4, Verse 129.

TOZIHOLMASSAEL: Massaleyeh 2410

——: Massaleyeh 2459.

MOSALMAN, Z RAHNAVARD TOLOUEH ZANEH: *The Dawn of Muslim Women:* Nashreh Mobasher, Tehran n.d., and Seyed R. *Pakzad Ezdevaj Raveheh Zandari,* How to Keep a Wife Within Marriage: Tehran, Afsat Company, (9th reprint), 1980.

QASSAS LAWS: art 6, September 9, 1982.

Ibid art 16.

Ibid art 92.

TABARI, A.: 'The Enigma of Veiled Iranian Women', *Feminist Review* No. 13, and H. Afshar, 'Khomeini's Teachings and Their Implications for Iranian Women' in *In the Shadow of Islam, op. cit.*, pp. 75, 90.

Zaneh Rouz: July 7, 1984.

——: July 7, 1984.

——: July 21, 1984.

——: August 11 and August 18, 1984

——: August 11, 1984.

——: August 18, 1984.

——: August 18, 1984.

——: August 18, 1984.

——: August 18, 1984.

——: August 18, 1984.

Op. cit.
——: August 18, 1984, and H. Afshar, 'Khomeini's Teachings . . .' *op cit.* p. 97.
——: August 18, 1984.
——: August 25, 1984.
——: August 25, 1984.
——: August 25, 1984.

NOTES ON CONTRIBUTORS

Haleh Afshar teaches Development at the University of Bradford, England. She has been a feature writer and researcher who has published several books and papers, with special emphasis on women, Islam and Iran. *Women, Work and Ideology* and *Women in Resurgent Islam* are two of her recent books, and she is currently editing a volume on Women and the State.

Bina Agarwal is an Associate Professor at the Institute of Economic Growth, Delhi. She was educated at the Universities of Cambridge and Delhi. She has been a Visiting Fellow at the Institute of Development Studies, and a Research Fellow at the Science Policy Research Unit, both at the University of Sussex, U.K. She has written extensively on rural development, technological change in agriculture, the fuelwood and environmental crises, and the position of women in India and other Third World countries. Her earlier books include: *Mechanization in Indian Agriculture: An Analytical Study based on the Punjab* (1983); and *Cold Hearths and Barren Slopes: The Woodfuel Crisis in the Third World* (1986).

Roushan Jahan is the president of a research and study group, Women for Women, in Bangladesh. She has been a literature and linguistics teacher and is now actively involved in research on the problems of Bangladeshi women. Her current research subject is violence against women in Bangladeshi families. Her forthcoming publications include papers on Identification of Priority Research Issues on Women in Bangladesh; Limited Participation of Women in Government; Eradication of Illiteracy among Bangladeshi Rural Women, and others.

Govind Kelkar is Senior Fellow at the Centre for Women's

Development Studies, New Delhi. She has taught Social History, Rural and Comparative Development at Miranda House, University of Delhi, Indian Institute of Technology, Bombay, and National Institute of Bank Management, Bombay. The author of *China After Mao* and numerous monographs and articles, she has been active in the women's movement in India. At present, she is a Fellow at the Nehru Memorial Museum and Library, New Delhi.

Chee Heng Leng is a teacher at the Department of Human Development Studies, Agriculture University of Malaysia. She is specially interested in issues and policies related to health and biology, and to Malaysia's family planning policies. She has co-edited *Designer Genes: I Q, Ideology and Biology* and contributed essays and papers to several books and journals. She is a member of the Sub-committee on Primary Health Care of the Malaysian Government Taskforce on the Status of Women, Federation of Family Planning Associations, Malaysia.

Maznah Binti Mohamad is a lecturer in Development Studies at the School of Social Science, Universiti Sains Malaysia. She worked as Principal Investigator in KANITA (Women and Children in Development), a project sponsored by UNICEF and NACIWID—Prime Minister's Department. She has written several papers on rural women.

Cecilia Ng teaches at the Department of Extension Education, Centre of Extension and Continuing Education, University of Agriculture, Malaysia. Her areas of interest are women and development, rural development and adult/development education. She has been a consultant to the Young Workers Community Education Project at Penang, and has published widely in academic and other journals, on women in agriculture.

Pasuk Phongpaichit is an economist who has taught in Australia and Thailand. She has served as a member of the task force responsible for the formulation of a perspective women's plan, National Economic and Social Development Board, Thailand, and is currently a member of the employment committee for framing Thailand's employment plan. She has written extensively on women, employment and economics.

Joke Shrijvers teaches courses on feminist anthropology and women and development in the Netherlands, and is co-founder of the Research and Documentation Centre on Women and Autonomy at Leiden State University. The subject of her field research has been the changing conditions of women in the North Central Province of Sri Lanka, and her ongoing research focuses on the feminisation of poverty. She is the author of *Mothers for Life: Motherhood and Marginalization in the North-Central Province of Sri Lanka* (1985), and numerous scholarly papers on women and development.

Amrit Srinivasan is Senior Lecturer in Sociology at the Hindu College, Delhi University. Educated at the Delhi School of Economics and Cambridge University, her doctoral research focussed on the politics of women's reforms in colonial India. Her special interests lie in the field of comparative and historical sociology. Within this broad area she has published papers on themes relating to gender and society, kinship and the study of mythological texts.

INDEX